Management of Collegiate Education in the 21st Century: Some Insights

Management of Collegiate Education in the 21st Century: Some Insights

Editor

Srinivas K. Saidapur

FASc., FNA, FNASc., FTWAS

GYAN

Published, 2019

Published by

Gyan Publishing House
5, Ansari Road
Daryaganj, New Delhi-110002
Phone: 011-47034999, 9811692060
www.gyanbooks.com
E-mail: books@gyanbooks.com

Printed at: G. Print Process, Delhi.

Cataloging in Publication Data—DK

Courtesy: D.K. Agencies (P) Ltd. <docinfo@dkagencies.com>

Management of collegiate education in the 21st century : some insights / editor, Srinivas K. Saidapur.

pages cm

Contributed articles.

ISBN 9788121214735

1. Education, Higher—India. 2. Universities and colleges—India—Administration. I. Saidapur, Srinivas K., editor.

LCC LA1153.M36 2019 | DDC 378.54 23

OPINIONS ON THE BOOK

"Prof. Saidapur has edited a book on a topic of great importance and relevance to the present and future of the country. The articles have been written by people with expertise and experience in higher education. I do hope that teachers, administrators and planners will go through the book for a proper understanding of the issues".

Bharata Ratna Prof. C. N. R. Rao, FRS

Jawaharlal Nehru Center for Advanced Scientific Research, Jakkur, Bangalore.

"This book, edited by Prof Saidapur, one of our most respected and distinguished educationists, is an extremely valuable contribution. Valuable, because it is timely in terms of the education reforms on the anvil in India. Valuable, because it gives the readers the benefit of the distilled wisdom of stalwarts who have excelled in the field of education. Valuable, also because it is so comprehensive, so holistic, covering every single aspect of the educational ecosystem. Professor Saidapur deserves both our congratulations as well as grateful thanks for this yeoman service to the future of our society, since, after all, education is our future."

Padmabhusan Dr. R. A. Mashelkar, FRS

National Research Professor & President, Global Research Alliance, Former Director General, CSIR, & President, INSA, New Delhi

"Management of Collegiate Education provides many critical insights for invigorating higher education. The faculty members as well as the educational administrators (Vice Chancellors / Registrar / Directors / Principals) of Universities and Colleges will find the book very valuable in revitalizing higher education"

Dr. D. P. Singh

Chairman, University Grants Commission, New Delhi

About The Editor

Srinivas K. Saidapur is a former Vice Chancellor of Karnatak University (2006-2010) and Founder Director of Higher Education Academy (2015-2017) established by the Government of Karnataka, Dharwad for training Principals and Faculty of Degree Colleges as in Administrative Training Institutes. He is a Fellow of Population Council, New York (1976-77), USA and Alexander von Humboldt Stiftung, Germany (1988-89), Visiting scientist at National Institute for Basic Biology, Okazaki (1999-2000) Japan. He is a recipient of the India's prestigious *Shanti Swarup Bhatnagar Prize* (1991), Sir M. Vishveswaraya Award of Government of Karnataka for Lifetime Contribution to Science & Technology (2012) and many more. He is a Fellow of the Indian Academy of Sciences, Bangalore, Indian National Science Academy (INSA) New Delhi, and National Academy of Sciences of India, Allahabad, and Third World Academy of Sciences, Italy. He also served as Vice President of INSA (2012-14).

He has previously edited two books: *Reproductive Cycles of Indian Vertebrates* (Allied Publishers, New Delhi, 1989) and *Frontier Lectures in Biology by INSA Fellows* (e-Book, 2015: http://www.insa.nic.in).

— — —

Dedicated to
All those striving to improve
Higher Education

Contents

ALL-ROUND DEVELOPMENT OF COLLEGES

Preface

A relentless decline in the quality of higher education and its relevance to industries has become apparent in recent decades. The degrees awarded by the Universities have lost their credibility as evident from the dismal performance of even the rank holders, Gold Medallists, those securing distinctions, first classes in their Master's Degrees in national level eligibility tests like NET/SLET examinations, oral tests and interviews for jobs. The graduates often depict poor knowledge of skills and also fundaments in their own subjects. Therefore, it is time that the country looks at the ailing education system and reforms it thoroughly, so as to arrest and reverse the declining trend. This is important because progress in any sphere depends on qualified, highly competent, committed expert personnel to man the responsibilities efficiently and effectively. Besides, the education system has undergone visible changes from the conventional classroom teaching (allowing passive absorption by the learners) to complex digitized system coded as education 1.0-1.4. So far three major industrial revolutions (IRs) have taken place (IR 1.0-1.3) and fourth one (IR 4.0) is ongoing. The education system and IRs depend upon each other and also they impact each other. Therefore, the prevailing education system must be in tune with the current needs of the time so as to facilitate IRs through innovations and get prepared to face challenges arising out of the IRs. For instance, coping up with the technology driven job disruptions is a major global challenge of the 21st century. So much so, it calls for a total redesigning of the education system. At the same time, it is equally important to imbue value based education that has roots in the country's ethos, culture and spirituality. Thus, in providing quality education (knowledge and skills), teachers play the pivotal role. Hence, a college/ varsity teacher should be familiar with meaning, scope and objectives of higher education, evolution of education systems and their impact on industrialization and the impact of industries on education, and many other dimensions.

An important message of the book is that in view of a rapid and massive industrial revolution and associated technology driven disruptions in the existing jobs has become a real problem. Fortunately, any IR creates new opportunities as well that require new skills. Therefore, the present education system needs to be completely redesigned from the conventional classroom teaching (permitting passive absorption by the learners) to creative thinking, making innovations and empowering learners to innovate. Hence, future strategies of education system lie in triumphing over the challenges of IR 4.0; and any failure to do so will only destroy the demographic dividends of the country.

The book has 25 Chapters that cover different dimensions, integral to the management of college development vis-à-vis higher education. These are: *Higher Education and its Dimensions, Leadership, Governance and Quality assurance, Library Resources and Digital Literacy, Student Support Systems, All-round Development of Colleges,* and *Future Prospects*. The topics cover, meaning and history of higher education, role of teachers, art of teaching, aspects of good governance, fostering quality in education, leadership role of principals, preparation for assessment and accreditation of colleges, importance of digital literacy, library as a centre of learning, harnessing potential of Alumni, management of stress, importance of counselling, 'Right to Information Act', idea of a 'Green Campus', mobilization of resources for research and development, redesigning future education and, finally the ways of strengthening entire gamut of collegiate education.

Lastly, the opinions and contents of the various chapters belong to the respective authors. The Editor does not assume any responsibility for the same. Suggestions from the readers, particularly on the need to include new topics/chapters in future edition of the book are most welcome.

S. K. Saidapur
Editor

ACKNOWLEDGEMENTS

I am immensely grateful to Bharataratna Prof. C. N. R. Rao, Padmabhushan Prof. R. A. Mashelkar and Prof. Dhirendra Pal Singh Chairman, University Grants Commission, New Delhi, for their valuable comments on the draft copy of the book, suggestions and encouragement.

I thank the authors of the various Chapters of this book for their contributions.

Finally, with great pleasure I thank M/s Gyan Publishing House, India for amiably undertaking the publication of this book and for extending cooperation at every step.

S. K. Saidapur

Editor

List of Contributors

S. K. Saidapur

Former Vice Chancellor, Karnatak University and Former Founder Director Higher Education Academy (Government of Karnataka), Dharwad-580003. Email: saidapur@gmail.com

S. P. Thyagarajan

Former Vice Chancellor, University of Madras, Chennai.Email: profspt@gmail.com

A. B. Shanbhag

Professor of Zoology (Retd.), Goa University, Goa-403206. Former Dean, Higher Education Academy, Dharwad-580003. Email: abshanbhag@yahoo.com

R. S. Deshpande

Former Director, Institute for Social and Economic Change (ISEC), Bengaluru-560 0056
Email: rs.kalbandi@gmail.com

Sohan Prabhakar Modak, Dr. ès Sci.

Former Professor Zoology (University of Pune)
Open Vision, 759/75 Deccan Gymkhana, Pune 411004.
India. Email:spmodak@gmail.com

B. G. Mulimani

Former Vice Chancellor, Gulbarga University, Kalaburgi-580106 and BLDE University, Vijayapura-586103.
mail: bgmulimani@rediffmail.com

Jagdish Tonannavar
Professor of Physics
Karnatak University, Dharwad-580003
Email: jrtonannavar@kud.ac.in

S. S. Patagundi
Former Professor of Political Science
Karnatak University, Dharwad-580003
Email: patagundi53@gmail.com

S. Sivasubramanian
Former Vice Chancellor, Bharathiar University,
Coimbatore- 641046 (TN), India.
Email: profssn@hotmail.com

H. A. Ranganath
Former Vice Chancellor, Bangalore University,
Former Director, NAAC, Bangalore-560056,
Visiting Professor, IISc., Bangalore-560012
Email: haranganath@gmail.com

H. M. Kasinath
Former Professor and Dean Faculty of Education,
Karnatak University, Dharwad-580003.
Email: drhmkasinath@gmail.com

Prof. J.S. Bhat
Director, Indian Institute of Information Technology
Surat - 395007, Gujarat, INDIA
Email: jsbhat.iiits@gmail.com

N. V. Sathyanarayana
Informatics India Ltd. Bangalore.
Email: sathya@informaticsglobal.com

Anupama Joshi
Deputy Librarian, Prof. S.S. Basavanal Library,
Karnatak University, Dharwad-580003.
Email: anuyadavaraya@gmail.com

Farzana M. Pathan,
Former Dean, Higher Education Academy,
Dharwad-580003.
Email: farzana.bmp@gmail.com

C. S. Patil
Professor of Law, Karnataka State Law University,
Hubli-580009.
Email: patilcrs@gmail.com

Manika Ghosh
Former Professor in Psychology and Director,
Eudaimonic Center, Bangalore
Email: manikaghosh9@gmail.com

CHAPTER - 1

INTRODUCTION

— S. K. SAIDAPUR

The only important thing in a book is the meaning that it has for you.
— W. SOMERSET MAUGHAM

My association with higher education has spanned for over 5 decades; as student, as teacher and finally as administrator-cum-leader (as Chairman of the PG department and later as Vice Chancellor). Besides, I had the good fortune of visiting several good universities and colleges in different parts of India: Jawaharlal Nehru University, Delhi to modest colleges remotely placed in rural and tribal belts with their own unique set of problems. These visits were actually for assessment and accreditation of institutions, an opportunity provided by the National Assessment and Accreditation Council (NAAC), Bangalore. And, more recently I had the opportunity to serve as the founder Director (2015-17) of Higher Education Academy, established by the Government of Karnataka at Dharwad for training teachers of the Degree colleges on the lines of Administrative Training Institutes (ATI) established for training the bureaucrats on administrative matters. The above assignments gave me excellent opportunity to understand the scenario of both collegiate and university education in the country.

In my 50 years of close association with the higher education system I had, call it a fortune or misfortune of seeing the rise and fall of several higher education institutions (HEIs), the Universities and some prestigious constituent colleges. Luckily, if I may say so, I was associated with the growth and ascent of these institutions for most part of my academic career. I remember quite vividly how the teaching fraternity worked hard to build the reputation of the institution and served the alma mater with dedication and devotion despite the lack of promotional avenues, and non-lucrative salaries. At that time, even a second class Masters Degree holder enjoyed great credibility. Today, no degree or rank by itself enjoys the same credibility as before since performance of the students in State/National Eligibility Tests and interviews has become unequivocally dismal. The dismal performance continues even after they assume teaching positions. Most teachers appear to lack motivation, aptitude and competency to teach. In addition, they exhibit little concern, commitment, honesty and integrity. Yet, faculty involved in higher education and heads of the institution, the Principals and Vice Chancellors draw handsome salaries, but sadly, enjoy publicity for all wrong reasons.

Returning to the main objective of the book, it is to address diverse issues confronting collegiate education. Essentially, similar issues confront the varsities. The book is designed to provide basic and critical insights about the meaning and basic objectives of higher education, brief history of higher education in modern India, summary of various education commission reports, role of teachers and their obligations, governance, quality assurance and leadership, appointment of faculty, catering to the needs of stakeholders (e.g. counselling, mentoring, stress management, placement cell, add on courses, holistic development), resource mobilization and so on. After all, everyone (Professors, Principals and even Vice Chancellors) associated with higher education ought to know the different dimensions of education system in addition to having sound knowledge of fundamentals and advances in the chosen subjects of interest. Keeping this 'core theme' in mind the book has been designed. An additional concern addressed in this book (various chapters) pertains to the future education system; a need to redesign education system so as to match the requirements of the 4th industrial revolution (IR 4.0). This includes overcoming the technology driven disruption in jobs, promotion of creative thinking, making innovations and acquiring new skills and so on.

Faculty members of both colleges and varsities need a proper orientation about the core objectives of *higher* education, its different dimensions (historical perspectives to modern education system), rapidly changing higher education needs and patterns all over world vis-a-vis changing roles of teachers, governance, quality sustenance and, overall development of HEIs in tune with the new challenges that emerge from time to time, due to technological advancements in various fields and their impacts. The book serves as a primer to orient faculty members of both colleges and Universities in fulfilling their explicit as well as implicit obligations in furthering the cause of higher education. Such 'Orientation' courses are indeed given by the Academic Staff Colleges, Teacher Training Institutions, and Higher Education Academies.

The book has six thematic sections: *Higher Education and its Dimensions, Leadership, Governance and Quality Assurance, Library Resources and Digital Literacy, Student Support Systems, All-round Development of Colleges,* and *Future Prospects* which comprise of 25 Chapters.

The Chapter 1 entitled 'Introduction' highlights the contents of all 25 chapters in brief so that the reader can have an overview of the entire book. The 2nd Chapter explains the very meaning of 'higher' education and its core objectives, as well as role of teachers in capacity building, providing value based and holistic education, and building a humane society. At the same time, in view of the evolving education systems and industrial revolutions, the changing roles of teachers in future, are highlighted. Conceivably, future education will have to be more and more learner centric involving creative thinking, innovating and empowering learners to make innovations. The Chapter concludes by underscoring the need and urgency to match the future education to changing paradigms so as to avoid a possible raze of demographic dividends.

A sound knowledge of historical perspective of higher education is vital for future developments. The 3rd Chapter by S. P. Thyagarajan provides a brief history of how higher education took its roots in India, its status before, during, and after the culmination of British colonial rule. Anyone connected with higher education ought to have a sound knowledge of how higher education took roots in this country, and its subsequent growth. Therefore, both young and old faculty must be aware of the evolution of education system in India.

In the 4th Chapter A. B. Shanbhag takes the reader through a delightful tour of trailblazers that lit the evolutionary path of modern higher education in the country. Describing salient features of these very exhaustive reports concisely is not easy. Yet, the author has done ample justice in abridging the essence of various education commission reports and put them in a capsule form for easy assimilation by the readers.

The 5th Chapter by R. S. Deshpande reviews the state of the art of teaching practices with particular reference to Social Sciences and the influence of Western thoughts on the same. He emphasizes unambiguously the need for radical rethinking and evolving more appropriate pedagogies for teaching social sciences keeping in mind the Indian context and contemporaneous requirements.

In Chapter 6, S. P. Modak eloquently reveals that teaching is in fact reaching out to students. He recalls his own experiences all through his school, college, doctoral and postdoctoral sojourns. This chapter enlightens on how to inspire students and focus on learner-centric teaching and encourage students to think and understand the basic concepts through (group) discussions and student's own efforts.

The Chapter 7 by B. G. Mulimani and J. Tonannavar focuses on the importance of developing scientific attitude and rationale in teaching process so as to inspire students for creative thinking. The authors cite many quotes of Indian and foreign scientists of great eminence that inspire any reader. The authors also draw the attention of readers to the 'words of wisdom' from the exalted early Indian thinkers. The central message is that only inspired teachers can inspire their pupil. The Chapter is therefore highly motivating.

In Chapter 8, S. K. Saidapur deliberates on the importance of leadership role of Principals / Heads of the institutions in fostering overall development of HEIs. He describes what leadership is all about and how it makes huge difference in building institutions of higher learning. He makes a case to say that the administrators and Principals are primarily facilitators and not the rulers, and that the fate of a HEIs, be it a college or the university, largely depends on the leadership qualities of the person in charge of the institution. He vividly explains the importance of academic, administrative and finance reforms in all round development of the Colleges. Further, the Chapter stresses on the need for value based and holistic education. It thus underscores the crucial role of leaders in steering the HEIs to greater heights.

Growth of any institution is a reflection of good governance which plays a key role in building and maintaining reputation. The governance issues are dealt in Chapters 9-12. The Chapter 9 by S. S. Patagundi describes the imperatives of good governance and their significance. After that, Siva Sivasubramanian explains in detail on how to foster quality in higher education (Chapter 10). In the next, Chapter 11, H. A. Ranganath reflects on the role of Quality Assurance Systems (QAS) in HEIs and the way forward. This is followed by Chapter 12 in which H. Kasinath deals with Internal Quality Assurance Cell (IQAC) and its functions in detail. Indeed the IQAC plays a key role and serves as a think-tank of the institution. In a way, accomplishments of HEIs are reflections of quality assurance systems of the institution.

All HEIs are required to undergo Assessment and Accreditation (A&A) periodically. The methodologies for A&A of NAAC are revised and updated from time to time based on the feedbacks from the assessors and the stakeholders. The new methodology of NAAC is in effect since July 2017. It relies more on quantifiable and less on qualitative matrices. Therefore, colleges and varsities desirous of undergoing A&A need to start preparation well in advance. The Chapter 13 by S. K. Saidapur describes nuances of aligning the institutions for A&A well in advance and avoid last minute hassles and mortifications.

As per the mandatory requirement of the State/Central governments, every institution must have a 'Right to Information' (RTI) cell. In Chapter 14, C. S. Patil enumerates setting up and functioning of RTI cells. All institutions need the basic knowledge of RTI cells. This Chapter explains the significance of RTI cell and its importance exceedingly well.

In institutions engaged in teaching and research, the libraries constitute important components. The Chapter 15 by N. V. Sathyanarayana lucidly traces evolution of libraries from clay tablet to digital tablet and movement towards ideal library. This is ably followed by Chapter 16 in which Anupama Joshi describes library as a learning resource, methods of accessing literature, and modern trends in libraries. Readers can thus get to know the changing trends in the functioning of libraries and their importance in education through these Chapters.

In Chapter 17, J. S. Bhat explains the importance and inevitability of *digital literacy* in the 21st century and, its significance in the globalized context to stay relevant and overcome challenges of the industrial revolutions as well as technology driven job disruptions. The author highlights how adoption of information technology can help not only in efficient and transparent administration of institutions but also in adopting to the changing paradigms in teaching, learning and evaluation processes. The author's plea to adopt ICT in all spheres of the college/varsity activities at the earliest is more than timely.

In this 21st century, besides knowledge skill development and entrepreneurship abilities play a key role. Chapter 18 by Farzana Pathan describes the various skill development projects initiated by the Government of India and their importance in imparting skills and entrepreneurship talents of our youth, and, at the same time, make an impact on the country's economy. These initiatives like the 'Skill Development, Make in India, Stand up India, Start-up India' are for harnessing the great demographic dividends from the growing youth population. Therefore, the author makes a case for apprising students about such programs and emergence of new opportunities envisioned by the India's most admired Prime Minister, Shri Narendra Modi.

The Chapters 19-20 by Manika Ghosh deal with the management of stress (Chapter 19) and importance of counselling (Chapter 20). Both these aspects are quite essential as growing number of students are experiencing stress due to anxiety, tension and trauma and the resulting unpleasant consequences. She explains how to undertake stress management and counselling even by the existing faculty members who are empathetic and feel concerned about the welfare of their wards. She stresses on the significance of timely counselling in saving and shaping the lives of students who may otherwise go astray.

The Chapter 21 authored by A. B. Shanbhag and S. K. Saidapur provides insights for resource mobilization for the institution from diverse resources. Indeed, resource mobilization is very important considering the fact that the expenditures on higher education are rising day by day but the support from the governmental agencies is generally not commensurate with the actual needs. The authors enumerate possible ways of generating funds.

In Chapter 22, A. B. Shanbhag describes the concept of a 'Green Campus' and its development. This is important especially in view of the fast deteriorating environment following industrialization, rising pollution and poor sanitation. The ideas provided in this Chapter will go a long way in developing model green campuses in colleges and universities that can serve as the lungs for people living in and around the area.

Harnessing the potential of Alumni Associations (AA) is largely unexplored domain in both colleges and varsities in India. Evidently, potential of AAs in developing colleges / varsities is a fertile area. In the Chapter 23 A. B. Shanbhag describes the importance of involving the Alumni in all-round development of colleges by facilitating formation of AAs and their vibrant functioning.

The Chapter 24 on 'Education in the 21st Century' by S. K. Saidapur conveys the central message of the book that in view of a rapid and massive ongoing industrial revolutions and the resultant disruptions in the existing jobs and creation of new opportunities, the present education system needs to change from the conventional classroom teaching approach (letting passive absorption by the learners) to creative thinking, making innovations and empowering learners to innovate. As a matter of fact, future strategies of education system lie in triumphing over the challenges of IR 4.0 and any failure to do so will only destroy the demographic dividends.

The Chapter 25 on 'Redesigning Higher Education: a few titbits' by the editor is in effect an *epilogue* that briefly portrays the existing higher education scenario and provides ideas that are central to designing a 'plan of action' for resurrection of collegiate education in tune with the contemporaneous needs. It is followed by a list of 'Abbreviations' that appear in various places of the text.

LAST WORDS: The book is intended to generate awareness on the prevailing scenario of higher education that is characterized by the loss of credibility of degrees, quality of teaching and learning, uninspiring management of HEIs, declining quality of faculty, inadequate or obsolete infrastructure, and unworthy leadership on one hand, and on the other, to inspire both young and senior faculty to imbue the true spirit of higher education, its importance in human resource building and development of the nation. Furthermore, the book emphasizes a need and urgency for redesigning education system (up gradation of infrastructure, use of flexible curriculums, learner centric teaching, fostering creative thinking and empowering the learners to innovate etc.) in tune with the IR 4.0 and its foreseeable consequences. To ensure a harmonious society, in addition to imparting skills and knowledge, value based education becomes equally important. For this reason, the book lays stress on the importance of promoting citizenry, a supreme objective of higher education. It is hoped that the central message embodied in this book spreads across the length and breadth of the country and reaches the policy makers who bear the moral responsibility of shaping the new education system. Lastly, it is fervently hoped that the book inspires teachers, promote leadership and good governance and help in sustained progressive growth of HEIs in the country.

Chapter - 2

Value of Higher Education and Role of Teachers

— *S. K. Saidapur*

Education is the training of mind, heart and soul.
– Aurobindo

This chapter deals with (1) the true meaning and spirit of higher education, (2) evolution of higher education in India, (3) pivotal role of teachers and, (4) future education. Eminent scholars like Swami Vivekananda, Aurobindo, Ramana Maharshi, Rabindranath Tagore, S. Radhakrishnan, Mahatma Gandhi, Jawaharlal Nehru and several others have commented on the meaning of higher education. Evidently, higher education is for manifestation of perfection; ideally it should lead to a search for truth and higher objectives, meaning and purpose of life. Higher education is for life and not merely for living. A true higher education may show a way to attain Knowledge (*Jnana*), a way to Liberation (*Mokhsa* or *Mukti*) and true Enlightenment. Teachers play a pivotal role in shaping the life and destiny of innumerable number of disciples. However, it is a matter of great concern that the quality of higher education in India appears to be declining fast along with a perceptible loss of credibility of varsity degrees (UG, PG, and Ph.D.) in recent times. It is no secret that a good majority of teachers at all levels of higher education, more often than not lack professionalism with respect to their conduct, teaching and mentoring the students due to poor competency and commitment. The reading habits of teachers and, craving to acquire new knowledge, have faded over the years. Decline in the knowledge of fundamentals among teachers is another cause of great concern. The modern teaching aids have helped teachers more than the students. The performance of students in NET / SLET is shockingly dismal over the years; the pass percentage rarely touches double digit despite the fact that those who appear for these tests often hold first classes, ranks and Gold medals in their respective varsity examinations. This excruciatingly depicts a loss of credibility in university teaching, evaluation, marks and degrees.

Let us first reflect briefly on the meaning of 'higher' education and, the importance of teachers in imbuing the true spirits of higher education among their pupils, and major changes in the systems of education (coded as Education 1.0-4.0) in relation to the concomitant industrial revolutions (coded as IR 1.0-4.0). Obviously, education leads to development of technology which in turn leads to IRs. Any IR necessitates development of more and more skills and creativity. Therefore, education and IR are intimately interdependent and impact each other. A vital link between education system and IR is the teacher; a teacher with vision, competence and commitment. What makes one a good teacher? Teaching is an art. Those who love teaching alone can become good teachers. Most good teachers are born teachers. The others can become good teachers by acquiring the needed skills and appreciation for values and ethos besides keeping themselves up to date in the subject of their expertise. Teachers, who can be called great, are of two types: the brilliant and the inspiring. A brilliant teacher need not be an inspiring teacher. An inspiring teacher need not be a brilliant teacher. A combination of both is however rare. Most importantly, to earn respect of the students, one has to have the basic attributes like honesty, integrity, good moral character, as well as a sound knowledge of the subject matter.

It is quite remarkable that in India 500-1500 years before the Christian era (BCE), the so called Vedic period, the key role of teachers in imparting education and building a humane society was recognized. So much so, our wise ancestors evolved the concept of a Goddess, Saraswati and sought her blessings to become educated and knowledgeable person. Further, the culture of worshiping books, the invaluable sources of knowledge and wisdom was initiated. No other country in the globe has such a practice. A teacher was considered to be the most learned person in the society and highly respected even by the rulers, kings and emperors. So much so, a teacher, *Guru* in the Indian context, is considered to be an embodiment of three Gods,

'Brahma, Vishnu and Maheshwara'. The following Sanskrit verse aptly summarizes the idea of a teacher:

Gurur Brahma, Gurur Vishnu,
Gurur devo Maheshwara,
Gurur saakshaath Param Brahma,
Tasmai shree Guruve Namaha.

In India, it is widely believed that Lord Brahma is a creator; Lord Vishnu is a preserver and Lord Maheswara is a destroyer. The above verse teaches that "A teacher is like Lord Brahma who creates knowledge within us; like Lord Vishnu who helps in preserving the knowledge so acquired (in our mind); and like Lord Maheshwara who guides in destroying ill-conceived ideas, and thereby facilitating us to stay on the right path and enlightened. To such a Guru we offer our salutations". This vision of our worthy ancestors is indeed remarkable. Apparently, there was no dearth of fertile minds even 5000 years ago in our country that is well enshrined in the teachings of great many saints and writers from time to time. With such a profound philosophy and realization of the importance of true education since ancient times where did we go wrong? What caused the deterioration in our education system? Why have our moral and ethical values declined? To find answers to such questions we need to browse the legacy of educational policies practiced or advocated during the periods of sovereign rulers (Kings, Queens, and the British colonial masters), and after attaining freedom from the British Empire in the year 1947.

Prior to the British Raj (pre-colonial days), typically a teacher would go to the house of the pupil and teach reading, writing, counting and maintaining records. Later, with time, the pupils started going to the house of the teacher. The teacher and his family looked after them as their own children. During the British colonial days a need was felt to teach English to Indians to facilitate communication, record keeping and accounting works. The recommendations of Sir Thomas Macaulay and Sir Charles Woods (Woods' Dispatch, 1854) led to the starting of universities in Calcutta, Bombay, Madras, and later in Banaras, Aligarh and Lahore (1880-1920). Higher education in independent India began taking shape with Radhakrishnan Commission (1948-49) which considered all aspects of higher education (curriculum, examinations, funding, medium of instruction, quality, accessibility, excellence, inclusiveness and governance) exhaustively. The Kothari Commission (1964–1966), National Policy on Education (1986) and Yash Pal Committee (2008) provided additional inputs on higher education. The recommendations of Radhakrishnan and Kothari Commissions are relevant even today. Sadly, before implementing these recommendations fully new committees are set up from time to time (see Chapter 2-3 for greater details).

It is a matter of great pity, that in our own times we have been witnessing degradation of the higher education systems. There are colleges and varsities where faculty recruitment has not taken place for decades. When teaching faculty is appointed, consideration for merit, competency and suitability are often ignored. Thus, institutions may appoint qualified but not necessarily competent faculty. Favouritism, nepotism and other considerations along with the political interferences dominate the appointments for various positions which results in driving away the meritorious candidates to other greener pastures, often abroad. Most of the teaching is done by the part time teachers who are paid a paltry sum each month or per lecture basis. Uncertainties and fear of losing jobs loom largely on the minds of such teachers. Inbreeding in the appointment of faculty has also contributed enormously to the downfall of educational standards. Hybrid vigour and competitive environment are totally lacking in almost all educational institutions thereby precluding raising educational standards. Furthermore, for variety of reasons, we in India seemed to have developed appreciation for everything that is foreign and a disrespect for everything that is native. This attitude is detrimental to our education system, moral and ethical values as well as self-esteem. It is therefore, high time that we revive our education system to global standards and side by side promote inculcation of Indian ethos and thoughts, moral and ethical values, and more importantly, restore self esteem through a meaningful education. This can help us in restoring the past glory and image of India, the mother of all civilizations. All we need to do is to revive the wisdom enshrined in the inspirational ideas of great thinkers and philosophers that this country has produced. Of the many great thoughts about the meaning of higher education, I quote here Gurudev Rabindranath Tagore who said, "The highest education is that which does not merely give us information but makes our life in harmony with all existence". Likewise, Pandit Jawaharlal

Nehru in his convocation address delivered at Allahabad University, said and I quote - *"A university stands for humanism, for tolerance, for reason, for the adventure of ideas and for the search of truth. It stands for the onward march of the human race towards even higher objectives. If the universities discharge their duties adequately, then it is well with the Nation and the people."* The statement of Nehru eminently summarizes the importance of higher education. It also reveals expectations of the society from higher centres of learning, the colleges and universities. Quality enhancement in teaching and learning are indeed prerequisites for building good human resource needed for governance of the country, development of Science and Technology base, spirituality, nationalism and finally a humanistic and tolerant society. Attainment of these virtues is the major objective of higher education.

Let us further muse over the meaning of 'education'. Is there a difference between being literate and educated? Yes, there is a difference. For instance, a literate person can read and write; literacy by itself does not guarantee that it will make a person educated. Yet, it is a fine tool to become educated. On the other hand, an educated person is one who believes and strives towards the pursuit of higher objectives in life. He becomes a knowledgeable person with wisdom of life. Such persons are role models for overall development of a humane society and ensure harmonious living with people of all faiths. Precisely for this reason, we need to revive the basic Indian ethos, and wisdom of great thinkers and philosophers like Buddha, Basavaeshwara, Aurobindo, Ramakrishna Paramahamsa, Swami Vivekananda, Ramana Maharshi and S. Radhakrishnan to name a few. It is no secret that the West is looking towards east for peace and enlightenment. And, India is a rich source of such knowledge from time immemorial. Certainly, it is not very difficult to imbibe such a knowledge that can be regarded as ultimate. To succeed in life or attain highest education, all one needs to do first is to train the mind, heart and soul, so profoundly advocated by Shri Aurobindo.

An ideal teacher is not only an expert in his or her chosen area but also a person who will inspire and sculpt the career and beliefs of the pupils. He burns himself to lighten the lives of his disciples. Teaching needs to be done with concern, commitment and scholarly pursuit of knowledge. The teachers teach both inside and outside the class rooms.

Inside the class rooms they teach the subject. Outside the classroom they teach they teach a lot on personality development by their own conduct, and adherence to moral and ethical values. Therefore, teachers need to be very conscious of their behaviour and conduct outside the class room. Evidently, they have the great responsibility in shaping the destiny of any country. It is often said that a most developed country is one in which teaching community enjoys highest respect in the society. It is not surprising therefore that the Indian culture and ethos also teach us to respect teachers and hold them in highest reverence. Honesty, integrity can help earn respect for teachers. Meaningful teaching-learning can take place when done with devotion (*Shradha*) and only then there is a mutual respect between the teacher and the taught. Sadly, respect and reverence for teachers is vanishing. Yet all is not lost. If teachers carry out their responsibility with competency and dignity, concern and commitment they can hope to regain their lost status of "Guru" and in turn restore the glory of India. At the same time, the State and Central governments must support and nourish higher education in a most fitting way so as to ensure production of not only good human resource but also place the country on the pinnacle of the world a place it truly deserves.

Building a globally competent nation and a humanistic society education plays a key role. The importance of education is beautifully summarized in the following statements: 'collapsing any nation does not require use of atomic bombs or the use of long range missiles. It only requires lowering the quality of education and allowing cheating in the examinations by the students. This will only ensure the following. The patient dies in the hands of the doctor who passed his exams through cheating. And the buildings collapse in the hands of an engineer who passed his exams through cheating. And the money is lost in the hands of an accountant who passed his exams through cheating. And humanity dies in the hands of a religious scholar who passed his exams through cheating. And justice is lost in the hands of a judge who passed his exams through cheating. And ignorance is rampant in the minds of children who are under the care of a teacher who passed exams through cheating. The collapse of education is the collapse of the nation' (*source:* anonymous 'WhatsApp' message).

The foregoing passages clearly emphasize the urgency for restoration of high quality education. Therefore, it is high time that students, teachers and education managers understand the true spirit and significance of higher education. The primary goal of higher education is to teach for 'life' rather than merely for living. Any education is meant to produce gentlemen who do not inflict pain on others. It should also instil self-esteem and national pride in the minds of our students by holding our lingual, religious, ethnic diversities in reverence. Education must lead to realizing these objectives. Spirituality is the strength of India while material accomplishments are the strengths of the Western world. The entire western world is looking towards India to learn spirituality, yoga and meditation as the ultimate sources for happiness, health, peace and enlightenment. We in India have overlooked these aspects and they are not taught at any level. Consequently, our children do not know the importance of these. Let me recall the statement of D. S. Kothari who said "How can we lament lack of national pride in Indians without first acquainting them with the country's phenomenal scientific achievements in the dim distant past?"

The preceding sections briefly portrayed the meaning and importance of higher education in the backdrop of Indian ethos and culture. As far as the education systems are concerned they always remain in a state of flux and are subject to evolve in relation to the current needs of the time. Moreover, education systems and industrial revolutions are interdependent and impact each other greatly. Education leads to development of technologies which in turn lead to innovations. The innovations and automations often disrupt currently existing industries and jobs. Indeed, one can readily see the technology driven disruption in jobs and industries all over the world. Yet, some new opportunities have also emerged that however require top skills. Therefore, future education will be for acquisition of more and more skills and making innovations (see also Chapter 24).

The future education system (4.0) is poised to undergo drastic redesigning largely because of the ongoing fourth industrial revolution (IR 4.0) which is based on complex digitization (see Chapter 24). Future education will essentially revolve around development of technologies and making innovations. Hence, the traditional class rooms will have to be redesigned to facilitate self learning, group learning, blended learning, creative thinking and making innovations. In this process, HEIs have to adopt flexible curricula, flipped class room teaching and become totally learner-centric. To realize these objectives, the role of teachers will also change from class room lecturing to being a facilitator, guide, mentor, philosopher and friend of learners. And this may not be easy. In all probability, the digital divide between learners and teachers will widen with the former becoming smarter in using digital technology than the latter. Therefore, the teachers themselves have to become technology savvy, active in social media and innovative in their approach and remain life-long learners. This calls for a change in the mindset of teachers which can enable them to face the changing needs of the time. Further, as the barriers between man and machines (technologies) diminish, we need to redefine education for future generations; yet not losing sight of basic tenets like values, beliefs, national pride and ethos of the country that make us human.

Higher Education and its Dimensions

Chapter - 3

Brief History of Indian Higher Education

— S. P. Thyagarajan

Those who cannot learn from history are doomed to repeat it.
— George Santayana

The East India Company established its first major settlement in Asia at Fort St. George in 1639. In and around the Fort grew Madras (now Chennai), 25 years before Bombay (now Mumbai), or 50 years before Calcutta (now Kolkata). The three became premier cities of the British overseas territories until Delhi was made the capital of British India. It was in these cities, the British educational system got established first.

The Origin and Development

The origin and development of informal system of higher education in India can be traced to the establishment of the Calcutta Madrasa in 1781 by Warren Hastings, the first Governor-General of India. In 1792, Jonathan Duncan, the Resident at Banaras, established the Banaras Sanskrit College and Mount Stuart Elphinstone at Poona College for Hindu Learning. Raja Ram Mohan Roy founded Hindu College (now Presidency College) in 1817 to provide advanced European knowledge through English medium. In 1818, Baptist Missionaries founded a college at Serampore. The Church of England started the Bishop College at Sibpur in 1820. Alexander Duff established the Scottish Missionary College in 1830 in Calcutta. More colleges were then opened at Masulipatam (1841), Nagpur (1844), Krishanagar (1845),

Behrampur (1853) and at Agra in 1853. These institutions were quite different from the colleges of today.

Modern Higher Education in India

Modern higher education in India started in 1854, with the famous Despatch of Sir Charles Wood, which is known as the 'Magna Carta' of English education in India. On receipt of the Despatch of the Court of Directors dated 19 July 1854, the Government of India took up the task of setting up universities in Calcutta, Bombay and Madras on the model of London University. The Government of India passed Acts of Incorporation in 1857 of all the three Universities. Anglicize policies reflected the power and self-confidence of Britain at this time and were designed, in Sir Macaulay's words, "*to create, a class who would be interpreters between us and the millions whom we govern, a class of persons Indian in blood and colour, but English in tastes, in opinions, in moral and in intellect, who would be consumers of British goods, provide recruits for the subordinate ranks of the East India Company's civil service and be loyal to the Raj*".

In 1860, the Indian Universities (Degree) Act was passed, empowering the universities to confer diplomas and/or degrees. A proposal was made in 1856 to establish a university in Punjab, especially for oriental learning and instruction. The Punjab University was thus established in 1882 by a special Act of Incorporation. A University College was established in Lahore in 1869 and it achieved the status of a university in 1882. The Mohamedan Anglo-Oriental College at Aligarh was established in 1875 which later got transformed into Aligarh Muslim University in 1920. Establishment of a Central College at Allahabad in a rented building on 1 July 1872 and subsequently led to formation of Allahabad University.

Education Commission (1882-83)

The Government of India appointed an Indian Education Commission in 1882 but did not give it the right to inquire into the general working of Indian universities. The Commission, therefore, contented itself with making only a few observations in connection with the improvement of affiliated colleges. While drawing the attention of the local government to the need for providing or extending the means of collegiate education at several places; it recommended that the rate of aid to each college be determined by the strength of the staff, the expenditure on its maintenance, the efficiency of the institution, and the wants of the locality. Special grants were also to be made whenever necessary, for the supply and renewal of buildings, furniture, libraries and other apparatus of instruction.

Indian Universities Commission (1902)

Higher education in India was so chaotic and had such poor standards that Lord Curzon had to take personal interest to its reform at the beginning of the 20th century. For this purpose, he appointed an Indian Universities Commission on January 27, 1902 to inquire into the condition and prospects of the universities established in British India and to consider and report on proposals for improving their constitution and working. The Commission submitted its report in the same year and adopted the model of London University, as modified by the Act of 1898. It made five important recommendations: (1) the reorganization of university governance; second, (2) a stricter and more systematic supervision of colleges by universities and the imposition of exacting conditions of affiliation, (3) closer attention to the conditions under which students lived and worked, (4) the assumption of teaching functions by the university within defined limits, and (5) substantial changes in curricula and in the methods of examination. Curzon's attempt at reforms created more problems. The new regulations for affiliation were considered a hindrance to Indian private enterprise in the field of higher education. The immediate result was that the number of colleges declined from 192 to 170 in 1912. However, the public demand for higher education could not be curbed, as the restriction on the raising of new colleges only led to an increase in the enrolment in the existing colleges.

Higher education in India was alien in character but the response to it was eager, especially in the metropolitan cities of Calcutta, Bombay and Madras where there were opportunities for Indians to find jobs in the government or in other professions. Between 1855-1856 and 1921-1922, the number of general colleges increased from 21 to 172 and student enrolment in them increased from 4,355 to 58,837. By 1947, there were 19 universities and 496 colleges with 2, 37,546 students. The growth was mainly in privately managed colleges. In 1901-02, while there were 140 Arts colleges with 17,655 students in them, there were only 46 professional colleges with 5,358 students. Between 1886-87 and 1946-47, the number of Arts colleges increased from 86 to 420 but the growth in professional colleges was much slower.

From 1911-12 onwards, there was a growing disillusionment with the model of affiliating universities. The first university to deviate from the affiliating model was Banaras Hindu University (BHU) set up in 1916. It was a unitary, residential and teaching university. It was also different from the usual universities in its basic philosophy - it was established by Annie Besant and Pandit Madan Mohan Malviya to uphold Indian values and ancient traditions. The University of Mysore, established in the same year as BHU, was the first university in a princely state. Osmania University, established by the Nizam of Hyderabad in 1918 undertook the experiment of teaching through Urdu.

The Calcutta University Commission

This was instituted in 1917 under the chairmanship of Sir Michael Sadler. It made a thorough assessment of the entire university system in the country, Calcutta only serving as an example, and submitted its report two years later. One of its major recommendations was the need for unitary teaching and residential universities. If the first three universities of the country were modelled on London University, the Oxbridge model inspired Sadler and his colleagues. Of the universities set up in the decade or so after the Sadler Commission report, Aligarh (1920), Lucknow (1921), Dacca (1921), Delhi (1922), Nagpur (1923), Andhra (1923), Agra (1927) and Annamalai (1929) deserve mention. Of these, only Nagpur, Andhra, Delhi and Agra were affiliating. The rest were all teaching and residential. The Great Depression of 1929 was a watershed. Between then and Indian independence, only one university was founded in the princely state of Travancore which after Mysore and Hyderabad was the third university in a princely state. Further, three more universities were set up in British India; these include Utkal (1943), Sagar (1946) and Rajasthan (1947) universities.

With the establishment of new universities, the need for co-ordinating their work became so urgent that in 1924, the First All-India Conference of Indian Universities was held at Shimla and it decided to establish an Inter-University Board to act as an advisory body. It consisted of representatives of all Indian university centres. It did useful work in several directions. It has now become an integral part of the Association of Indian Universities (AIU).

Genesis of India-Specific Universities

Some people felt that the then existed schools and colleges were imparting education that did not inculcate either patriotic sentiments or pride of India. The Deccan Education Society was founded in 1880 in Poona to facilitate and make education cheaper by establishing schools and colleges. The first institution started by it was the Ferguson College in 1885 where the youth were motivated to serve their country. Mahatma Gandhi founded a series of national universities during the first noncooperation movement in 1920-1922. These included the Gujarat Vidyapeeth, Kashi Vidyapeeth, Bihar Vidyapeeth, Tilak Maharashtra Vidyapeeth and Jamia Millia Islamia. Hindi or the prevailing vernacular languages was the medium of instruction in these universities. Mahatma Gandhi found the British system of education as an "unmitigated evil". He felt it was impractical and destructive of the Indian imagination. It ignored everything that India had discovered in its edifying experience.

Rabindranath Tagore tried a different kind of educational experiment at Shantiniketan where he founded the Vishwa Bharati in 1921. He did not think of it as just another university but one that attempted to synthesize Asian and Western culture. He respected Western knowledge but his concern was that English education had alienated the Indian intelligentsia both from the common people and from its roots.

Private Initiatives

Interestingly, educational institutions were also established by the socio-religious reform movements of the late 19th century, partly in response to the Christian Missionary Colleges that were first in the field. Sir Syed Ahmed Khan established the Oriental College at Aligarh in 1877 to popularize English education among Muslims in North India. The Arya Samaj tried to modernize and strengthen Hinduism through educational institutions, particularly in Punjab and the then United Provinces. The Dayanand Anglo-Vedic College (DAV) was founded at Lahore in 1886. Subsequently more such colleges sprang up. These colleges were affiliated to universities and followed the prescribed curriculum but emphasized the study of Sanskrit and the Vedas. The Sikhs in the Punjab started the Singh Sabha Movement in 1873 and also the Chief Khalsa Diwan established Khalsa schools and colleges. They, too, followed the curriculum prescribed by the universities to which they were affiliated but laid greater stress on the study of religion and the language of the community.

All these institutions played an extremely useful role but could not provide a viable indigenous alternative to the system that had already got established. Moreover, there was a growing demand for higher technical education since the 1880s. Jamshedji Tata, one of India's pioneering icons of the early 20th century, was fully aware of the shortcomings of Indian universities. He saw that they examined but did not teach, and was particularly concerned about the lack of scientific teaching. Tata initiated a scheme in 1898 that finally led to the founding of the Tata Institute of Science (now known as Indian Institute of Science) at Bangalore in 1911. The leaders of the Swadeshi Movement in Bengal established a college of engineering and technology in 1907. It was later shifted to Jadhavpur. D. K. Karve started a women's university, the first of its kind, in 1918 at Poona, which later developed into the SNDT Women's University, now located at Mumbai.

Genesis of University Grants Commission

In 1943, the Central Advisory Board of Education drew up a national plan for the post-war development of education, popularly known as the Sargent Plan. The Sargent Report observed that there had been a *general lack of planning in University education* and that *both the Central and Provincial Governments had yielded to popular pressures in bringing universities into existence without providing the necessary resources to enable them to function on sound lines*. Hence, there was a felt need for an authority to coordinate university education in the interests of the country as a whole. Accordingly, it suggested that such a body be created on the model of the University Grants Committee in Britain. The main function of the proposed Indian University Grants Committee was to have supervisory role on the allocation of grants to universities from public funds and to ensure that they had enough resources to meet the demands that might be made. It was envisaged that such financial assistance would be given as block grants for a certain number of years, to enable the universities to plan ahead. All grants to universities for new developments would be made by the Central Government through the Grants Committee.

The Report further recommended that in addition to its main functions, the proposed Grants Committee should also be empowered to encourage private benefactions; coordinate university activities so as to avoid overlapping, and to adjust, as far as possible, the output of the universities to the economic needs of the country; prevent undesirable competition amongst them, ensure periodic visits to the universities in order to ascertain their needs; establish cultural contacts; remove all international barriers and arrange for the exchange of teachers and students with foreign countries.

The Government of India appointed a University Grants Committee by the letter of Department of Education, Health and Lands Resolution dated June 4, 1945 consisting of four part-time members to advise the government on the grants to be given to the Central Universities. The constitution of the Committee was amended and its scope enlarged by the Department of Education Resolution dated July 27, 1946, and the Ministry of Education Resolution dated December 16, 1947. It was empowered to deal with the other universities. Neither the Committee's Chairman nor its members were full-time and its functions were restricted to being basically advisory. It functioned as an intermediary body between the government and the universities. However, the Committee could not be very effective and was kept in abeyance for a few years till it was accepted by the Indian Government and 'University Grants Commission' (UGC) bill was passed in 1956.

The UGC Bill in Parliament

Dr. M.M. Das, Parliamentary Secretary to the Minister of Education introduced a Bill in Parliament on September 30, 1954 to make provision for the coordination and determination of standards in universities and for that purpose, to establish a UGC as a statutory body. Maulana Abul Kalam Azad introduced the statement of 'object and reason' on September 24, 1954. Both Houses of Parliament passed the Bill on March 3, 1956. The government then issued the notification and UGC became a statutory body with effect from November 5, 1956.

The Act sets forth the power and functions of the Commission under Article 12 as follows: It shall be the general duty of the

Commission to take, in consultation with the universities or other bodies concerned, all such steps as it may think fit for the promotion and coordination of university education and for the determination and maintenance of standards of teaching, examination and research in universities, and for the purpose of performing its functions under this Act, the Commission may -

A. Inquire into the financial needs of the universities
B. Allocate and disburse grants to universities established or incorporated by or under a Central Act for the maintenance and development of such universities or for any other general or specified purpose
C. Allocate and disburse such grants to universities for development purpose
D. Recommend to any university the measures necessary for the improvement of university education
E. Advise the central and state governments to allocate grants to universities for any general or specified purpose out of the Consolidated Fund of India or the state, as the case may be
F. Advise any authority, if required, on the establishment of a new university or expansion of activities of any existing university
G. Advise the central or any state government or university on any question which may be referred to the Commission by the Central or the State government or the University, as the case may be
H. Collect information on all matters relating to university education in India and abroad
I. Require a university to furnish it with such information as the case may be needed relating to the financial position of the university or the studies in the various branches of learning undertaken in that university; and perform such other functions as may be prescribed or as may be deemed necessary by the Commission for advancing the causes of higher education in India

The UGC Act of 1956 has been amended from time to time as situations have demanded by Parliament by Act No. 27 of 1970 (No.33

of 1972). It was further amended by the UGC Act, 1984 (No. 59 of 1984) and the UGC (Amendment) Act, 1985 (No. 70 of 1985).

The Radhakrishnan Commission

With the advent of India's independence from British rule, a University Education Commission was set up in 1948 under the chairmanship of Dr. S. Radhakrishnan. Its mandate was to report on university education and to suggest improvements and extension that was desirable both for the present and for the future requirements of the country. The University Education Commission recommended in its Report (1948-1949) the setting up of a Central University Grants Commission / Committee which, working through the Ministry of Education, would allocate sums made available by the Central Government in accordance with the special needs and merits of each university. It also considered it absolutely necessary to establish a greater coordination between the Central and State Governments.

The Radhakrishnan Commission felt that good governance of institutions for higher learning was possible if wide powers were given to the State Governments; yet initiative in public education needed to be taken by both the provincial and the central governments. However, coordination had to lie with the Centre to ensure that all states and union territories acted within certain limits and observed certain minimum standards. It was also necessary to ensure that gradually a coherent national policy would emerge on education. Joint planning by the Centre, States and Union Territories was needed in several areas. Therefore, it suggested that education should be placed in the *concurrent* list in the Constitution.

Education Commission (1964-66) Chaired by D.S. Kothari

Report of this committee made a realistic suggestion of phasing out the affiliating system. It suggested giving autonomy to some viable / credible colleges with critical potentials. Such autonomous colleges should eventually emerge as deemed Universities. Other suggestions of Kothari Commission include conferring autonomy to University Departments/Schools as well.

Since the inception of UGC, there have been continuous efforts to bring in holistic reforms in Indian Higher Education through Commissions and Committees: A list of important Commissions /

Committees constituted by the GOI and their terms of references are provided in Table 1.

Facilitated by the twelve 5-Year Plans, Indian Higher education has been dynamically evolving towards international standards. The most unassailable achievement is the growth rate of enrolment in higher

Table 1: Constitution of Committees / Commissions and their terms of reference on the subject of Higher Education in India

S. No.	*Name of the Committee / Commission*	*Year*	*Terms of Reference*
1	A. L. Mudaliar Committee	1967-68	Introduction of Healthcare Services in Universities
2	The P. Gajendragadkar Committee	1969	Governance of Higher Education Institutions
3(a)	P. B. Gai Committee	1969	Governance in Universities
3(b)	Rev. P. T. Chandi Committee	1969	Governance in Colleges
4	Rais Ahmed Committee	1971	Examinations Reforms in Universities
5	A. R. Wadia Committee	1972	Introduction of Centres of Advanced Studies and Research
6	Reservation Policy Committee	1973	Minimum qualifications for Appointment of Teachers in Universities and Colleges
7	V. S. Jha Committee	1974	Reviewing of the functioning of UGC
8	Madhuri R. Shah Committee	1982	Reviewing of the functioning of Central Universities
9	The Mehrotra Committee	1983	Pay revision Committee for Teachers in Universities and Colleges
10	Commission for National Policy on Education	1986	Policy Reforms on Indian Education
11	A Gnanam Committee	1990-91	Management and Governance of Higher Education Institutions
12	Punnayya Committee	1993-94	Funding of Higher Education Institutions
13	R. P. Rastogi Committee	1994-95	Pay-scales revision for Teachers of Colleges and Universities with 55% eligibility marks for appointment
14	Rajendar Sachar Committee	2005	Social, Educational and Economic Status of Muslim community
15	National Knowledge Commission (headed by Sam Pitroda	2005	Policy Reforms on Higher Education in India
16	Yash Pal Committee	2008	Renovation and Rejuvenation of Universities
17	Kasturi Rangan Committee	2017	New Educational Policy-2018

education as indicated by the National Gross Enrolment Ratio (GER) of 30.2% at the end of 12th Five Year Plan period, with about 30 million students through 730 universities and 4300 colleges of different nature. While we are successfully achieving the access and expansion requirement of higher education, the challenges have been in the areas of equity, quality and excellence in higher education. In spite of several

Higher Education Commission/Committees during the last 70 years after India's Independence, the agenda for reforms remain the same in the above challenging areas. It is to be seen whether the New Educational Policy under the Chairmanship of Kasturi Rangan being developed currently by Government of India will rejuvenate the Indian Higher education system!

Suggested Reading

1. Kaur, K. (2003) 'Higher Education in India (1781-2003)' published by University Grants Commission, New Delhi.
2. Muthiah, S (2006) 'History of University of Madras': *University News*: 44(36), 10-22 published by Association of Indian Universities, New Delhi.
3. Sharma, K. (2013) 'Sixty years of the University Grants Commission', published by University Grants Commission, New Delhi.

CHAPTER - 4

PROGRESSION OF HIGHER EDUCATION IN THE POST-INDEPENDENT INDIA

—*A. B. SHANBHAG*

Education, particularly the tertiary sector, is ever changing and ever expanding dynamic system, requiring to be assessed periodically to take stock of its achievements, failures, probable avenues to be adopted to make it beneficial enterprise for the society and the Nation at large. Therefore, it is natural that from time to time communiqués from the 'rulers' are issued based on the information on the scholarly reports of expert committees appointed by the federal or state Governments so as to orient the education system in right direction for the overall benefit of the denizens and the Nation in turn. When we look at the path of evolution of higher education in our country right from the days of rule of East India Company / Government of British India to the Government of Free post colonial Democratic Republic of India, reports of five Education/Knowledge Commissions listed hereunder can't escape the attention of anybody; they are the major milestones in the sojourn undertaken by the system. They are:

I. Woods Despatch (1854)

II. Radhakrishnan Commission (Indian University Education Commission, (1948-49)

III. Kothari Commission (Education Commission, 1964-66)

IV. Yash Pal Committee Report (Renovation and Rejuvenation of Higher Education, 2008-09)

V. Knowledge Commission of India (2005-2009)

I. Wood's Despatch (1854)

Though there are diagonally opposite views as to its cardinal influence on Indian education system as a whole, the Wood's despatch, a recommendatory letter of 19th July 1854 by Sir Charles Wood, the President, Board of Control of English, East India Company, sent to Lord Dalhousie, then Governor General of India is held at high esteem as the Magna Carta (Charta) of modern 'English' education in India. The synoptic specific recommendations in Wood's despatch are as follows.

- Setting up of Education Department in every province
- Opening of at least one Government School in every district
- Extending the Grant in aid to Affiliated Private Schools
- Training Indian natives, also in their mother tongue
- Establishment of Universities on the model of the London University in bigger cities like Bombay, Calcutta and Madras
- Making provision for a systematic method of education from primary level to the university level
- Supporting women education by the Government

If recommendations listed in Wood's Despatch, were to be implemented in their entirety they would have laid a uniform and irrefutable foundation of education across the length and breadth of the country. It is unfortunate that these recommendations were not implemented in entirety in letter or spirit. Some of the obvious shortcomings in the despatch and in its operations were: It had no reference to vocational or technical education. Secondly the elementary and primary education didn't get adequate attention of the Government compared to that of secondary and tertiary. Financial support didn't come through as desired either because of inadequacy of funds, or diversion of funds collected as education cess for other causes, or the stringent rules as to their allocation. Privately run institutions got step motherly treatment as to the grant in aid compared to missionary schools. Principle of religious neutrality embodied in the Despatch was thrown to winds and Christianity was indirectly forced upon the pupils. The state turned Nelson's eye towards issue of vernacular language as medium of instruction at primary stage, growth of local Indian languages and education of girl child. Some educationists feel that a finely crafted well designed policy on Education in the form of Wood's Despatch could have been instrumental in bestowing 'Right to Education' to Indians fairly early in colonial rule fell short in its synonymy as 'Magna Charta' of Indian Education, primarily because of faulty execution.

II. Radhakrishanan Commission (1948-49)

During the mid 20th century, when the world was struggling to wriggle out of treacherous recession following two World Wars, India was trying to overcome the impact of its long-drawn freedom struggle and also the trauma of partition that preceded its hard-earned freedom from colonial yoke. All the same the first national Government of free India lead by Prime Minister Jawaharlal Nehru adopted a policy with immaculate emphasis on education along with modern science and technology, agriculture with mega irrigation projects, and industrialization with heavy industries such as steel, chemicals, and manufactured products etc. In tune with this modern outlook, on the heels of freedom, in 1948, Government of India (GOI) instituted an Education Commission under the chairmanship of Oxford Professor S. Radhakrishnan to "report on Indian University Education and suggest improvements and extensions that may be desirable to suit present and future requirements of the country."

The commission consisted of 10 members, besides the Chairman in the form of well-known educationists and Education Administrators, few of them from abroad, to name a few Dr. Zakir Husain, Vice Chancellor, Aligarh Muslim University, Dr. A. L. Mudaliar, Vice Chancellor, University of Madras, Sir James Duff, Vice Chancellor, University of Durham, Dr. John Tigert, Former Commissioner of Education, USA, Dr. Meghanad Saha, Science Dean, University of Calcutta, and Dr. Tara Chand, Secretary and Education Advisor, GOI.

Activities of the Commission were given befitting momentum by inaugural address of Hon'ble Maulana Abdul Kalam Azad, then Education Minister (GOI) by appraising the Committee the intensions of the Government in regard to the purpose and the scope of inquiry. As a follow-up, 2900 copies of a comprehensive, well designed questionnaire covering all the aspects of terms of reference, were circulated to people with experience of university education or keeping interest in it such as members of Constituent Assembly, Premiers and Ministers of Provinces and States, Vice Chancellors of Universities, Directors of Public Instructions, Heads of Colleges, Heads of University Departments, Educationists and Rectors of Student Hostels. However, only six hundred responses with considerable inputs were received. The Committee also visited 27 university centres from 13th December 1948 to 19th July 1949, met all those who mattered in providing facts and necessary inputs to arrive at logical and practical recommendations.

The voluminous data gathered through responses to the questionnaires, and the personal interactions with the people at the university centres was analysed, deliberated and the findings were put in the final report of the Commission. The report ran in to a total of 700 pages having 18 chapters such as procedures, historical retrospect, aims of university education, teaching staff, standards of teaching, medium of instruction, examinations, student activities, women education etc. The main report covered 512 pages and gave a good coverage for the stages through which the education in India went through in ancient, medieval and colonial past in the chapter on historical retrospect before dwelling on its findings and specific recommendations.

A. General Observations

The Commission sensed deep awareness among the university community about the need of higher education for national growth, and also the uneasy sense of impeding inadequacies then existing in the system. It was rightly reflected that the democracy largely depends for its very existence on high standards in all forms of education - general, vocational and also professional. Therefore, it was implied that the universities must be able to produce learned men and women with ideas such as freedom of belief and expression, faith in reason and humanity, and deep obligation to promote human well-being. Further, the Commission recorded its recommendations on general education and professional education such as agricultural, commercial, engineering and medical separately.

B. Recommendations on General education

Graduation

With an eye on maintenance of higher standards of teaching certain steps were suggested. In the background of variations in the length of duration in various schooling stages in different states of the union, and also wide variety of nomenclature prevailing for these stages such as lower and higher primary, secondary, higher secondary, intermediate, pre-university etc, it was grossly suggested that the eligibility to admission to graduate courses in colleges or universities need be on completion of schooling for 12 years on the whole, including that in intermediate colleges.

Establishment of good number of vocational institutes also was suggested so as to divert adequate number of students towards vocational training after 10-12 years of schooling. To avoid overcrowding in universities maximum number of students in Arts and Science colleges was expected to be limited to 3000 in teaching-universities and 1500 in affiliated colleges.

In general education, the common practice of extreme specialization in intermediate and degree programs was recommended to be discontinued, without any further delay. The graduation courses in general education were expected to be developed appropriately so as to give the students the best possible acquaintance and mastery of the contents, methods of thinking and working in each field, in relation to other related fields.

Some additional expectations were tutorials in smaller batches to be integral part of teaching programs so as to enhance mental abilities of students rather than coaching them for facing exams. Improvement of university libraries, with larger grants, open access system, longer working hours, upgradation of science laboratories with better buildings, state of art equipment, and trained technicians were found to be absolutely essential.

Postgraduate studies and Research

Some of the major recommendations with respect to PG studies and research were:

- There should be uniformity in regulations for post graduate studies leading to M. A. and M. Sc. Degrees. A pass graduate should study at least for two years while a honours graduate should study for one year to complete the post graduate degree.
- The courses should include advance study of one special subject, training in methods of research, and laboratory work besides lectures.

- The admission to Ph. D. degree should be on all India basis and with great care. Tenure for Ph. D. degree should extend at least for two years. The candidate should have a grasp of his subject in 'breadth and depth' rather than be a 'narrow specialist'. Examination should include a thesis and viva-voce to test the candidate's 'general knowledge of whole field of the subject.
- Certain number of 'Research Fellowships' should be available in each university to be awarded to those candidates who have high degree of scholarship and competence to pursue research career.
- D. Lit. and D. Sc. degrees should be awarded on published work of outstanding quality and conspicuous originality.

To overcome then prevalent acute shortage of scientific man power and also quality teachers in science, recommendation was to train larger number of science students with the hope that we may get at least a few men of outstanding calibre in the stream. Some additional suggestions were

- Ministry of Education should institute large number of scholarships for bright students at the M.Sc. and Ph.D. stages with suitable mechanisms to select them and free-ships by way of "science talent search" process.
- Science departments of universities should be strengthened by the creation of additional professorships, readerships and lectureships. In selecting the personnel, emphasis should be on quality rather than on numbers.
- Fundamental research should be the primary concern of the universities, but they should not be precluded from taking up special applied problems concerning their own regions.
- Greater facilities should be provided for study and research in 'Border line"/ Interdisciplinary sciences like Biochemistry, Biophysics, Geochemistry, Geophysics etc.

Professional Education

Unlike earlier trend in the west, wherein theology, law and medicine were the only three recognised professions, with the passage of time many more disciplines such as engineering, architecture, dentistry, teaching and journalism entered the list. The commission nicely defined the professional education as against vocational education in the following words. Professional education is a process by which men and women prepare exacting, responsible service in the professional spirit. The term need be restricted to preparation for fields requiring well-informed and disciplined insight and skill of a high order. Less exacting preparation may be designated as vocational or technical education.

In consonance, the Commission dwelled on Agriculture, Commerce, Education, Engineering and Technology, Law and Medicine in the category of professional education. Some of the noteworthy recommendations made by the Commission are:

Agricultural education

The Commission was sensitive to the fact that India lived in villages, and it is this rural India that caters to the basic needs of food and fabric of the nation through agriculture. But because of heavy taxes and exactions during erstwhile rules, and as the National income didn't percolate to rural parts, the agrarian community languished in poverty and illiteracy. The Commission also felt promotion of literacy coupled with better and extensive agricultural education may lead to the prosperity of rural India and keep the bonds of rural folks with their profession intact, in turn the interest of the nation. Some of the prominent recommendations on agricultural education were as follows.

- Agricultural education be given as far as possible in rural setting, so that it includes direct participation and experience with agricultural life and practice
- The existing Agricultural colleges need be strengthened with infrastructure, better equipped labs, adequate staff and state of art curriculum inclusive of related areas such as agriculture credits and co-operatives.
- New agricultural colleges to be associated with rural universities, wherever possible.
- A widespread network of experimental farms may be established with the support from provincial and central support, where trained personnel are available and, the research

students get an opportunity to provide labour as first-hand experience besides their research work. All the rural educational institutions like elementary, secondary schools, colleges and rural universities, wherever possible be having their own experimental farms

- Indian Council of Agricultural Research (ICAR) need be the overall clearing house and coordinating body for all advanced Agricultural Research Centres, source of publications and publicity of disseminating material.
- A panel for Agricultural Education and Research shall function in UGC for apportioning and judicious utility of the available resources for the purpose.
- The UGC along with ICAR look in to merits of public policy involved in levying the cess on specific cash crops like cotton, sugar and jute as a source of research and, educational funds as against the block grants from UGC
- Careful inquiry be made as to the wisdom of rapidly developed and far ranging research on ocean resources as a possible means of speedier and augmenting support to the nation's food and fertilizer supply complementing and supplementing with the agricultural output.

Commerce

The Commission observed that the objectives of then existing courses in commerce were not clear as to whether they were intended to train students for professions like accountancy, banking or insurance or meant to raise graduates proficient in general principles of business organisation to take secretarial or junior administrative posts in commercial concerns. The commission also wondered in what way a commerce graduate at that point of time was better than the arts graduate who had studied economics, statistics and other allied subjects. Anyway, the commission suggested few specific recommendations listed below for improvement of the situation.

- A commerce student during graduate study be given opportunities for practical work in three or four different kinds of firms

- After graduation some of them be advised to specialise in particular professions like accountancy and receive the requisite practical training
- The training at master's degree be less bookish and, confined to comparatively a small number

Education (Teaching)

The Commission indeed lamented that it may take little longer for the general populace in the country to recognize that Education/ Teaching is also a profession by itself for which intensive preparation is necessary as in any other professions. The course structure then in Education with compulsory papers in the form of principle/theory of education, methods of teaching, history of education, school management and hygiene; practical teaching in the form of Criticism lessons and demonstration lessons along with the optional subjects was balanced and satisfactory in the eyes of Commission.

The graduate training in education/teaching was primarily to meet the requirements of secondary school teachers. The Commission recorded without any reservation that enrolment for training in education or teaching was more because of lack of better alternatives than out of wilful choice in most cases. One, if not the only reason for the scenario was said to be poor salary structure for the teachers in the sector, that failed to attract better talent.

In this background the commission recorded few concrete recommendations as listed below to improve the situation.

- The courses should be remodelled and more time given to school practice and more weight given to practice in assessing the students' performances. Suitable schools be used for practical training
- The bulk of a staff of the training colleges be recruited from people who have first-hand experience of school teaching
- Students be encouraged to proceed to the master's Degree only after some years of experience of teaching

Engineering and Technology Education

On the basis of the survey of the then existing Engineering and Technology institutions in the country, observations of the Commission in general were that in most of the cases equipment is insufficient, the staff small and underpaid, and courses of study too few and stereotyped. It further felt that yearly output of engineers was too small in comparison to the demands of the country growing out of the various schemes of industrialisation and development undertaken by GOI. In the light of these observations the recommendations were as follows:

- The existing engineering and technological institutes of the country should be regarded as national assets, and steps should be taken to improve their usefulness according to the recommendations of the Advisory Panel of Engineers and Technologists to be set up
- Increase the number of engineering schools of different grades particularly to train grade 4 and 5 technicians such as foremen, craftsmen, draftsmen, overseers, etc.
- Training should cover a larger number of fields and branches of engineering to meet the increasingly varied needs of the country. If there is unemployment among competent engineers, it is because too many are trained in some disciplines and too few in others.
- As effective engineering education requires works practice along with academic study, this be secured as work during vocational or as post-graduate works training, or as participation in work and study programme during the under graduate years.
- Wherever possible, the existing engineering and technological colleges be upgraded for PG training and research in selected subjects.
- Steps be taken to start without delay the higher technological institutes as recommended by the Higher Technological Education Committee, for training much needed engineer-scientists and design and development engineers
- In establishing new engineering colleges or institutes there be fresh, critical inquiry as to the types, of engineering service needed in India. Uncritical repetition and imitation of existing institutions here and abroad should be avoided. Especially consideration should be given to training which will prepare

students to become competent, self-reliant, and courageous to take initiatives to start new industries, even if on a very small scale.

Law

Some eminent practitioners of law and excellent judges appeared before the Commission and made valuable suggestions concerning the improvement in legal education. It further noted that law gave us great leaders and men in public service, conspicuous being Mahatma Gandhi. The commission also regretted that our colleges of law didn't hold a place of high esteem at home or abroad but wanted that the profession gets transformed in to one of profound scholarship and enlightened research. With this goal in view, some of the recommendations by the commission were the following:

- Three-year degree course in pre-legal and general studies be required for admission to law courses
- Three-year degree course in law be offered in special legal subjects, the last year to be given over largely to practical work, such as "apprenticeship in advocates' chambers"; that the staff shall be whole-time and part-time.
- The whole-time staff should teach largely in the fields of fundamental subjects and the part-time staff more largely in the fields of practical application and procedures.
- Law classes be scheduled only during the regular hours of teaching
- Opportunities for research be available in every law faculty, particularly in Constitutional Law, International Law, Administrative Law, Jurisprudence and our systems of Hindu and Muslim Law

Medicine

Medical Colleges were in existence even before the early universities in India came in to being in 1857 in three principal centres, Calcutta, Bombay, and Madras granting 'degrees'. But bulk of practitioners went through medical schools established in different parts of the country, granting diploma, of which some were maintained by State governments and others were in private control, especially missions. Those passing out of the schools were to serve as Medical Assistants/ Support staff and didn't have personal responsibility to treat any major ailment.

Apparently, the standards of medical degrees given by the Indian universities differed. Therefore, in 1931 Indian Medical Council was established with the objective of laying down minimum qualifications for teaching and practising. Another problem confronting the profession was to take in to account what should be the role of indigenous systems of medicine such as Ayurvedic and Unani practices, which were considered blindly traditional. Some of the inherent weaknesses of the systems were lack of concept of sanitation and aseptic conditions amongst the native healers and little or no scientific knowledge of anatomy or physiology. Taking all these aspects in to consideration the recommendations by the commission were:

- Maximum number of admissions to a medical college be 100, provided the staff and equipment is adequate
- All the departments of studies which require hospital facilities be located in a single campus
- There be 10 beds in the associated hospital per student admitted to a college
- Training in a rural centre be required both in the under-graduate and graduate stages
- Post-graduate training be offered in certain colleges, taking into account the personnel and the equipment essential for the purpose
- Public Health Engineering and Nursing be given greater importance
- Facilities for research in indigenous systems be provided
- History of Medicine with special reference to Indian systems be taught in the graduation course in Medicine

The Commission also introduced the idea of working on new professional disciplines such as Business Administration, Public Administration and Industrial Relations besides the conventional ones in Higher Education Institutes (HEIs) so as to train men and women to guide, manage, and conduct economic affairs in complex economic society.

Medium of Instruction

The Commission was well aware of the legitimately hurt National pride at the idea of English, an alien language occupying a dominating position in the education scene of the country. National opinion was flowing with increasing force in the direction of the replacement of English by an Indian language. The replacement of English by any other Indian language was also not an easy task primarily because of the greater diversity of languages in India than in any other country.

The Commission invested a vast amount of time and energy to arrive at solutions to this vexed issue and give balanced recommendations given below.

- Pupils at the higher secondary and university stages be made conversant, with three languages: the regional language, the Federal language and English; Higher education be imparted through the instrumentality of the regional language with the option to use, the Federal language as the medium of instruction either for some subjects or for all subjects
- Federal Language (Hindi with Devnagari script) be developed through the assimilation of words from various sources and the retention of words which have already entered into Indian languages from different sources, thereby avoiding the dangers of exclusiveness
- For the medium of instruction for higher education English be replaced as early as practicable by a modern Indian language
- Immediate steps, be taken for developing the Federal and Regional languages. Provincial Governments be required to take steps to introduce the teaching of the Federal language in all classes of higher secondary schools, in degree colleges, and in Universities.
- English, be studied in high schools and in the universities in order that we may keep in touch with the global living stream of ever-growing knowledge.

Examinations

The Commission recorded that the examinations as they have been functioning, have been recognised as one of the worst features of

Indian education. The Commission was convinced that if it must suggest one single reform in university education it should be that of the examinations. If examinations are necessary, a thorough reform of these is still more necessary. It was emphatic that valid, reliable, adequate objective examinations be introduced in the universities at the earliest possible time. They need be designed in such a way that their results should be helpful in choice of students, their counselling and guidance, measuring their progress, diagnosing present conditions and devising remedial measures and finally in assessing educational achievement. The two broad categories of examinations are Intelligence and Achievement Tests. Aptitude tests discover future possibilities while achievement tests reveal past attainment.

The Commission in general professed for the use of objective tests at length because of their multiple advantages such as objectivity, accuracy, and speed in administering the examination, evaluation and also unambiguous and noncontroversial results as against the tests with long answers or essays, more so for admission or entrance tests. But it didn't wish to create the impression that objective testing should necessarily rule out the essay-type of examination altogether. Some specific recommendations made by the commission are listed below.

- Each university should have a permanent full time Board of Examiners with a small staff of assistants who can do clerical and routine work.
- A battery of psychological and achievement tests, be developed for use with higher secondary school students for the final test at the end of twelve years of schooling. This will, together with other relevant information, serve the purpose of an admission examination to the 1st degree course at the university.
- A set of objective progress tests for guidance and for evaluating class room progress should also be developed immediately.

Some additional suggestions of the Commission to correct the evils then prevailing in the examination system were the following.

- A university degree is not required for administrative services at lower cadres. Special examinations for recruitment to the various services should be organized that are open to all.

- Due credit be given for class-work. One-third of the marks allotted to each subject be reserved for work done during the course of instruction and this be adopted forthwith in the teaching universities for UG and PG examinations.
- In view of three years involved for the first degree it is not desirable that all that work should be subjected to one examination at the end of the period. That would entail unnecessary mental strain to the students.
- Examiners should be selected with great care. No one should serve as an examiner in a subject which he has not taught for at least five years. Three years should be the limit of continuous service as an external examiner for the first-degree examination.
- The standards for success at the examination should, as far as possible, be uniform in the various universities and should be raised. It was suggested that a candidate should get 70% or more marks to secure a first class, 55 to 69% for a second and at least 40% for a third. The system of awarding grace-marks was recommended to be abolished for the first degree and all higher examinations.
- Viva-Voce examinations should be employed only for PG and professional degrees. They should be designed, however, to test the candidate's competence in the fundamentals of the field of study.

Students, Their Activities and Welfare

The opening statement of the section by the commission is a clear indication of pivotal importance attached by it to the student community in the education system as a whole.

"The student is not created for the university, but the university exists for the student and, therefore, it must spare no effort and omit no devices which may promote the fullest and most complete realization of the students' possibilities on all planes, physical, intellectual and spiritual". The statement speaks loudly as to what type of wholesome training the Commission desired for the students in our colleges and universities. Thus, the Commission also dwelt in finest detail on all those matters that ought to be taken care by the institutions of higher learning towards physical welfare of our young men and women. It also emphasized on the importance of sports, physical education, National Cadet Corps (NCC) and Social Cadet (NSS in present terminology).

Selection and Scholarships

- Admission to universities and colleges be based on merit without discrimination of any kind.
- In the 1st degree stage, the widest possible variety of courses should be offered to enable local students, qualified to benefit by an education, to have opportunities which would otherwise be denied.
- Scholarships may be awarded following examinations, on the basis of merit to gifted but financially needy students.

Health

- All students, both men and women, be required to take at no cost to themselves, a thorough physical examination at admission and periodically thereafter, at least once a year.
- All universities, with or without Medical Colleges must have hospitals and dispensaries for student service.
- Each university / college remote from a university centre shall have a Director of Physical Education with the status, pay and training comparable to heads of other departments.
- All physical education activities and courses of study to be under the Director of Physical Education.

National Cadet Corps (NCC) and Social Service

- Institutions which have not been allotted Units or Sub-Units of the Cadet Corps should be provided with one.
- The Centre should take over from the Provinces and States, the responsibility for the administration of the National Cadet Corps.
- The Centre should detail Regular Officers of the Army, Navy and Air Corps for instruction in the universities and colleges.

- There be manoeuvres in the summer in which Army and Air Units work together; that Naval Units take cruises in the summer.
- Enlistment in the Cadet Corps to be continued on a two-year, voluntary basis.
- The Social Service be encouraged and remain on a completely voluntary basis.

Hostels and Residence

- Universities establish reasonable standards for hostels, residence and corporate activities as a condition of college affiliation. These standards be enforced, and no affiliation be granted in the future until standards have been met
- All hostels be cosmopolitan in character and the present communal hostels be abolished.
- Playgrounds and corporate activities be convenient to students living in hostels, and also in off-campus lodges
- All lodges and off-campus residential units be rigidly inspected for sanitation, social desirability, location and other pertinent considerations.

University Unions, Discipline and Student Welfare

- University Unions be as free as possible from political activities.
- The Union be the principal centre of Student corporate activities and the federative link of all student organizations
- The Union be operated 'by students and for students' without interference of University authorities
- Students be encouraged to take interest in good governance, but not in party politics
- An office of Dean of Students, be set up in colleges and universities
- An Advisory Board of Students Welfare be in place in all universities

Women's Education

The Commission categorically stated that 'There cannot be an educated people without educated women'. Though general education for interesting and intelligent living and for citizenship in large part can be the same for men and women, Commission clearly held a strong view that 'though men and women are equally competent in academic work, and though many subjects are equally interesting and appropriate, it does not follow that in all things men's and women's education should be identical.' It also expressed dissatisfaction as adequate thought and planning has not gone in formulating the areas of disciplines fitting with the soft treading the women and making their education useful, rewarding and making them contented equal partners for the growth of learned society without making them bear the brunt of roughshod situations. Expected approach was to familiarize women with problems of home management and the skills needed to meet them in addition to provide equality of opportunity. Therefore, the report dwells on certain specific areas of specialisation suiting women like Teaching, Home economics, Nursing, and Fine Arts etc. The Commission was clearly for co-education and in no way precluded women from entering in to disciplines of their liking. The Specific recommendations on women education were as follows:

- The ordinary amenities and decencies of life should be provided for women in colleges. There should be no curtailment in educational opportunities for women, but rather a great increase.
- There should be intelligent educational guidance, by qualified men and women, to help women to get a clearer view of their real educational interests, to the end that they shall not try to imitate men but shall desire equally good education. Women's and men's education should have many elements in common but should not in general be identical in all respects, as is usually the case today.
- Women students in general should be helped to see their normal places in a normal society, both as citizens and as women and to prepare for it, and college programmes should be so designed that it will be possible for them to do so.
- Through educational counsel and by example the prevailing prejudice against study of home economics and home management should be overcome.

- Standards of courtesy and social responsibility should be emphasized on the part of men in mixed colleges.
- Where new colleges are established to serve both men and women students, they should be truly coeducational institutions, with as much thought and consideration given to the life needs of women as to those of men. Except as such colleges come into existence there are no valid criteria for comparing segregated education with coeducation.

Besides gross curricular framework, teaching programs keeping pace with futuristic national needs, student welfare, health, physical wellbeing, scholarship avenues for the meritorious and needy, gender equality with a conscious tilt so as not to push them in to rough shod life, the commission also concisely dealt with the wide range of corollary aspects relevant to higher education such as constitution, administration, and finance.

Constitution and Control

On the basis of the analysis of broad spectrum of institutions, like merely Affiliating Universities, Teaching Universities, Teaching and Affiliating Universities and likewise different types of colleges such as Constituent Colleges, Affiliating Colleges, Government Colleges and Private Colleges the Commission made clear recommendations, some being stern and firm towards promoting higher standards of education, in turn safeguarding the interests of stakeholders as listed:

- The university education be placed on the Concurrent list
- The concern of the Central Government with the universities be with regard to finance, coordination of facilities, adoption of national policies, ensuring minimum standards of efficient administration and liaison between universities and national research laboratories and scientific surveys etc.,
- There be no university of the purely affiliating type
- Government colleges be gradually transformed into constituent colleges of the universities
- Private colleges be recognised only on satisfying the university on the laid down conditions
- The number of colleges affiliated to a university be limited

- The aim of an affiliated college be to develop into a unitary university and later into a federative one

The Authorities of the University

The suggested broad frame of authorities and regulatory bodies of universities was to have: The Visitor (The Governor-General); the Chancellor (generally the provincial Governor); the Vice-Chancellor (a whole-time officer appointed); the Senate (Court); the Executive Council (Syndicate); the Academic Council; the Faculties; the Boards of Studies; the Finance Committee; and the Selection Committees.

Finance

The passage in the report quoted herein is a poignant revelation of the pathetic state of the financial position of universities in India at that point of time. "A careful perusal of the budget statements presented by the universities in India reveals the fact that the financial position of most of the universities is far from satisfactory. In most cases the universities are working on a, deficit budget and in all cases, it is seen that the revenue from the different sources is hardly sufficient to meet the average present needs of the universities, and in no case are there sufficient funds either for expansion or for improvement in the many directions needed".

While the finances of a university were largely drawn from endowments, from examination fees, tuition fees and grants, the affiliated colleges didn't generally derive any financial assistance from the universities directly. The major source, the endowments, at times liberal from provincial rulers and leading industrial houses also failed to meet the requirements owing to downward interest rates on the endowments.

The financial assistance given to affiliated colleges varied from province to province; in some it amounted to 50 per cent of the salaries of sanctioned posts but in some provinces no grants were given by the Government to the private colleges. Besides many of the colleges, especially private ones treated the institutions as the commercial ventures even at the cost of dismal salary packages to teachers, so as to make adequate profits.

The GOI constituted the University Grants Committee (Later named as University Grants Commission) to advise on grants to be given to Central Universities. At one time it was proposed that the University Grants Committee established by the Government of India should also be responsible for the grants to be made to other universities, endorsed also by the Conference of Inter-University Board. In this background, the recommendations in a nutshell of the Commission to ameliorate the situation were as under:

- The State should accept its responsibility for the financing of higher education.
- The aid to private colleges should be for buildings and equipment as also for the recurring expenditure, the latter to be on a uniform basis, say half of the present teachers' salaries and a third of other approved expenditure.
- Steps be taken to amend Income-tax Laws to encourage donations for educational purposes
- Additional grants be made to colleges and universities to enable them to give effect to our recommendation
- The Government should contribute an additional annual amount of about ten Crores for the development of university education during the next quinquennium.
- University Grants Commission be set up for allocating grants

Following the nascent independence of the country from colonial rule after a long-drawn struggle and sacrifices of the leaders and the masses, it was but natural for the early Governments to strive to lead the country to economic independence, increase in general prosperity, effective democracy, liberation from the distinctions of cast and creed, rich and poor and the rise in level of culture. Naturally, it was not any surprise in Commission's perception that right type of education can only be a powerful weapon to accomplish all these successfully.

III. Kothari Commission (Education Commission 1964-66)

Towards the end of the Third Five Year Plan, Government of India felt a need to hold a comprehensive review of the educational system with a view to initiating a fresh and more determined effort at educational reconstruction, and hence the Education Commission (1964-66) was formed to advise the Government on the 'national pattern of education' and on the general principles and policies for the development of education 'at all stages and in all aspects'.

The GOI constituted a Commission in 1964, to advise the Government on the national pattern of education under the Chairmanship of Dr. D. S. Kothari, Chairman of UGC. The commission had a team of 14 members, four of them being overseas educationists, a member secretary and an associate secretary with comprehensive terms of reference from primary to tertiary stages. The Commission started functioning from 2nd October 1964 and submitted its report on 29th June 1966, following extensive data gathering and deliberations.

In the process, the Commission set up twelve Task Forces to work on School Education, Higher Education, Technical Education, Agricultural Education, Adult Education, Science Education and Research, Teacher Training and Teacher Status, Student Welfare, New Techniques and Methods, Manpower, Educational Administration and Educational Finance. In addition, it set up seven Working Groups to work in depth on areas like Women's Education, Education of Backward Classes, School Buildings, School-Community Relations, Statistics, Pre-Primary Education and School Curriculum.

True to the comprehensive terms of reference on education as a whole, the Commission seems to have not only succeeded in putting the entire educational program on a unified pan-India frame, but also indicating deadlines for implementation of certain steps within specific earmarked five-year plans giving adequate time margins for changes to fall in line.

The Guiding Principles for Educational Reconstruction

The following are the core principles on which the Commission heavily leaned for guiding educational reconstruction.

- Developing unified educational pattern of structure across the nation
- Making science a basic component of education and culture
- Making work-experience an integral part of general education
- Vocationalisation of education, especially at the secondary school level, to meet the needs of industry, agriculture and trade; and

- Improvement of scientific and technological education and research at the university stage with special emphasis on agriculture and allied sciences.

The Educational System - Structure

The Commission was of the firm opinion that if there is uniformity in the educational pattern and an extension in the total period of schooling, it will be possible to bring about an upsurge in the attainment of better standards. The approach was of considerable importance and merited close examination in view of the wide range variations that existed in the structure and pattern of education among the States and the union territories across the nation.

Earlier report of the Secondary Education Commission (1952-53), prescribed a national pattern of school classes covering eleven years- five years of lower primary, three years of upper primary and three years of higher secondary classes. This was to be followed by a three-year course for the first degree in arts and science and a further two-year course for the second degree. The Education Commission visualized a flexible educational structure covering:

- A pre-school stage of one to three years;
- A primary stage of 7-8 years divided into two sub-stages a lower primary stage of 4 or 5 years and a higher primary stage of 3 years;
- A lower secondary or high school stage of 2-3 years in general education or of 1-3 years in vocational education;
- A higher secondary stage of 2 years of general education or 1-3 years of vocational education;
- A higher education stage having a course of three years or more for the first degree, followed by courses of varying durations for the second or research degrees.
- The first 10 years of schooling, covering primary and secondary stages shall provide a course of general education without any kind of specialization.
- The primary stage shall be preceded, wherever possible, by pre-primary education of one to three years; The age of admission to class I will ordinarily be not less than 6+ years;

- The commission envisaged a 20 percent dropout after the primary stage
- Likewise the commission envisaged that around 20 percent may step out of the stream of general education into different vocational courses whose duration may range from 1-3 years;
- Remaining shall continue further in the stream of general education;
- 10 years of school education will be followed by all external examination.
- No attempt of specialization should be made till class X.
- The idea of upgrading secondary schools to the higher secondary status to be abandoned.
- The pre-university, intermediate or junior college courses should be transferred from higher education to school education in a period of 10 years (1966-75).

Vocationalisation at the Higher Secondary Stage

The Commission emphasized the need to vocationalise higher secondary education and to expand the vocational courses to cover about half of the total initial enrolment in the education. It suggested organizing a large variety of terminal courses varying in duration from 1-3 years. They need to include courses for the training of primary and pre- primary teachers; courses conducted by the industrial training institutions for different trades for which the completion of studies in class X should be the minimum qualification; courses in agriculture and industry which will train the middle level of personnel needed; courses for training paramedical / health personnel; courses for secretariat work; and courses in home science. In short, the higher secondary stage should be of two years and be located exclusively in the schools and steps to be taken to implement this reform through a phased programme spread over the next 20 years (1966-85); As a first step in this direction, the pre-university course, irrespective of its duration, should be transferred from the colleges to the schools on a high priority basis within the next 10 years.

Reorganization at the University Stage

The duration of the first-degree course was recommended to be not less than three years. Further it was suggested that strong 'graduate schools' in some universities may provide a three-year M.A. /M.Sc. / M.Com, and also degree courses in certain subjects. For the sake of convenience, these courses may be designated as honours courses or they may be given some other suitable name. It was felt that if they are properly organized and a careful selection of students is made, they will be able to produce excellent personnel for the teaching faculty and for high-grade research.

Utilization of Facilities

It was generally agreed that the facilities in our educational system, deficient as they were, are not utilized to their full advantage. There is much that can be done to improve standards even in existing circumstances by lengthening the school days, increasing the number of working days, curtailing long vacations and so on.

Medium of Instruction and Development of Regional Languages

With respect to regional languages the committee opined that the energetic development of Indian languages and literature is a *sine qua non* for educational and cultural developments. The commission advocated taking steps to adopt regional languages, already in use as media of education at the primary and secondary stages, as well as at university stages.

Furthermore, the commission suggested that at the secondary stage, the State Governments should adopt, and vigorously implement, the three-language formula which includes the study of a modern Indian language, preferably one of the southern languages, apart from Hindi and English in the Hindi-speaking States, and of Hindi along with the regional language and English in the non-Hindi speaking States. Every effort should be made to promote thc development of Hindi as the link language across the nation.

Recommendations on General Aspects of Educational Reconstruction

Excerpts of important resolutions put out by the GOI following the Report of the Education Commission for educational reconstruction are as shown below:

(1) The educational system must produce young men and women of character and ability committed to national service and

development. Enough efforts should be made for the early fulfilment of the Directive Principle under Article 45 of the Constitution seeking to provide free and compulsory education for all children up to the age of 14.

(2) It will be advantageous to have a broadly uniform educational structure in all parts of the country. The ultimate objective should be to adopt the 10+2+3 pattern, the higher secondary stage of two years being in schools, colleges, or both according to local conditions.

(3) Strenuous efforts should be made to equalize educational opportunity. The education of girls should receive emphasis. More intensive efforts are needed to develop education among the backward classes and especially among the tribal people. Educational facilities for the physically and mentally handicapped children should be expanded.

(4) The school and the community should be brought closer through suitable programmes of mutual service and support. The students should avail opportunity for work-experience and national service, by participation in meaningful and challenging programmes of community service.

(5) With a view to accelerating the growth of the national economy, science education and research should receive high priority. Science and mathematics should be an integral part of general education till the end of the school stage.

(6) Special emphasis should be placed on the development of education supporting the needs of agriculture and industries. There should be at least one agricultural university in every State.

(7) Immediate steps should be taken for the production of high quality textbooks for schools and universities. Frequent changes of textbooks should be avoided.

(8) A major goal of examination reforms should be to improve the reliability and validity of examinations and to make evaluation a continuous process aimed at helping the student to improve his level of achievement rather than at 'certifying' the quality of his performance at a given moment of time.

(9) The number of whole-time students to be admitted to a college or university department should be determined with reference to the laboratory, library and other facilities and to the strength of the staff. Centres of 'advanced' study should be strengthened and a small number of 'clusters of centres' aiming at the highest possible standards in research and training should be established.

(10) The liquidation of mass illiteracy is necessary. Teachers and students should be actively involved in organizing literacy campaigns, especially as part of the social and National Service Program.

(11) The success of all education endeavours ultimately depends on the quality of teachers' personal qualities and character, his educational qualifications and professional competence. Teachers' emoluments and other service conditions should be adequate and satisfactory, having regard to their qualifications and responsibilities.

(12) The universities and colleges should assist the secondary schools in improving their efficiency. For example, each college can be functionally related to many secondary schools in the neighbourhood and provide extension services and guidance to them to improve their standards. A similar programme for the colleges themselves could be developed through the universities. The universities can conduct special diploma courses, for improving the competence of either pre-service or in-service secondary teachers. These can preferably be correspondence courses, requiring only short-term personal attendance.

(13) Rural areas have about 65,000 higher primary schools and about 360,000 lower primary schools. In other words, in a rural area having a radius of five to ten miles, there are: one secondary school, about five higher primary schools and 28 lower primary schools. The total number of teachers may be about 80 to 100. This is a fairly small and manageable group which can function in a face-to-face relationship as a functional 'school complex' with mutual interaction within easily

accessible distance for the benefit of education system as a whole.

IV. Yash Pal Committee Report (2008-09)

The Ministry of Human Resource Development (MHRD) constituted a Committee to review the functions of statutory bodies like UGC and AICTE in the wake of changes in Higher Education and Technical Education through its letter dated 28th February 2008 with a team of 24 members including the Chairman, Prof. Yash Pal, former Chairman of UGC. Subsequently, on the suggestion of the Committee, MHRD renamed the committee as the Committee to advise the Government of India on '*Renovation and Rejuvenation of Higher Education*' through its letter dated14th October 2008.

The Committee put its report primarily in three major sections. The first section dealt with the '*Idea of a university*'; the second '*Challenges of the higher education sector*' recorded problems faced by the sector because of the decisions of the past, leading to unwanted fragmentation of the system incapacitating it to deliver the goods for the national good in a globally competitive scenario; and the third, '*Recovering the idea of university: a roadmap*' outlined solutions towards renovation and rejuvenation of higher education sector justifying the terms of reference to the Committee.

The Committee defined idea of a University thus: *"A university is a place where new ideas germinate, strike roots and grow tall and sturdy. It is a unique space, which covers the entire universe of knowledge. It is a place where creative minds converge, interact with each other and construct visions of new realities and established notions of truth challenged in the pursuit of knowledge"*. The quote precisely puts up the notion that must have been at the back of the collective mind of the learned Committee all through its sojourn in crafting its remedies towards fulfilling the goals ascribed to it.

Challenges in Higher Education

The committee considered the following eight aspects as the major challenges in the higher education sector.

1. Cubicalization: The conventional universities are centres where there is scope to learn and do research in whole range of

disciplines. It is also known that often, the cutting-edge research comes from interdisciplinary fringe areas where more than one disciplines meet and merge. However, as it happens most of the time, there are invisible walls between disciplines. Universal approach to knowledge demands that boundaries of disciplines be porous and scholars be constantly on guard against the tendency towards 'cubicalization' of knowledge. But of late in our country more and more universities with unitary disciplines such as Law University, Health University, and Technical University are coming up with least scope for day to day interdisciplinary interactions routinely possible within the multidisciplinary university campuses.

2. Distances and Disconnects: Some universities have remained to be centres for conducting examinations and awarding the degree certificates for professional courses such as medicine and engineering, but ironically not having powers to determine whether the institutions that claim to produce professionals like engineers and doctors have the wherewithal to do so. Nor they have any say in designing academic programs in professional courses because of control of independent discipline specific statutory bodies such as All India Council of Technical Education (AICTE) and Indian Medical Council (IMC) etc.
3. Divide between Research Centres and Universities: Historically the universities were considered to be the centres wherein teaching and research go hand in hand. With the passage of time, teaching and research have come to be separate activities. While universities remained to be the centres to teach and examine masses, more and more elite research institutions were created, where researchers had no occasion to interact with the young minds being trained in teaching institutions. The Committee opined that it will be beneficial if all premier research institutions such as National Chemical Laboratory (NCL), National Physical Laboratory (NPL), Indian Space Research Organisation (ISRO), Centre for Cellular and Molecular Biology (CCMB) etc get connected

with the universities in their vicinities, thereby creating opportunities to their research scientists and manpower to avail teaching opportunities in teaching institutions. At the same time, young and energetic minds in these teaching institutions will be benefitted by the research milieu and the inquisitive minds of researchers thereby creating a win-win situation for intelligentsia.

During the early years of independent India, national leaders and planners with their long-range foresight, established institutions like IITs and IIMs outside the purview of traditional university structure to give them a free play so as to be able to generate and groom excellent engineering and managerial pool for nation building. With the bestowed autonomy, the institutions succeeded to guard zealously, contributed to a large degree to their impeccable success. The Committee ardently felt that a rethinking may be necessary as to such isolation in the form of insulated isles of unitary discipline institutions away from the mainstream universities, and wondered whether this will be conducive for the interdependent wellbeing of the system in the long run.

4. Mushrooming of Deemed Universities: Provision of 'Deemed University' was primarily intended with a noble cause for the institutions, unique and distinct in character to be able to enjoy a university status without losing their distinct character and autonomy. But some private institutions adopted the 'deemed-to-be university route' to get degree granting powers. In 35-year period between 1956 and 1990, while only 29 institutions were in the said category, rose to a whooping 99 within a period of 15 years that followed. Many of these were not established solely for the educational purpose, and some of them went to the extent of declaring 'guaranteed' degrees including Ph. D. for a price.
5. Teacher Education and Vocational Education: As on date, partially the teachers' training and the entire vocational training were not in the purview of colleges and universities. It was felt that teacher education involving curricular framework and imparting communication and assessment skills to teachers

at all levels need be under university control, instead of limiting it to teachers at secondary school level and above, owing to its significant role in shaping the society through well trained teaching community. Secondly, though vocational training post-matriculation or pre-university stages being in practice for decades, neither the quality push nor the quality up gradation with changing skill requirements with advancing times had taken place.

6. Private-Commercial Provides: For quite some time in our country, private enterprises evinced interest in opening the higher education institutions, especially professional colleges such as medical and engineering colleges, of late the universities also. Though, it may not be auguring well to paint all private initiatives with the same paint and the brush, Committee Report gave a grim and dismal picture of some of the privately run Professional institutions.

   Many private institutions charge exorbitant fees, beyond the prescribed norms in the form of many kinds of levy, not accounted for by vouchers and receipts, and are often unable to provide even minimum competent faculty strength. The non- affordability of the programs of such institutions to a clear majority of eligible students was a matter of public concern. In many private educational institutions, the teachers were appointed at the lowest possible cost, and were treated with scant dignity, thereby turning away competent persons from opting for the teaching profession. Thus, all these anomalies persisted in many private institutions as there are no policies or guidelines to measure the competence of private investors in starting and managing a technical institution other than the requirement that it should be registered as a non-profit or charitable trust or society. Most decisions on admission of students in the management quota in private institutions fell under the control of family trusts or societies. Specific studies were expected regarding the sources of funds utilized by such family trusts or societies as there are allegations that such funds are either unaccounted wealth from business and political enterprises or from the capitation fees charged from the students in addition to a plethora of unexplained fees charged whimsically by the managements. Therefore, no doubt that the participation of the private sector need be encouraged in the process of doubling of the higher education capacity from the present level, but at the same time, it must be emphasized that governments cannot afford to abandon the responsibility for further augmentation of the existing capacity entirely to the private sector.

7. Foreign Universities: Universities are expected to function in an area with organic links with the society geographically, socially and culturally, and then only they can do the justice to the cause of education. If they start functioning as extension counters in foreign countries, they may not be doing as best, as expected. The universities from abroad, not known in their own countries if get licences to open their 'shops' in India would end up in siphoning profits to their parent institutions, if not, to the share holders of the enterprise. However, Committee had no reservation if any, that the internationally known universities intend to establish universities in India, provided they gave Indian Degree and functioned as per the rules and regulations applicable to the Indian universities.
8. Need for Rehabilitating Professional Education in the University: Over a period, professional education has been segregated from universities and the medical and engineering colleges or institutes have been functioning as isolated islands insulated from general university setup. As a result, the universities have merely remained to be degree granting and certification authorities with regard to these professions. In Committee's view these actions caused substantial damage to the university system and so also to the professional education. The new trend to establish 'stand alone' universities in restricted and narrow areas like law, information technology, pharmacy, catering, yoga, music and fashion technology etc, is the antithesis of required interdisciplinary cooperation promoting interactions for the growth of knowledge and cutting edge research. Furthermore, over fifteen different statutory agencies such as All India Council of Technical

Education (AICTE), Medical Council of India (MCI), Bar Council of India (BCI), Council of Architecture (COA), Indian Nursing Council (INC), Pharmacy Council of India (PCI), Distance Education Council (DEC) besides University Grants Commission (UGC) are entrusted with the responsibility of establishment and monitoring of performance of a large number of professional institutions in the country. The regulatory provisions of various acts are substantially different from one another, as they were established at different periods of time by different legislations. Further, the overall responsibilities for the entire higher education system assigned to UGC were not validated in the provisions of other acts. This has lead to very little coordination among the statutory bodies in respect of degree durations, approval mechanisms, and accreditation process etc., pushing the regulatory bodies in to legal battles ending up in embarrassing situations. Considering all these aspects, the Committee was of the strong view that professional institutions are returned to universities in a complete administrative and academic sense by the abolition of intermediary bodies set up to issue licenses to professional colleges alone, and to inspect them.

Recommendations for Rejuvenating the Higher Education

In the background of challenges faced by the higher education in the recent past as reflected in concise form in foregoing account, the Committee chalked out specific recommendations for renovation and rejuvenation of this apex sector of education. Some significant recommendations are listed below:

(1) All universities must be teaching-cum-research universities. All research bodies must connect with universities in their vicinity and create teaching opportunities for their researchers

(2) There is a need to expose students at the undergraduate level to various disciplines like humanities, social sciences, aesthetics, irrespective of the discipline they would like to specialise subsequently

(3) All syllabi should require teachers and students to apply what they have learnt in their courses, on studying a local situation,

issues or problems. There should be sufficient room for the use of local data and resources to make the knowledge covered in the syllabus come alive as experience. Universities must study areas that are relevant in their immediate social and natural milieu and create knowledge bases in those areas

(4) It should be mandatory for all universities to have undergraduate programs. All teachers in universities must teach at the undergraduate level also.

(5) There should be no discrimination between Central and State funded universities. All benefits extended to Central Universities must also be extended by State Governments to the State universities and the Centre must incentivise the States to do so.

(6) National tests like the GRE must be organised round the year. Students from all over India must be allowed to take the tests as many times as they like, and their best score can be sent to the universities for admission.

(7) Urgent measures are needed to attract good people who enjoy teaching and research back to the university and offer them a positive and motivating environment

(8) Teacher training for all levels of school education (from primary to higher secondary) must be carried out by institutions of higher educations. The absence of university-level interest in teacher training has resulted in poor academic quality. Similarly, all vocational institutions must also be part of universities.

(9) All professional institutions must be part of a comprehensive university in a complete administrative and academic sense. We must abolish intermediary bodies that have been set up solely to issue licenses to professional colleges alone and inspect them. This will also help new interdisciplinary courses and research to evolve in the comprehensive universities. We must prevent isolation of study of engineering or management.

(10) To double higher education capacity, we need all three kinds of universities: state-funded and run universities, private universities and those funded and run by public-private

partnerships. All of them should work efficiently overseen by a transparent regulatory mechanism.

(11) Private degree-granting universities must not be confined to select areas like technology, medicine, management, finance etc. They must be required to be comprehensive universities covering the arts, social and natural sciences too.

(12) There must be tight regulation of private universities in terms of auditing of accounts, payment of minimum salaries to teachers, certain percentage of seats reserved for meritorious students who are also to be provided scholarships etc.

(13) Granting of Deemed University status should be put on hold. All existing Deemed Universities are to be given three years to shape up, failing which their Deemed University status is to be withdrawn.

(14) If the best of foreign universities (amongst the top 200 in the world) want to come to India, they should be welcomed. Such institutions should award an Indian degree and be subject to all the rules and regulations that would apply to any Indian university.

Effective Governance of Higher Education System

The Yash Pal committee unambiguously opined that we need to improve governance of universities by developing expertise in educational management and, avoid burdening good academics with administrative chores. We must have a separation between academic administration and overall management (including fund raising). State governments must abandon the trend of appointing civil servants as university administrators.

We need a *de novo* regulatory body - the National Commission for Higher Education and Research (NCHER) under which the various functions of the existing regulatory agencies would be subsumed. The NCHER would be an autonomous body created by making a suitable amendment to the Constitution, accountable only to the Indian parliament and drawing its budgetary resources from the Ministry of Finance. It would have a seven-member board with a full-time Chairperson. Of the seven members, one would be an eminent professional from the world of industry and one with the background of a long and consistent social engagement. All other five members would be academic people of eminence, representing broad areas of knowledge. The status of the Chairperson of the commission should be analogous to that of the Chief Election Commissioner and that of the members should be comparable to the Election Commissioners. The Commission will be independent of all ministries of the GOI. It will have the autonomy to hire talent at various levels within and outside the government. It will also have the autonomy to define the compensation of its employees.

Given the federal nature of our country and the role of states in education, there must be Higher Education Councils (HECs) in the states which will co-ordinate with the NCHER, to allow different institutions created and funded by the Centre and States to grow on equal footing.

There should be a fast-track statutory mechanism in place for the adjudication of disputes between teachers, employees and management of institutions and universities in respect of matters concerning service conditions, as well as in matters of disputes relating to fee, admissions etc. A suitable law could be enacted to establish a National Education Tribunal along with State Education Tribunals or appropriate number of Benches of the Apex Tribunal for such adjudications.

The NCHER should galvanize research in the university system through the creation of a National Research Foundation. It should identify the best 1,500 colleges across India to upgrade them as universities and create 'clusters of other potentially good colleges' to evolve as universities.

V. National Knowledge Commission of India (2005-2009)

National Knowledge Commission (NKC) of India was an Indian think tank, primarily launched to evolve policies and advise the prime minister on the reforms to be undertaken in education sector, research institutions and intellectual property legislations such that the country attains competitive edge in the knowledge-based economy in the 21st century, globally recognised as 'Knowledge Century'.

NKC was constituted drawing eight members from leading knowledge dependent sectors such as universities, industrial concerns, research institutes, and information & communication arena headed by Mr. Satyanarayan Gangaram Pitroda popularly known as *Sam Pitroda* a technocrat and former adviser to late Prime Minister Rajiv Gandhi who led the revolution of computerisation and telecommunication access in the country. NKC was commissioned on 13th June 2005 by the inaugural address by then Prime Minister Dr. Manmohan Singh. Initially earmarked tenure of 3-years for the Commission was extended by another year, with an intension that the Commission could take the good job done by it to the logical conclusion. Apart from reports and the advises tendered by the commission to the Prime Minister on annual basis, it's final comprehensive report as published by Govt of India in March 2009. The terms of reference made to the commission were to evolve policies and plans towards:

- Building excellence in the educational system to meet the knowledge challenges of 21st century
- Promoting creation of knowledge in science and technology laboratories
- Improvement in the management institutions engaged in Intellectual Property Rights
- Promoting knowledge applications in Agriculture and Industry
- Promoting knowledge capabilities in making Government an effective, transparent and accountable service provider.

The Commission formed working groups drawing the experts, conducted relevant surveys, held workshops and seminars, deliberated the issues and formulated the recommendations and policies within the paradigm of: *Access to knowledge, Knowledge concepts, Creation of knowledge, Knowledge applications* and, *Delivery of services.*

'Affordable, quality education for all those who deserve' is the approach adopted by all knowledge-based economies to equip their human resource with requisite knowledge ensuring societal progress and economic prosperity. Hence, while dwelling on educational policy the NKC was sensitive to stick to guiding principles of 'access, excellence and equity'.

Here, I have confined to important recommendations pertaining to education made by the Commission which are given below:

(1) Right to Education: As per the 86th constitutional amendment act, right to education is a fundamental right. To provide

advantage of this amendment, the Commission advocated a Central Legislation affirming right to education so that universal access to quality education to all Indian children up to standard VIII or age of 14 becomes a reality.

(2) English Language: Without getting in to vexed issue of medium of instruction NKC strongly recommended that, English being an international language becomes a determinant of access to knowledge so also to educational and employment opportunities, it need be taught in schools as a language along with first language right from first standard. The need to reform the pedagogy of English language teaching and suitable training of the English language teachers was emphasised.

(3) Access to quality education: To provide access to good school education at elementary and so also secondary stage, NKC suggested major expansion in number of these schools and so also upgradation of their quality as they lay the foundation to the education process, as a whole.

(4) Vocational Education and Training (VET): NKC felt that it is necessary to ensure a robust regulatory and accreditation framework, along with proper certification of VET. As only 7% of the skilled labour force is working in formal sector, a partnership between public and private sector was envisaged towards VET upgradation strategies, so that productivity potential of bulk of our skilled and semiskilled work force is enhanced for benefit of all.

(5) Higher Education: NKC recommendations centred on expansion, excellence and inclusion and increase in General Enrolment Ratio to above 15 by 2015. This was believed to be possible by increased public spending and private participation and philanthropic contributions. Another cardinal suggestion was creation of 1500 universities. Establishment of independent Regulatory Authority for Higher Education (IRAHE) functioning at arm's length from all stakeholders. Regular curricular revisions, Course credit systems, adequate reliance on internal assessment, and encouraging research were some of the measures indicated by NKC for attaining

excellence. It also stressed the need for ensuring that all deserving students get access to higher education irrespective to their economic background and affordability.

(6) Professional Education: A radical recommendation of NKC pertains to replacing existing independent regulatory bodies by discipline- based subgroups unified under a common regulator for all professional streams- medical, legal, management, and engineering with a greater autonomy for institutions in adopting contemporary curricula, examinations and research programs.

(7) Open and Distance Education: Owing to limitations on providing physical infra structure principally in terms of adequate space in urban areas, the commission felt that around one fifth of enrolment can be under open and distance education system. Such a system will primarily depend on ICT base, and hence dependent on ICT infra structures, web based common open resource, credit bank and National Testing Service. Production of quality content and leveraging global open educational resource is essential to enhance the efficacy of the system.

The present Chapter provides brief summary and major highlights of the various education committee reports. For more details, one must read the original reports that are indeed very thought provoking and scholarly. They also make enjoyable reading. These reports should have been taken seriously and the recommendations implemented fully. However, this has not happened. At best they are considered partly, as per the wisdom of the Central Government in vogue when such reports were commissioned. Undoubtedly, India needs a holistic approach for overhaul of the higher education system. It also needs courage to initiate certain steps for which there will be enormous opposition. After all it is easy to do than undo. As everyone knows by now that the country is going to have around 35% of its population representing youth. Therefore, mechanisms are needed to channelize and harness their energy for meaningful utilization. Otherwise, these young men and women without proper education and avenues for decent living can become a liability and antisocial elements. Hence, we need to tread the path rather carefully and urgently. In this process, the wisdom enshrined in the various education commission reports can come handy.

Suggested Reading

1. The report of the University Education Commission, Volume I, Ministry of Education, Government of India, 1962.
2. General Problems, Education and National Development, Report of the Education Commission, 1964-66, National Council of Educational Research and Training, 1970
3. Report of the Committee to Advise on Renovation and Rejuvenation of Higher Education. http://mhrd.gov.in/sites/upload_files/mhrd/files/document-reports/YPC-Report.pdf
4. Dahiya, B. S. (2009). The Yash Pal Committee Report: A review, Mainstream, 157(39)
5. https://en.wikipedia.org/wiki/Wood's_despatch
6. http://www.publishyourarticles.net/knowledge-hub/education/importance-of-woods-despatch-to-educational-system-of-colonial-india/5346/
7. https://en.wikipedia.org/wiki/Kothari Commission
8. National Knowledge Commission, Report to the Nation 2006-2009, National Knowledge Commission, Govt. of India, New Delhi

CHAPTER - 5

TERRAIN UNDER SHADOW: TEACHING SOCIAL SCIENCES AT COLLEGE

— *R. S. DESHPANDE*

International Social Science Council recently brought out an exhaustive report titled "World Social Science Report (WSSR)", bringing together a kaleidoscopic view of Social Sciences world over. An interesting view is expressed in the preface of the report by the President of the International Social Science Council Professor Gudmund Hernes that "*Never before have the social sciences been so influential: economists run Ministries of Finance, Political Scientists staff public administrations and MBAs run corporations. Indeed social scientists have not just entered boardrooms, but since Kinsey also bedrooms. Never before have social scientists, had such an impact on public opinion, in terms of both how the world is seen and how it is acted upon. Terms that were once specialised-for example, 'competitive advantage' or 'self-fulfilling prophecy'-the media have entered everyday language*" (UNESCO, 2010, p. vi). It is known fact that in the overall knowledge domain Social Sciences did not receive equal importance as that of Physical or Natural Sciences. The World Social Science Report brought this out and besides dealing with many facets of social sciences in an effort to bring out the essence of the increasing demand of social sciences in every field of human activity. WSSR also emphasised the homogenising and globalising social sciences. The irregular internationalisation and unevenness within social sciences are also indicated as matters of concern. It is not surprising that among the plethora of contributors to the report we can see only one Indian contribution. This is the most expected possibility as in Indian context we always have strong hierarchy among knowledge disciplines, something like differentiated levelled respect in the domain of knowledge. In the cultural ethos of India we have the strong presence of hierarchical caste system, but that seems to have percolated in the branches of knowledge where some of the sciences top the hierarchy and social sciences come closer to the bottom. For example, Nuclear Physics is above the Physical Chemistry and Rural Sociology searches for a place at the bottom rung. Can we say contents of teaching as also books are responsible for this? In this Chapter, I am trying to bring out the position of social science teaching under the portals of higher learning in a critical perspective. I have no intention to compare social sciences with any of the other disciplines and that is not my brief here. I will be focusing on the teaching and the methodology of teaching followed broadly in social sciences in majority of the teaching institutions in India. I am quite aware, that there are exceptions and truly these exceptions are just countable and non-imitable. A few islands of excellence do exist in the set of a few institutions teaching Social Sciences, but these haves shun reaching to their peer and the most needed dialogues between them are absent. I am trying to look into the house of social sciences in order to suggest some ways to set right unwarranted practices that we have adopted and have stayed with us for a century.

History and Spread

Indian thinking in social sciences can be traced back to its culture and civilisation, right from Mahabharata to Kautilya's Arthashastra. The Bhisma Purana in Mahabharata provides the basics of public administration including the duties and functions of the King. In contemporary thinking during those days all the branches of knowledge in social sciences had merged into the 'administrative art of running the state'. The components of knowledge collapsed around the concept of 'welfare' as understood by the rulers or the Kings. Keeping pace with the religious under-currents in all walks of life, social sciences inevitably picked up the religion as the crust of its philosophy. The administrative system of *Mouryas*, *Chalukyas*, the *Rajputs* or the Hindu kings of Delhi, was largely dominated by the religious thinking and the stratification of the knowledge streams as dictated by the religious Scriptures. This was also true in the medieval period when the treatise were written on administrative systems (*Aine Akbari)* during Akbar's regime and therein provided an Indian version of understanding Social structure interfaced with economic organisation. There was a little scope for analytically confronting any of these ideas as the ideas elaborated here had a strong religious backing and came from the seat of the then power. Thus social sciences historically emerged out of centrifugal point of welfare of the masses and strengthening of the administrative systems largely available in Arabic and Sanskrit languages. Different components of the administrative systems were neither separated razor sharp nor were efforts made to understand these independently.

The real transformation in the spread of social sciences in the context of society and economy entered India along with the British Rule. British brought along with them the 'box of knowledge' that contained the divisibility of social sciences as defined by the Western social science thinkers. This onslaught rejected the earlier monolithic structural idea of Social Sciences. British system defined knowledge emanating from different branches of social sciences that was considered advanced stage in the Western world. Therefore, this was accepted readily by the Indian academics, as we strongly believed that the Western System is the only abode of development. Systematic efforts were made by the British to plough in the Western ideas in social sciences in Indian education system and it began with the minutes of Macaulay Committee to which William Bentinck gave full concurrence (Macaulay, 1835). The Macaulay report was the major turning point in learning and understanding through the prevailing languages in India. Macaulay was certainly stressing on the language of learning and at that time the entire learned writings in India were either in Sanskrit or Arabic. His first task was to dump this into garbage therefore in his report Macaulay writes *"It is argued, or rather taken for granted, that by literature the Parliament can have meant only Arabic and Sanskrit literature; that they never would have given the honourable appellation of "a learned native" to a native who was familiar with the poetry of Milton, the metaphysics of Locke, and the physics of Newton; but that they meant to designate by that name only such persons as might have studied in the sacred books of the Hindus all the uses of cusa-grass, and all the mysteries of absorption into the Deity"* (Macaulay, 1835, p.1). The minutes go further to record that the money spent on learning through Arabic and Sanskrit would mean to create champions of errors. By the end of that report he is quite piquant in stating that *"I conceive that we have at present no right to the respectable name of a Board of Public Instruction. We are a Board for wasting the public money, for printing books which are of less value than the paper on which they are printed while it was blank- for giving artificial encouragement to absurd history, absurd metaphysics, absurd physics, absurd theology- for raising up a breed of scholars who find their scholarship an encumbrance and blemish, who live on the public while they are receiving their education, and whose education is so utterly useless to them that, when they have received it, they must either starve or live on the public all the rest of their lives*" (Macaulay, 1835, p. 11). That sealed the path of Indian academics to work and develop in the field of sciences or social sciences including languages. It was not a bad move of shifting to learn through English every subject and every branch of knowledge, but that should not have buried the indigenous emergence of knowledge and development of sciences or social sciences. Tacitly, we followed the British education system that included their books, journals knowledge and methods of teaching and learning. It is at this turning point, India got on to the path of western methodology and philosophies in teaching and learning. I hasten to add that this path was not erroneous and could have supplemented the existing stock of knowledge but totally entombing the indigenous thinking was not needed. It is interesting to understand the views of the builders of independent India in this context. Dr Maulana Azad said "*A truly liberal and humanitarian education may transform the outlook of the people and set it on the path of progress and prosperity, while an ill-conceived or unscientific system might destroy all the hopes which have been cherished by generations of pioneers in the cause of national struggle"* (Maulana Abul Kalam Azad, Lecture on February 18, 1947). In following the British system of learning and teaching we gave a circumvented the humanitarian angle of our teaching of social sciences. Let me examine how this was contributed by the policy as also with the practice.

Proliferation and Divisibility

In social sciences, the first phase in Indian knowledge system began on the Western model broadly with economics, political science, sociology, geography law and education. Most of the schools of learning and teaching had wider coverage of subjects and the teaching also combined across the subjects. One can broadly visualise a few broad game changing points of developments in social sciences. The first phase began totally on the footprints of the Western world almost copying the same departments, books, syllabi and methods of teaching (Nadkarni and Deshpande, 2011). The initial teachers of social sciences preferred to get training in the Western Universities as had added prestige attached to it. It was natural that these academics who were trained under the Western system, copied the schema in totality to apply in our universities and colleges. During the second phase, the teachers thus trained imparted knowledge to the next generation of teachers and as a result the method of learning and teaching continued to flow unabated with fragmentary changes. Even the books and teaching material, were copied and reproduced from the Western books including the examples. The references were often made to the systems and culture of the Western countries. We learnt "Indifference Curve" having given choice between Apple and Oranges, when neither of them was available in small towns in India except in a few metropolitan cities and accessible only to the rich, who were expected to make a choice between the two. Sociology often described the 'Family and Caste' system that was written and articulated by the Western sociologists. Therefore, understanding of the simple concept of Indifference Curve was a difficult proposition for a student of economics during those early years. Similarly, 'Indian Sociologist' being published from London by Dr Shyamji Krishnavarma from 1905 onwards and included contributions that addressed to basic understanding of Indian Society but that proved as knowledge to the Westerners. It really did not develop analytical Sociology and the entire subject went towards a descriptive analysis. Books of a few Western authors translated by the Indian authors followed this discipline of the subject. These were made available during the third phase and the translations or to be truthful "copying" was very crude especially in economics. These books were written in Western formats and transliterated into Indian language formats, without changing anything substantial. Under this shadow, the teaching of economics, sociology, political science and other social sciences began in the third phase. Over years, the social sciences proliferated and today we have 2382 schools / departments / centres teaching various social sciences (see Thorat and Verma, 2017). There are 18 social sciences listed by Thorat and Verma in their study and the distribution across the country is not quite equitable. The number of universities in India increased from 25 in 1956 to 431 by 2008 and during the same period the colleges increased from 700 to 20677 whereas, enrolment reached to 11.6 million students. The gross enrolment ratio in the age group of 18 to 23 increased and reached to 11% by 2006-07. Large part of this increase can be attributed to the entry of private players in the higher education sector. Most of these however, have been in the field of medical sciences, engineering, and other professional courses. Very few private institutions dared to enter into teaching of social sciences. Relatively, the institutions imparting education in social sciences did not increase substantially. The proliferation of institutions was skewed towards non-social science institutions and therefore, inherently education market was truncated against social sciences. These subjects were not treated as respectfully as medical sciences, and other sciences including engineering. Every knowledge discipline soon reflected the mirror image of the hierarchical society outside and social sciences largely relegated to the place at bottom rung. An inherent Caste system got concretised across various branches of knowledge disciplines with a definite hierarchy. Admission to Social Sciences were taken as the last resort and "*if and only if*" admission to the other courses is not possible. As a result the teachers in Social Sciences were also those who did not come from the top deciles of the intelligentsia. The fourth phase was ushered in with the policy changes towards neo-liberalism. Educational institutions imparting training were commercialised and the market forces dominated the teaching and learning systems. New courses and new disciplines were introduced keeping in view only the marketability of the graduates of the subject. Placement cell became the most important and sought after 'holy place' in every institution. As monetary gains seemed feasible in the education sector, many new colleges and universities were started by the private players. Presently, there are 311 private sector universities that include State Sector, Deemed Universities and Open Universities, as against 345 Public Universities (see table 1). This proliferation has occurred in the last 15 years whereas; the network of Public Universities took almost a Century to come to the present level. Many new 'education barons' emerged on the scene and education became the most attractive business preposition. Employability became a *mantra* of the future of education and seeking of knowledge was relegated to the corner of learning. Many colleges and institutions began their placement cells and even the admissions depended more on the success of placement cells and not necessarily on the academic standing of the institution. All this new employment market was accessible largely to the non-social sciences and to Management graduates. Focus on good teaching took a beating and teachers focused on students passing the examination. Such a philosophy gave birth to what became famous as "Latur Pattern" or "Kota Pattern". Large numbers of students appearing for 12th examination from this small town in Maharashtra or Rajasthan were assured of scoring the best marks and getting to the professional colleges. Students studied more through the Coaching classes than the regular colleges and schools. The graduates passing out of the University in Social Sciences had a big question of employability and the choices faced by them are quite limited as against the Commerce or Management subjects. Social Science teaching and learning never focussed on seeking employment or placement and hence honing the skills of applications was not considered at all. Following the trends in other subjects Social Sciences also had branched out in sub-disciplines and this splintering of the monolithic science of the Society diluted the knowledge content in teaching and learning.

Table 1: Shows number of Public and Private Universities in India

S. No.	*Institutions*	*Number*
1.	Central Universities	44
2.	Central Open Universities	01
3.	Institute of National Importance	100
4.	State Public Universities	345
5.	Institute under State Legislature Act	05
6.	State Open Universities	13
7.	State Private Universities	233
8.	State Private Open Universities	01
9.	Deemed Universities-Private	79
10.	Deemed Universities-Government	33
11.	Deemed Universities-Government Aided	10
	Grand Total	**864**

Source: All India State of Higher Education Report: 2016-17, New Delhi.

Fencing the Commons

As a result of splitting the core subjects into smaller specialisations, in Indian education system we have now a large number of social science subjects which add up to close to 250. Some of the disciplines are absolutely obscure and have little relevance with the mother discipline. This fact is not properly understood by the policy makers. Traditional 'Indian Social Sciences' culture draws up on a monolithic knowledge from many historical books and authors; however, these are largely locked safely in the library cabinets. Most of these were not easily accessible to the readers before the internet revolution. In the absence of these, teachers and students relied on the western sources of teaching and learning, where the monolithic nature of social sciences was already shattered into fragments. Many new subjects and disciplines were being added every day and these kept distances from each other. We had many resources in our rich libraries but rarely, we turned around to get to know that in India we treated Social Sciences as one discipline, an amalgamation of all components. Following the western methods we constructed such boundaries around the disciplines and fenced the commons from within.

I had an experience of serving in a very reputed institution in the country (Gokhale Institute of Politics and Economics) which has an excellent library and a huge collection of vintage Social Sciences documents that loudly make it clear that Social Sciences are internally connected. This library also has the documents in the Post-independence India like Radhakrishnan Commission report of 1948-49; Mudliyar Commission of 1952, Kothari Commission of 1964-66 and strangely all these have emphasised only on the curriculum development than methodologies in teaching and learning. These Commissions dealt largely with infrastructure, other facilities, curriculum, teacher training, finance etc but did not touch upon the inter-dependences of Social Sciences nor attempted anything about the learning and teaching processes in Social Sciences. In fact these Commissions treated Social Sciences very curtly and one finds only casual reference to Social Sciences learning or teaching. National Policy on Education (1986 and 2016) also does not even mention the teaching-learning methodologies. Often the making of the smart classroom, sprucing of classrooms and some additions to the curriculum based on western universities occupied the central attention of the educational scientists. This disallowed the students to break the walls between disciplines and enter into other spheres of knowledge closer to the Society. Their attention was entirely focused on getting higher marks and grades rather than learning and understanding the subject. This is not universal observation but it is certainly a generalised observation of teaching and learning process in the Indian universities. In this context it is necessary to understand what Professor Yash Pal had stated in his report and I quote "*We have overlooked that new knowledge and new insights have often originated at the boundaries of the disciplines. We have tended to imprison disciplinary studies in opaque walls. This has restricted flights of imagination and limited our creativity*" (Yash Pal Committee, 2009). He further stated that "*...it is important that the universities relate to the world outside and the walls of disciplines are porous enough to let other voices be heard. It would also be necessary that university education is seen in its totality and the subject areas are not designed in isolation*" (Yash Pal Committee, 2009). This undoubtedly emphasises the necessity to increase the porosity of the walls built for separating disciplines and branches of knowledge. One can achieve this either through a design by the policy makers or by the desire of the learner. I searched purposively all the reports on education policy mentioned above including the National Education Policy documents and found that Social Science as a word has not been used in any document more than ten times and that too incidentally or accidentally. Therefore, the focus on Social Sciences teaching and learning was largely taken for granted or ignored.

Stuck into School Pedagogy

The foregoing passages abundantly show that teaching and learning processes in social sciences have received least attention at the hands of education policy makers. The first generation of social scientists got trained at the institutions of learning outside India. They brought with them the stock of knowledge, the curriculums, books and references and followed these very religiously. No divergences were permitted and full control of teaching and learning of these basic social science disciplines was in the hands of those who were trained under the shadow of a different culture and society. They also prepared the next generation of teachers in social sciences who followed exactly the same routines in the coming years. A few changes were made on the way which too reflected the analogous changes in the Western world. The drill was so perfect that the Indian trained teachers and students received the second grade treatment at the hands of the Western trained social scientists. This group of westernised social science teachers at Universities also influenced the teaching and learning methods and often emphasised pedagogy. Herbart coined this term to incorporate a few steps in the methods of teaching that included preparation, presentation, association, generalisations and the applications of the knowledge collected. This is well said than done in teaching social sciences and largely the teachers of social sciences followed these steps meticulously from the earlier books, outdated notes of their teachers. It was expected that the students must repeat exactly the same material in the examinations, if they deserve better marks. In the entire process and the steps like association generalisation and applications were totally absent and this flaw was neither noted nor emphasised any time in teaching and learning methodology of social sciences. We were stuck into a primary school pedagogy, wherein teacher explains the lesson; dictates the methods / notes and students follow verbatim the diktats of the teacher. In the process this morphed pedagogy of learning and teaching killed many innovative minds of teachers and students. The schoolbooks, college books and notes and carrying the material to the school and colleges increased multi-fold without any analogous development of the brain of the child. No wonder we have proliferated in social sciences only at a pedestrian level without any innovations. It is essential for us to graduate from this '*school pedagogy*' to the true meaning of pedagogy or more towards "*andragogy*" which was actually the learning and teaching method in the old Indian teaching system.

Teacher Quality and Enhancement

The commissions and committees planning for enhancing the quality of education have emphasised teacher quality and enhancement in teaching materials. In social sciences, the approach was precisely to meet the suggestions provided in a complete mechanical manner. In order to improve the teacher quality and refresher courses of all sorts as well as capacity building programmes were started in the entire country in almost every university and college. These were tagged with a carrot of promotion to the next grade, if a teacher completes two / three such programmes. There was no attempt however, to locate the influence and impact of these courses in the quality of teaching and the changing of the teaching material in the colleges and universities specifically in social sciences. As a member and quite a few times Chairman of NAAC peer review team, I found that there has hardly been any improvement due to the refresher courses attended or capacity building courses undertaken by the teachers in the colleges and universities. The books and the notes continued exactly the same which I saw four decades ago as a student. Albeit some of them are printed through computers. With the availability of computer the new faculty members give strong emphasis on "*power point*" presentations. This revolution has not deepened our knowledge seeking behaviour but brought in strong laxity in preparation and delivery of the lectures. Teachers have totally forgotten about bringing in applications of various theories and connecting to the current events around the world. As a matter of fact, every day we have a large amount of new material coming out that relates to the theories in most of the disciplines of social sciences. Rarely do the teachers take advantage of this new available material and knowledge bank to deliver the latest information to the students (Deshpande and Shaha, 2011). Therefore, the entire emphasis of our educational planners and policymakers on the quality improvement of teachers and changing of the learning process seem to have got stuck finally to providing a white board in the classroom and changing the nomenclature of the classroom to a smart classroom, without inculcated smartness of applications in social sciences among the students.

Neo-liberalism and Position of Social Sciences

Privatisation in the education field began quite early in the country. Initially it got into medical sciences and then slowly proliferated through engineering and management sciences to other disciplines. It is true that the public investment in education was always inadequate and needed support from the private sector. Initially the private sector educational institutions had contributed significantly to the enhancement of quality in teaching and learning, brought in new forces of knowledge and new methodologies in establishing institutions. All this was done by philanthropies by investing their wealth and personal efforts. They dedicated life for building such institutions of excellence. The clue was taken from here to introduce privatisation in education but totally with a different motive of commercialisation. After the process of liberalisation had set in India, the proliferation of private educational institutions has been phenomenal. Somewhere, in this journey of neoliberalism, the goal towards reaching excellence in education became secondary. Today we have a large number of engineering colleges, medical colleges, management institutions, arts and science colleges and massive number of schools. In this entire process social sciences remained as one of the willy-nilly packages along with the other disciplines. One of my recent experiences of establishing a Centre for Social Sciences in the reputed privately funded institution in the electronic city of Bangalore met with miserable consequence. Every privately funded body is interested in making money out of education and not in enhancing of knowledge frontiers. Universities and colleges proliferated under private domain unabatedly and are expected to match the number of public funded institutions soon.

We have now 233 Private Universities and 79 Deemed Universities. Some of the towns like Raipur in Chhattisgarh have many Private Universities in a single city. Totally we have 313 privately run institutions, only 32 short of the 345 Universities in public domain. These do not include the unrecognised privately owned tuition classes which have a massive spread across the country and run a parallel teaching and learning sector. The only difference is that they do not provide Degrees and for that the student has to join the recognised institutions at least for name sake. The entire focus of the commercial education sector (e.g. Kota Classes, Chate Classes, Rao Classes, etc.) is to train a student to score high marks and grades. In the entire development acquiring of knowledge took a corner seat and students passing out do not have basic understanding of the subjects. We had an excellent programme anchored by Mr Shahrukh khan asking well learned persons questions from fifth standard text books and many 'highly educated' failed miserably. This is the pathetic story and we have to live with it.

In the best social science institutions, even though the top functionary of the institution happens to be a trained social scientist, the emphasis was more on process of earning than the process of dissemination of knowledge. The quality control and regulatory authorities are also hoodwinked with standard methodologies. Therefore, neoliberalism did not do great service to the improvement of knowledge delivery system in the country; this needs to be carefully analysed. We have a long way to go making some headway towards enhancement of teaching and learning process of social sciences; it began in the shadow of the Western trained social scientists and continues under the shadow of the present generation of market oriented social science teachers. Drastic change in the pedagogy and integration of different social science subjects is urgently warranted. Examples include integration of (1) Sociology, Social Works and Social anthropology (2) Economics, Statistics and Mathematics (3) Economics, Commerce and Business Management, (4) Political Science, Public Administration and Rural Development and so on. The artificial boundaries created between the disciplines for our convenience must now vanish.

References

1. Deshpande, R. S. and Shaha, K (2011). Social Science Research in India: A Summary of discussions, in Nadkarni and Deshpande (Eds.)
2. Govt of India (1970). Education and National Development: Report of the Education Commission of India (Chairman DK Kothari), New Delhi National Council for Educational Research and Training.
3. Govt of India (2009). Report on the committee to advise on renovation and rejuvenation of higher education (Yash Pal Committee). New Delhi: Ministry of Human Resource Development.
4. Government of India (2016) (1986). National Policy on Education,-1986, New Delhi Ministry of Human Resources Development (MHRD).
5. Government of India (2017). All India Survey on Higher Education (AISHE), Ministry of Higher Education, Govt of India, New Delhi.
6. Habib, I. (2010). Maulana Abul Kalam Azad and the National Education System, National University of Educational Planning and Administration, New Delhi.
7. Nadkarni, M. V. and Deshpande, R. S. (20110. Social Science Research in India, New Delhi, Academic Foundation.
8. Thorat, S. K. and Verma, S. (2017). Social Science Research in India: Status, Issues and Policies, New Delhi, Oxford University.
9. UNESCO (2017). New Education Policy 2017; Incorporating Social Responsibility and Community Engagement in Higher Education, UNESCO Chair in Community Based Research and Social Responsibility in Higher Education, New Delhi.
10. (Macaulay minutes) http:// www.mssu.edu/projectsouthasia/history/ primarydocs/ education/Macaulay001.htm

Chapter - 6

Teaching is Reaching Out

— *Sohan Prabhakar Modak*

The mediocre teacher tells. The good teacher explains. The superior teacher demonstrates. The great teacher inspires.

— William Arthur Ward

Artistic creations hide behind patient learning, designing and hearing, negotiating and talking during a lengthy period of trial and error to negotiate till the quality of the outcome is pleasing. The 'Art of Teaching' is not like preaching but mimics stitching embroidery with many coloured threads articulating a design with flair and flourish. Teaching demands constant attention to the detail so that not even a stitch goes wrong.

Mentors Galore

As a child, Bhate Gurujee tutored me in Sanskrit verse, pronunciation, rhythm and linguistic complexity. My mother would work on my English and my father on Marathi, handwriting and reading. The science teacher in my school, Shree S. A. Savarkar, would show how to observe shapes, their movements, let me experiment with a Cartesian Diver and pack me off to a metals workshop to learn handicraft. At the Fergusson College, Prof. B. G. Shirole, teaching frog anatomy and behaviour, would become a frog, while Prof. Karekar would be tracking the migratory salmon. In the University, we squinted into the microscope with Prof. D. N. Kamat to understand how living or painted cells and tissues looked like, just as Prof. K. R. Karandikar with his extraordinary clarity, conviction and creativity exposed us across the length and breadth of the structural and functional edicts of the great comparative anatomist, E. S. Goodrich.

At the University of Geneva, my doctoral guide Dr. Jerzy Gallera walked me though all methods for culturing chick embryos outside the egg shell. He showed how to practise microsurgery on living embryos to understand the injury and the healing process. My skill in French language being non-existent then, we would communicate by drawing pictures and flow charts on blackboard and using jargon taught by Prof. Leela Mulherkar during M.Sc. As I picked up French, he would spend hours telling stories of his life as the prisoner of war after fighting German army during the resistance of Warsaw. Gallera would talk about philosophy, explain and criticise Kierkegaard's writings, extol Aristotle. He would spite Chamberlain for having sold Poland to Hitler. He would tell jokes on Hitler and Himmler and then offer afternoon coffee and pastry to reenergize me and Gerard Nicolet, another doctorate student, to continue our lab work late into the night. His vigil on our learning the living history of embryology, with all its nuances, failures, successes, rough and touch, generosity, treachery, smiles, laughs, teas and sorrows, were cornerstones for acquiring aptitude for questioning, digesting what others were telling, acquiring skill sets on old and new techniques and technologies while experimenting on embryos. With the bonhomie, love as well as occasional burst of anger, the desire for more trust turned on the faucets for fountains for being curious without fear.

As a postdoctoral fellow at Oak Ridge national laboratory, Prof. Tuneo Yamada, a Japanese Samurai, with his inscrutable oriental smile, asked me riddles, tugged and poked at my thoughts, concepts, the known, the unknown, what lay on the horizon, denied me opportunity to fly without permit, and then let me float on my own under a careful watch till one day, in 1969 when I studied lens cell nuclei on a Zeiss scanning microspectrophotometer in Richard Kimball's lab, told me that I have discovered the molecular basis of programmed cell death, a subject on which I published more than 10 research papers, nearly a decade before the process was rediscovered, fine-tuned and represented by planting a Greek term Apoptosis, which unfortunately means *falling off* (like falling off a cliff), which has nothing to do with programmed death. Here was my first encounter with how by sheer muscle power some scientists create even bad terminology to claim credit for discovery. Apoptosis is now being routinely being used for even un-programmed necrotic or pathological cell death; for nearly 10 years hardly anyone would cite our work. Whatever, Tuneo's earlier comments had struck a chord and I learnt to fly Cessna aircraft at Knoxville airport, first with an instructor and then solo for nearly forty hours!

At Oak Ridge National Laboratory, Charlie Steinberg revived the memories of lessons in Prof. Werner Arber's Biophysics course in Geneva. During the summer 1968, I learnt how Ultraviolet radiation affects Haemophilus influenza in Jane Setlow's lab. And then, there was Ram Uppuluri, inimitable statistician, who took me on merry go around with numbers to show me, instead of just visual records, how to assess the probability of occurrence of events, shapes, or biological processes from the available data.

At the University of Kentucky, Prof. Jesse Sisken, the cell cycle specialist, and Prof. Fred Bollum, working on mammalian DNA polymerases, helped me crawl over DNA during replication. As we incubated lens sections in polymerases, with some cells actively dividing, some in a steady state and a few undergoing programmed cell deaths, we found that DNA in dying cell nuclei contained breaks. Later, P. L. Biochemicals commercialized this assay as Tunnel assay.

In 1970 at the Swiss institute for Experimental cancer Research in Lausanne, I encountered Cecilia Leuchtenberger who had done the pioneering work on nuclear pycnosis, and Klaus Scherer, co-discoverer of pre-messenger RNA in eukaryotic cells let me lose on a wild goose chase of the so called cytoplasmic informational DNA, I learnt and used every major technique to study DNA, except crystallography, to find that these molecules are produced by radiation damage caused by isotopes used to tag it. This, five years' of a disastrous stint, ended by turning me into a molecular biologist. By 1972, I had my own research group and I had the taste of becoming boss for the first time. I would blame my post-doc, student, assistants and technicians for mistakes in their work, scold them for laziness until in one group meeting, they asked, "Hey, you are constantly nagging us on what to do and not to do, you are setting deadlines and finding faults, but how come you are not in the lab"? That shook me up. There, my juniors were telling me what was wrong with me! I began fidgeting in the lab after everyone had left for the evening. I squirmed, my head churned and one day, Eureka! An idea struck me and I developed 2-dimensional electrophoresis for nucleic acids and showed how DNA broke down with sequential single strand breaks during programmed cell death. I called a lab meeting thanked my group members for opening my eyes and explained what I had found. From that day, I knew that to guide others, I had to listen and take them along while actively engaging myself in the process of enquiry.

Mentors galore unassuming, never hungry for power or prizes, but always listening, ready for dialogue, questions and answers, negotiations on the probabilistic thought and bitten by the bug for the quest of the unknown. In Switzerland and France, the scientific enquiry merged with fascination for taste for architecture, languages, poetry and pleasures of culinary delights along with a return to the politics and fantasies of youth. As a young Indian, I never became despondent with identity crisis as my mentors, friends and colleagues kept building bonds for lifetime.

Teaching- Tremors

In January 1967, Dr. William MacArthur from Knoxville College asked if I could teach embryology to undergraduate class. I jumped at the opportunity. In Tennessee, spoken English is a slang laden with a drawl and singing accent that took me a while to assimilate. Unlike India where people think that speaking fast is smart, at the Knoxville College it took me a while to learn to listen to the questions and answers from students, just as I had to struggle to get my point across to them. Fortunately, during my first months in Switzerland when I hardly knew French to communicate with my Guide and colleagues, I had learned that I had started by drawing diagrams of embryos and flow charts for work on blackboard. In Knoxville College, I espoused the same strategy of dialogue while simultaneous discourse and drawing on blackboard to get my point across, something Prof. Shirole had made into an art form at the Fergusson College.

In the Swiss Cancer Institute in Lausanne, scientist staff felt that our doctorate students should have an advanced course on recent development and I was roped in to organize and initiate a course in Cell Developmental Molecular Biology. It included visiting lectures from eminent scientists like Lucien Caro, Max Birnstiel, Rudolf Weber, Charles Weismann, Walter Gehring, Francois Gros, Richard Setlow, Jim Regan and others who mixed the known with the unknown with dexterity, discussed hypotheses and new techniques to ask and deal with questions and how discoveries are made. Two years later, the French speaking Universities in the western Switzerland got together and converted it into a postgraduate course that became a rewarding experience both for students and scientists.

Teaching: tremors, trauma, tantrums

Seventeen years earlier, before leaving India for studies abroad, Shri M. S. Golwalkar Gurujee had told me, be like a Roman in Rome, but come back and work in India. After short stints, first at the Radiobiology group at Ohio State University in the USA and then at the Biophysics laboratory at the Centre for Nuclear Energy in Grenoble France, I refused the offer from Nuffield Laboratory for ophthalmology at Oxford and joined the University of Poona. Well, my American accented English raised question marks on faces of many students. Indian students are ultra-polite and shy with teachers and it is difficult to know whether they really understand what is being said or they are just waiting for the discourse to end. It was disconcerting that they simply won't ask any, questions. So after every 8-10 minutes into the lecture I would pause and invite questions again finding none forthcoming. So, I introduced the practice of asking them a question and waiting till each student had its turn, but to no avail. Silence from students means either they do not know the answer because they hadn't followed the discourse, or that they were afraid to give a wrong answer while worrying what would their peers think, or simply that my lecture was incomprehensible. In India, most teachers do not like being interrupted probably due to their weakness in the ability to communicate as well as their knowledge and comprehension of the topic at hand, let alone the issue of false pride of being The Teacher who can't be questioned! Well, when I found that even after a full round of waiting, I couldn't get a correct answer, I formed small groups of 4-5 students each picked out randomly and to discuss among themselves to find the answer and I left the classroom for 5 minutes. Amazing, on most occasions, the trick worked and when I was back, most of them had the answer. In Indian classroom, students come from all types of cultural, linguistic and economic groups with social diversity across the spectrum. In small groups, soon the divide began disappearing with increased flow of communication and they began socializing. The method allowed students to discuss together by crossing over cultural and linguistic barriers to compose a cogent answer and it took a few more sessions to perfect the practice. I wish I had figured out the gimmick earlier, but then there is always the first time somewhere. In every class there are habitual backbenchers who avoid eye contact with teachers so that no questions are targeted towards them. I had to engineer their switching places to the front row, not liked by some initially, but with the formation of groups to solve questions, it paid dividends.

Finally, there is the matter of classroom acoustics. If a teacher cannot be heard, most students go to sleep. If the volume is too high, very few can remain alert through the noise. Therefore, it is necessary to adjust the acoustic coordinates with respect to the size of the classroom and number of students. Sometimes, I would even skip a classroom and hold the class on the lawn in the garden.

Teaching: tremors testing and tuning

Teaching is one of the most daunting tasks in communication. A teacher should be the primary source of information to catalyse learning and integrating the information into knowledge. A good teacher is motivated to connect and induce the student to drop the barriers in communication, something that requires good presentation skills, correct use of language, and speed of delivery that allows students to grasp the contents without being bored to death. A teacher has to articulate, be grammatically correct and focussed on the audience reaction.

A good teacher must continually update the contents and subject comprehension to a level of expertise required to answer most queries from students. Learning is like solving puzzles where the final picture emerges through recalls and time-lapse integration through trial and error, intuition, pattern recognition, general knowledge, creativity and enterprise. It takes a lot of personal involvement in learning the subject matter by asking oneself questions on the contents before exposing oneself to the curiosity of students who are honed to care and dare asking questions. Every question student asks has a reason to be. There are no stupid questions and no stupid students. Indeed, every question from a student reveals which part of contents was not clearly explained during the lecture and must be part of the self-learning experience. Every student has the right to understand and question the contents, the logic, logistics and context.

An ideal teacher should be skilled and involved in the process of enquiry and should have the mind set with scientific temper without the loss of empathy and self-respect. The teacher must know that information is not knowledge and that creative teaching involves inductive dialogue, not dictations, to promote learning. A good teacher knows that Humanities and Sciences are introvert superposing philosophy. Creative learning involves high level curiosity to question, analyse, synthesize and even disagree to promote the mind-set in the search of truth at any cost. These are the minimal conditions to establish the scientific temper.

A teacher should know that Technology is extrovert and requires skills and aptitude for execution, innovation, management and enterprise. On a ten point scale, 5% of undergraduate teachers will score 7 or more, the next 20% between 5 and 6. Clustering into Poor, Fair, Good, Very Good and Excellent on a horizontal scale will not affect this situation. Here, the postgraduate teachers will fare only marginally better. In actual practice, examination scores should reflect on the ability of students to absorb, assimilate and reproduce subject contents as well as the ability of the concerned teachers to transmit the contents. Whatever, the students' scores are often high due to the manipulation of the process of examination. The present sorry state of undergraduate and postgraduate education in India and most countries, east or west, is due to the deplorable quality of employable work force that gives the lowest choice to the profession of teaching among available employment opportunities. The problem lies in the fact that teaching is one among the least preferred employment option for most. Teacher quality can be improved only marginally through makeshift operations such as refresher courses, monetary incentives. It has to begin in schools and colleges where, those who have not learnt, therefore not knowledgeable cannot articulate, explain and transmit the contents, should not be in this profession.

Teaching, testing, assessing, raising the bar on curiosity and course correction

In Pune, I spent a lot of time trying to figure out how to get my point across to students, how to assess their reactions and finally ended up tabulating an assessment protocol that would ask about a dozen questions and seek answers on a point scale of 1 to 5 from each student.

Compiling answers from all gave me an idea about what was satisfactory, and where I went wrong in my teaching. I discussed the Table with my peers; some liked it and while some didn't, all agreed to use the method (Table 1). At the end of each semester, the questionnaire is distributed and assessed and results are compiled separately for each teacher and communicated individually. Indeed, being a voluntary activity, it produced dramatic results with some faculty.

Table 1. Teacher Evaluation Questionnaire

Name of the Teacher:
Course Title:

S. No.	*Parameter*	*Score 1-5 [Poor=1; Fair=2; Good=3; Very Good=4; Excellent=5]*	*Comments*
1.	Course Content		
2.	Subject Content		
3.	Up-to datedness		
4.	Communication in English		
5.	Audibility		
6.	Body Language		
7.	Ability to Explain		
8.	Visuals/PPTs		
9.	Visuals- White Boards		
10.	Asking Questions		
11.	Answering Questions		
12.	General Demeanour		
13.	Punctuality		
14.	Course Completion (%)		
15.	Comments on Lacunae		
16.	Comments on Strength		

Learning is like solving puzzles where the picture emerges using memory base for recall and integration in real time by recognizing patterns through a trial and error, general knowledge and multiple choice selections, through intuition, desire to learn and common sense. There is also the other side of the coin where the student is the centre piece. Every teacher assumes that she/he has the ability to be ready to accept/understand whatever is coming its way and therefore transmit. The teacher assumes that the target student is able to read, write, listen and speak, able to observe, recognize shapes, patterns and relationships between those through recall and retrieve from the memory base. In actual practice, it is the job or the objective of the teacher to establish the path to recognize and discriminate truth from beliefs and falsities. The student should have the opportunity to acquire skills to analyse and synthesize how to be logical in thinking and to question beliefs as well as test truths which happen to be established norms at any given time. She/he should be on constant lookout for the recent developments with fearlessness and hard work matched by acquisition of necessary skills. Information based appreciation of quality and quantity and unfazed curiosity and desire to overcome the hurdles in the process of enquiry and learning are minimum requirements to succeed. Indeed, recognizing the need to expose students to the latest in science and technology, delivered by the experts themselves, I organized 3 international symposia, 3 national meetings and 4 technology training workshops through support from the University Grants Commission, Departments of Science and Technology, Atomic energy, Biotechnology and the Council for Scientific 7 Industrial Research and the Asian Molecular Biology Organisation. There, students and faculty heard and interacted with stalwarts like John Gurdon, Jim Smith, Ruth Bellairs, David Ede, Bob McKinnel, Ron Hart, Mukund Modak, Tuneo Yamada, Tokindo Okada, Makoto Asashima, Goro Eguchi, Masahiko Muramatsu, Jean Jacques Laurence, Yves Courtois, Klaus Scherrer, Georges Spohr, Walter Wahli, Adolf Graessman, Eyal Giladi, V. Sasisekharan, T. Ramasarma and many other Indian and Foreign scientists, And, there were those who led the charge in changing the structure and organisation of teaching and conduct of science in India, namely, Obeid Siddiqui, Pushpa Bhargava S. Ramachandran, KK Govind Menon, to name a few. The upshot, thanks to my teacher colleagues, especially, V. Sitaramam, K. Kannan, M.V. Joshi, not a single student during my stint in Pune, remained unemployed. About 45% settled abroad, 35% joined industry or business in India and the rest joined either National laboratories or the teaching profession. I, too, evolved, not just in teaching and research but also as an inventor having obtained U.S. and European Patents for a box to hold objects in sterile conditions and an Indian Patent for a special comb to set agar agar gels for immune-electrophoresis, and even launched an enterprise to manufacture gel electrophoresis apparatus. That is how the handicraft, feeling and learning about living systems, dissecting these to the level of cells, organelles, molecular complexes and molecules, talking and writing about these and finding new ways to examine them and make them available for scientific enquiry have helped me converge along a somewhat elliptical path that even crossed the frontiers of languages, literature and poetry.

College and University education are expensive propositions for students and their parents and the situation has worsened since the advent of private institutions that have increased including those with hit-and-run practices for monetary gains. In 1985, I proposed a Biotechnology Training programme, and first the National Biotechnology Board under Department of Science and Technology, followed by the Department of Biotechnology, under the able leadership of Dr. S. Ramachandran, a biochemical engineer, not only supported the idea but proposed its inception at six academic institutions. A major transformation involved sanctioning a monthly stipend to students selected for the course. Here, this issue concerns the need that students feel autonomous which makes them far more proactive in the learning processes (Modak 1996).

Teaching and learning is a two-way street. The teacher has to teach but also learn from students what and how. It is only then that the exercise will bear fruit that ripens slowly, sometimes over the life time!

Already in the school, students discriminate between descriptive and numerical sciences; they love one and hate the other. In life sciences, it is important to recognize the subject relevance with a need to link Molecular biology, Genetics, Cell-developmental biology, Biochemistry to Biophysics and quantitative methods through statistics and mathematics along with communication skills. In collaboration with Prof. Chandar Daswani, a specialist in English language teaching, I developed a course to promote the proficiency in spoken and written English with emphasis on reading, writing, analysing and presenting science texts, as a critical requirement.

A teacher is not a "know it all". Therefore, it is necessary to ensure that students get exposure to other teachers from the same as well as other institutions of learning and to avail of varied methodologies. I have seen this practice instituted already in sixties in the USA, where Associated Universities conduct a summer training programme for undergraduates. At ORNL, I had summer students for 2 years who performed extremely well. I introduced the summer training programme for first year Zoology and Biotechnology students in 1985 and it was received enthusiastically by National Laboratories, Industry, other Universities and IITs in India. This practice exposes students to varied work practices and methods and the receiving institutions are exposed to potential future recruits.

Acknowledgements: I am eternally grateful to my mentors, teachers, colleagues and students alike for never losing faith in me and always subjecting me to the humiliation of being someone who had to find the answer and for making this exercise worthwhile. I am grateful to Prof. Tangirala Ramasarma and Prof. Srinivas Saidapur who have helped retune parts of the text and been a huge inspiration.

Suggested Reading

Modak, S.P. (1996). Science Education in Indian Universities: Proposal for a 5-year integrated M. Sc. course in Life Science. *Curr. Sci.* 71, 960-967.

Modak, S.P. and Sauna, Z. (2018). A Negotiated Assessment of Teachers in Institutions of Higher Education (Manuscript in Preparation).

CHAPTER - 7

NURTURING EXCELLENCE IN SCIENCE EDUCATION AND RESEARCH

— B. G. MULIMANI AND J. TONANNAVAR

Imagination is more important than knowledge
- ALBERT EINSTEIN

Frontiers of knowledge, in every branch of science, are on the move at an unprecedented rapid pace. Science is the base for the development of every nation. Let us not forget that it is our mathematicians – Brahamagupta, Bhaskara and others' fundamental contributions to mathematics including the 'Number – ZERO', have been the greatest inventions of man. Notwithstanding a rich intellectual tradition, today we are in a dilemma as to how to promote 'excellence' in science education and research. This dilemma has been apparent in the recent proliferation of publications in predatory research journals. The UGC ought to set a baseline of standard for research in India. While India is going through the era of liberalization, privatization and globalization, there is an urgent need for nurturing excellence in science teaching and research. Attaining excellence in science education is a must for producing such human resource as required, among others, for the successful implementation of Science and Technology Policy initiatives by the Government to realize the vision of a developed India. Higher education in India is a complex landscape rooted in the socio-cultural setting and the present article is an anthology of motivations and sayings of the eminent scientists including our perspectives and broad suggestions.

For long, the human life and society have been dominated by the forces associated with religion and authority. It is very recently, the emergence of new way of thinking – scientific method, has changed the way we think and live. Science has become integral part of our living. Science being knowledge of a certain kind arrived on the horizon in the 17th century in full scale, bringing with it an attitude of cool rational outlook. Today, the impact of science on the lay-person has more to do with its technological spin-offs rather than stimulating him to cultivate scientific temper. Scientific method as we know it today comes down to us from Galileo, who, in its essence established *'Observation of significant facts, framing of hypothesis, which if true, explains the facts and predictions as consequences from it are verified'* as the basis. Best example for the scientific method comes from Newton who cast his laws of motion in mathematical forms, making them logical, verifiable and predictable. On the other hand, the biologist Charles Darwin provided a huge mass of evidence in favor of a mechanism he proposed that explains the theory of origin and evolution of species. He propounded that, *'From so simple a beginning endless forms, most beautiful and most wonderful forms have been, and are being evolved'*. Since Darwin, the theory of evolution has passed several tests, proving its scientific merit. In the words of geneticist Theodosius Dobzhansky, *'Nothing in biology makes sense except in the light of evolution'*. Matt Ridley in his recent book *'The Evolution of Everything'* opines that we can now gradually understand or explain evolution of everything: be it education, culture, morals, religion, money or internet. Another new dimension added to the scientific method is due to Albert Einstein who demonstrated the power of *thought experiments,* that is, situations are imagined in a new way but bound by the laws of physics. In his own words, 'I was sitting in a chair in the patent office at Bern when all of a sudden a thought occurred to me: If a person falls freely he will not feel his own weight. I was startled. This simple thought made a deep impression on me. It impelled me toward a theory of gravitation'. Today the scientific method has essentially remained the same since the 17th century though in some cases its application and practice are more complex. Physics is more exact science because its laws obey the principles of mathematics. This is also true of Chemistry whose base is now molecular and its practice is as much science as it is an art. Being a fundamental science, chemistry is, in a way, at the heart of every branch of science. Different branches of social sciences are increasingly becoming scientific on account of the application of scientific method.

Scientific temper is an attitude of mind to be adopted from the scientific method as a mental habit. It is supposed to free the mind from blind beliefs and dogmas. Scientific outlook refers to the role of scientific method in so far as it can influence religion, ethics, society, psychology, education, public policy and governance. There is no denying the fact that a nation's intellectual and economic prowess is measured by its scientific progress. While art in the life of the world civilizations is very ancient, science, by contrast, is recent but the impact of science on the modern civilization has been deep and wide and will continue to be so. The explosion of scientific knowledge and technological advancement as its spin-offs has had influence on social, cultural, intellectual and economic life of the modern man. Industrial revolution demonstrated what Francis Bacon had said, 'Knowledge is Power'. Modern science began with Copernicus, Kepler, Galileo and Newton as an act of understanding the motions of heavenly bodies by asking right kind of questions by them with a penetrating intellect that challenged the authority and Aristotelian world-view, thereby unraveling nature's secrets. Bertrand Russell says of these men, 'Unprejudiced observation without regard to aesthetic prejudices required therefore, at that time, a rare intensity of scientific ardor'. These men of science did not concern themselves about the immediate practical applications of their discoveries; instead, they sought to deduce an impersonal world-view of the underlying fundamental laws of motion of the celestial bodies, subject to verification and interpretation. With further scientific progress, it was soon realized in the 18th and 19th centuries that the values of science are: To enjoy studying nature, to gain certain knowledge and to put it to utility. These values constitute what may be called 'scientific outlook' which deserves to be treated as a culture on par with those imparted by liberal education. According to the American Association for the Advancement of Science, '*ideally, a liberal education produces persons who are open-minded and free from provincialism, dogma, preconception, and ideology; conscious of their opinions and judgments; reflective of their actions; and aware of their place in the social and natural worlds*'. It was believed until the 19th century that teaching of literature, ethics, philosophy, and so on, refined the human mind to the highest form of culture. The teaching of science in the context of liberal education clearly did not find its rightful place due mainly to misplaced notion that it deals with utilitarian aspects such as motors, airplanes, telegraphy and medicines and therefore, these aspects cannot refine the human mind in a manner that art and literature do. However, the educational value of science is the mental excellence which is as great as that of literature. From a utilitarian view-point, the teaching of science prepares men and women to be a desired skilled human resource for practical and economic goals. The teaching of Science, Technology, Engineering, Art and Mathematics, popularly shortened to STEAM, is emphasized in the contemporary higher education, since, the importance of these subjects in school and college pedagogy is directly associated with training human resource for the successful implementation of science and technology policies.

Science, as noted, is a certain kind of knowledge derived by observation of significant facts and from the facts we arrive at general laws. Therefore, the scientific method in essence involves, firstly, observation of facts; secondly, framing a hypothesis to account for these facts; thirdly, if the hypothesis is true, deductions from the hypothesis are verified experimentally. By the method of induction, a certain general law follows from the facts. Using the general law, we proceed in reverse order deductively until we arrive at the particular facts with which we started inductively. The scientist discovers a law by the method of induction and the teacher in the class room uses deduction to demonstrate the truth of the law. The scientist has a child-like curiosity and it is his business to ask right kind of questions. What is it? Why is it? How is it? Finding answers to questions leads him to solutions. It is said of Einstein that as a young boy he asked 'What would I see if I moved with the speed of light?' In his quest for the answer, he discovered 'Theory of Relativity'. Eminent physical chemist E. Bright Wilson Jr. says, 'Many scientists owe their greatness not to their skill in solving problems but to their wisdom in choosing them'. In this context, the story of Bharat Ratna Prof. C.N.R. Rao, is exemplary. In his autobiography, '*Life in Science*', he recalls, 'When I started my career, I tried to pick an area of research where I could contribute significantly. I looked for an area which was not crowded and was guided by Robert Frost's famous poem:

Two roads diverged in a yellow wood
And sorry I could not travel both
I took the one less travelled by
And that made all the difference

Picking a lonely road is a still a good way to choose a research area, but this is becoming increasingly different nowadays'. The cultivation of science by scientists is many-sided. Let us look at what different scientists have to say what science is for, how it is pursued and what it means to them. Eminent scientist Raghunath Mashelkar says, 'The first grand challenge before Indian science is that of building some *irreverence*. Our students are too reverent'. We must encourage students to question authority which has no place in science. On this the IISc's scientist Gautam Desiraju concurs: 'The Indian is too scared to question authority of any form. He would rather swim along with the current. He does not dare to differ. All this runs counter to the scientific disposition, which proceeds systematically along the route of questioning, formulation, experimentation and verification'. Polish-born, British scientist and author Jacob Bronowski says that the essence of science is to '*ask an impertinent question and you are on the way to a pertinent answer*'. Japanese-born-American Nobel Laureate Leo Esaki was inspired by the following words at the bust of Alexander Graham Bell which stands at the main entrance to the Bell Labs: *Leave the beaten track occasionally and dive into the woods. You'll be certain to find something that you've never seen before*. Inspired by these words, Esaki joined IBM T. J. Watson Research Centre, New York, where he invented a diode that demonstrated electron tunnelling, a novel quantum mechanical result thought to be realizable only in special conditions. So choosing an unbeaten path makes all the difference. On another level, what science seeks to achieve? English philosopher Herbert Spencer stated: 'science is organized knowledge'. American microbiologist Cornelius van Neil defines: 'In essence, science is a perpetual search for an intelligent and integrated comprehension of the world we live in'. Austrian zoologist Konrad Lorenz thinks of search for truth as - 'Truth in science can best be defined as the working hypothesis best suited to open the way to the next better one'.

In the making of a scientist, motivations play a decisive role. It would be inspiring to consider the early life of C. N. R. Rao. Born and educated in Bangalore, he not only had the benefit of his learned parents but also was taught by very motivating physics and chemistry teachers at school. After his graduation at a very young age of 17 from the Central College, Bangalore, one of his teachers advised him to enrol for a postgraduate degree in Physics and Chemistry at Banaras Hindu

University instead of his desire to join the Indian Institute of Science (IISc.). After M. Sc, he had a brief stint at IISc, and then he joined Indian Institute of Technology (IIT), Kharagpur for doing his Ph.D. degree. He was impressed by Nobel Laureate Linus Pauling's famous book, *The Nature of Chemical Bond.* The book's approach to chemistry through the structure of atoms and molecules appealed to him. His desire to work in modern chemistry as instigated by Pauling combined with the suggestion of Sir J. C. Ghosh, Director of IIT to pursue higher studies outside the country took him to the USA (1954). After securing admission to both Massachusetts Institute of Technology (MIT) and Purdue Universities, he chose the latter because it gave him a chance to work with a professor who had been from Linus Pauling's research group. After his post-doctoral stint at the University of California at Berkeley, he joined the IISc, Bangalore. His life has been defined by three coordinates: (1) Science as a way of life; (2) Faith as source of energy and (3) Institutions as magnets for harnessing new knowledge. Nobel Laureate Ahmed Zewail aptly describes Prof Rao's scientific life: 'A voyage of success and a man who believes in excellence but disbelieves in mediocrity and bureaucracy'.

One is fortunate enough to be raised by educated parents as is true of Niels Bohr, Homi Bhabha and Sir C. V. Raman who found themselves in favorable circumstances like good school and college, parents' academic habits and accidental meetings with eminent persons while they were children. Bohr's father was an academic and his brother became a distinguished mathematician. Bhabha was the son of a wealthy lawyer, who, with a wonderful collection of books, encouraged young Bhabha who became a voracious reader. Highly talented Bhabha studied the theory of relativity at the age of sixteen. While his parents wished him to be become an engineer to run an industry, he was repulsive of the idea and said this to his father, 'I'm burning with a desire to do Physics. I will and must do it some time. It is my only ambition'. With this burning desire, Bhabha went on to become not only an exceedingly successful nuclear scientist but also built two institutions, one for pursuing peaceful uses of nuclear energy, now called Bhabha Atomic Energy Research Centre (BARC) and another for pursuing fundamental research, called Tata Institute of Fundamental Research (TIFR). Of the many books Raman read as a student, the three books that greatly influenced his spiritual and intellectual outlook include: Edwin Arnold's *The Light of Asia* on Lord Buddha, *The Elements of Euclid* and the great German scientist Hermann von Helmholtz's classic *The Sensations of Tone*. Of the first book Raman says, 'I remember being powerfully moved by the story of Siddhartha's great renunciation, of his search for truth and of his final enlightenment. This was at a time when I was young enough to be impressionable, and this reading of the book fixed firmly in my mind the idea that this capacity for renunciation in the pursuit of exalted aims is the very essence of greatness'. Of the second book, the young Raman's evaluation of it is indeed remarkable, '...my early reactions to the compulsory study of Euclid were anything but favorable. The reason for this is, I think, to be found in the excessive emphasis placed on the subject as an intellectual discipline and the undue attention given to details as distinguished from its broader aspects. He finally concludes, 'The pages of Euclid are like the opening bars of the music of the grand opera of Nature's great drama. So to say, they lift the veil and show to our vision a glimpse of a vast world of natural knowledge awaiting study'. About the last book, this is what Raman has to say, 'I discovered this book for myself and read it with the keenest interest and attention. It can be said without exaggeration that it profoundly influenced my intellectual outlook. For the first time, I understood from its perusal what scientific research really meant and how it could be undertaken. I also gathered from it a variety of problems for research which were later to occupy my attention and keep me busy for many years'. Clearly, Helmholtz's master piece, like an inspiring teacher, profoundly influenced the young Raman, to say the least, to become a scientist. Nuclear physicist Raja Ramanna too had similar upbringing due to his father, a learned judge and a mother with a taste in English literature. If the upbringing and books to which some scientists partly owe their success, teachers, accidental incidents, meeting and hearing eminent scientists too have their share of influence. One of the India's great scientists of the 20th century, Sir Jagadish Chandra Bose had come under the influence of his physics teacher, Father Lafont at St. Xavier College, Kolkata, who molded him to be a scientist. Likewise, many scientists as teachers at the University of Cambridge influenced the young Bose. It was Sir Raman's inspiring lecture at the school and an opportunity to visit his lab at the Indian Institute of Science made Rao to say 'My god, how wonderful it would be to be like Raman. It was probably then the seed of my becoming a scientist was sown'.

Born in a wealthy family and his father being a practicing lawyer, James Clerk Maxwell, was tutored and educated at the University of Cambridge. His electromagnetic theory is one of the greatest discoveries in science. There are exceptions to these stereotypes of making a scientist. Albert Einstein though was born in a middle-class family, received modest education at a gymnasium in Switzerland (his mother taught him to play violin). In the case of Charles Darwin whose father was a doctor, he was encouraged to follow in the footsteps of his father but chose to be a naturalist. Despite just a pass degree from the University of Cambridge, Darwin went on to become a greatest biologist thanks to his revolutionary theory of evolution. 'Evolution' is now is a core theme in biology and it serves to unify all its branches. Isaac Newton came from a farming family with no early advantages but rose to become the greatest scientist ever on account of his fundamental discoveries in mechanics and optics. He ushered in a *Newtonian era*. Mathematical genius Srinivasa Ramanujan whose parents were by any measure not learned but he turned out to be once-in-a-millennium mathematician with such discoveries that have kept mathematicians busy even today.

The history of science since Galileo, Newton, Darwin, Einstein and others has amply demonstrated that, the pursuit of science is also equally important for the culture of man and his society. In the words of the great mathematician Henry Poincare' *'The scientist does not study nature because it is useful to do so. He studies it because he takes pleasure in it; and he takes pleasure in it because it is beautiful. If nature were not beautiful, it would not be worth knowing and life would not be worth living'*. While science has impacted our world-view, its bond with religion is delicate and often seen as confrontational. At the core of religion lies faith. In science too beliefs are held by scientists. Science is bound by verifiable evidence which is transcendental in religion. It is pertinent to consider what Einstein has said: 'A religious person is devout in the sense that he has no doubt of the significance of those super personal objects and goals which are neither required nor capable of rational foundation. A legitimate conflict between science and religion cannot exist. Science without religion is lame, religion without science is blind'. There is probably a need to blend scientific outlook with ancient wisdom and modern science, the teaching of which would produce a strong India. In this context it may be noted the Indian Constitution was amended (42nd Amendment Act, 1976, incorporating Article 51A) making provision for, among the Fundamental Duties for citizens of India, '(h) to develop the scientific temper, humanism and the spirit of inquiry and reform'.

It is said that 'India is a rich country where poor people live, because we have not understood the wealth creating potential of knowledge'. We have become consumers of knowledge, not creators of knowledge. How do we address the need for a paradigm shift in our higher education system? There is a need to grow the culture of creativity embedded in Indian culture and ethos without the feeling of being inferior to the West. Raman has expressed this lack of confidence with admirable lucidity: *We have abundant human material in India. Speaking as a teacher of 24 years' experience, I can assert, without fear of contradiction that the quality of the Indian mind is equal to the quality of any Teutonic, Nordic, or Anglo-Saxon mind. What we lack is perhaps courage, what we lack is perhaps driving force which takes one anywhere. We have, I think developed an inferiority complex. I think what is needed in India today is the destruction of that defeatist spirit. We need a spirit of victory, a spirit that will carry us on to our rightful place on this planet. If that indomitable spirit were to arise, nothing can hold us from achieving our rightful destiny.*

It is educative to note that the great Astrophysicist S. Chandrashekar attributed the phenomenon of sudden emergence of greats like J.C. Bose, C. V. Raman, M. N. Saha, S. N. Bose, P. C. Ray and others during the period from 1920 to 1925 with the motive for self-expression *–to show to the West that Indians were equal to them in their own realm*. It must be acknowledged that since Raman, India has had men of eminence -Vikram Sarbhai, Verghese Kurien, Satish Dhawan, A. P. J. Abdul Kalam, M. S. Swaminathan, Yash Pal and R. A. Mashelkar to name a few whose impeccable zeal, vision and commitment have transformed India into a nation of many achievements. The legacy of space science and communication are due to the pioneers: Vikram Sarbhai and Satish Dhawan. Verghese Kurien unleashed the largest dairy program as 'White Revolution' and creating 'Amul' brand that has successfully countered international brands. Abdul Kalam provided leadership for the missile development program. India owes 'Green Revolution' to M. S. Swaminathan. Mashelkar has been the architect of the legislative framework of patents and intellectual property rights, replacing 'publish or perish' dictum with 'patent, publish and prosper'. He strongly advocates *Science led Innovation* to achieve social and economic transformation in India. He cites success in biotechnology, medical science, business, pharma and telecom sectors as exemplary to achieve the same in indigenous technology in which we are weak. A culture of think-out-of-the-box in science, he argues, would create technological innovations. As the Director of National Chemical Laboratory, Mashelkar introduced this culture by way of *kite flying fund* which promoted new potential ideas regardless of their success. At CSIR as its Director General, he initiated a similar munificent *New Idea Fund* which brought to light a dearth of new ideas! Hence, Mashelkar has proposed *a new value system... that respects science that solves problems, technology that transforms and innovation that impacts the society* resulting in scientific knowledge convertible into monetizable knowledge. Apparently all this points to a need for revamping our education system. The thesis in the article is very succinctly expressed by one of post-independent India's eminent breed of scientists and science educators Prof. Yash Pal: 'If I were asked to name one major direction that could drastically change the nature of our education and research enterprise from kindergarten to the university level I would say: 'Build on individual competence and exploration and couple with the life around you. If this advice were taken seriously, it would imply that: Learning is not delivered; it is created'. Way back in 1990 at the inaugural session of the Indian Science Congress on the theme 'Self-reliance, Non-alignment and Innovation in Science and Technology', Prof. Yashpal, who delivered the address, said, 'What does being innovative in science and technology mean?' He answered the question saying: 'It means that our teaching should specifically address our problems irrespective of whether it is very simple or highly sophisticated'. We need to retrospect our achievements in this direction now. This requires, as has been emphasized by Mashelkar and others as the most important challenge before us, promoting irreverence, i.e. the questioning attitude which will lead to creating an 'Innovation Eco-system'. The questioning attitude coupled with right thinking would encourage students to become creative/innovative scientists. It may well be said that the ability to ask the right kind of questions, even imaginatively, is more important than solving problems. 'Imagination is more important than knowledge' says Einstein.

In his vision for building India, Raman has precisely and eloquently said: *Unless the real importance of pure science and its fundamental influence in the advancement of all knowledge are realized and acted upon, India cannot make headway in any direction and attain her rightful place among nations of the world*; further he emphasizes *what India needs is science, more science and still more science*. Celebration of National Science Day to commemorate discovery of 'Raman Effect' is best served if the true spirit of Raman's approach is realized. In view of the rapid advances in every field of knowledge, science should be taught as *a process of thinking*. And, science teaching now must be viewed as a process of learning - a way to learn and as thinking how to think '*Thinking about thinking is thinking*! It is equally pertinent to recall our ancient words of wisdom '*Na hi jnanen sadrasham' (Nothing comparable to Knowledge); 'Jnana Vijnana Vimukataye' (knowledge liberates)* the motto etched at UGC office, and *'Aa no bhadra kartavo yantu Viswatah' (let noble thoughts come to us from all sides),* to guide us in our endeavour.

In summary, it may very well be said that, to prepare the students to pursue excellence, they be taught or exposed to the works of the great minds before they embark upon research career. On this Einstein clearly says, *the essential of the being of a man of my type lies precisely in what he thinks and how he thinks, not what he does or suffers*. The teacher must organize teaching-learning as a process to develop a passion in the students toward a culture of innovation. Our colleges and universities must become centres of discovery, invention and innovation that would produce solutions for the problems of India.

Suggested Reading

1. Abdul Kalam, A.P.J. with Rajan, Y. S. (1998). India 2020: A vision for the New Millennium, Penguin Books India.
2. Abraham P, (1982). Subtle Is the Lord: The science and the life of Albert Einstein. Oxford University Press, New York.
3. Basu, B. and Yash Pal. (2006). A Life in Science. Vigyan Prasar, Dept of Sci. and Tech., New Delhi.
4. Desiraju, G. R. (2008). Science Education and Research in India. Economic and Political Weekly, 37-43, June 14.
5. Kurien, V. (2005). I Too Had A Dream. Rolli Books.
6. Mashelkar, A. R. Reinventing India. Sahyadri Prakashan, Pune. www.mashelkar.com.

7. Rao, C. N. R. (2016). Life in Science. Penguin Random House India, 2016.
8. Ridley, M. (2015). The Evolution of Everything. Fourth Estate, London.
9. Russell, B. (1931). The Scientific Outlook. George Allen and Unwin Ltd, London.
10. Venkataraman, G. (1994). Bhabha and His Magnificent Obsessions. Universities Press, Hyderabad.
11. Venkataraman, G. (1998). Journey in to Light. Indian Academy of Sciences, Bangalore.
12. Wali, K. C. (1991). Chandra: A Biography of S. Chandrasekhar. Viking Penguin India.

LEADERSHIP, GOVERNANCE AND QUALITY ASSURANCE

Chapter - 8

Leadership Role of Principals

— *S. K. Saidapur*

Effective leadership is not about making speeches or being liked; Leadership is defined by results not attributes. — Peter Drucker

Literally 'Principal' means chief, first in command, head, leader etc. A Principal is primarily concerned with the all round development, and governance of the college. It includes, among other things, building the institution in terms of infrastructure (e.g. laboratories, library, sports and gym facilities) and ensuring appointment of good faculty. The Principal needs to be a visionary, competent, committed person and works with a missionary zeal. He needs to take all sections of the stakeholders, the students, staff, parents and general public in to confidence, involve them in decision making processes, promotion of both quality education and credibility of the institution. Therefore, qualities of a dynamic leader are needed in a Principal.

As a rule the college Principals face many expected and unexpected problems almost every day. They need to overcome such challenges skilfully and efficiently. The nature of challenges varies from one institution to the other. For example, problems of the new colleges differ from that of the well established ones. Likewise, problems of Government, Private and Autonomous Colleges differ. However, challenges are not to be regarded as hurdles as nothing can be accomplished in life without them. Indeed, they provide opportunity to realise ones' potential and gain confidence. Hence, heads of institutions should welcome challenges and triumph over them using their skills and ingenuity. A dynamic principal can make a big difference to the college. He should be aware of his role as a leader, understand the challenges before him and devise ways to triumph over them. This chapter highlights the major challenges that generally confront Principals as well as opportunities they hold for all round development of the institution. First, let me detail some important issues before the principals.

Major Challenges

Following are some of the major issues confronting most principals. However, it all depends on the college, financial status of the institution, geographic location, and many other factors.

1. Creating Academic Ambience

First and foremost, this includes providing good class rooms that are well furnished with comfortable desks and chairs, black/white boards, and modern audio-visual gadgets. Where feasible, one could have smart boards as well. Though seemingly trivial, the class rooms should have cosy ambience with well painted walls that look fresh and sober, plenty of air and light. Science courses require good laboratories equipped with all needed instruments, chemicals and glassware in proportion to the prescribed intake and the curriculum.

2. Faculty

Adequate number of well qualified permanent faculty with competence and dedication to the cause of education is needed in all educational institutions starting from primary to higher education. Unfortunately, most educational institutions throughout the country face the problem of faculty crunch in terms of both number and quality. Further, we need competent teachers rather than merely qualified teachers. In government institutions teachers are transferable, and they are also transferred frequently from one college to the other; at times without replacements. This can severely affect sustenance of quality education in a given college. It is the responsibility of the State governments to ensure that adequate number of faculty positions is provided to the college.

3. Library

A good library, housing required books and journals, facilities for photocopying, browsing and downloading the needed reading materials is needed. The atmosphere in the library is often shabby. Good ambience can attract more and more students to library. Ideally, library should have separate sitting areas for teachers, boys and girl students. It should have high speed Wi-Fi and browsing as well as photocopying and printing facilities. Libraries should subscribe to INFLIBNET / N-LIST which will help in accessing most needed literature for both teaching and research.

It is good to create a small section housing *'inspiring books'* in the library. The inspiring books may be in the form of: biographies of eminent personalities in diverse fields, books depicting noteworthy Indian contributions in the area of Science, Literature, Spirituality, teachings of Indian great saints, great ancient scriptures, books on freedom fighters and notable achievers in various fields (including sports), personality development related self help books, as well as carefully chosen fictions. Creating a *'section of inspiring books'* can be an innovative practice. Also, it will go a long way in promoting reading habits among the faculty and students.

4. Indoor/Outdoor Sports and Gym facilities

Most colleges lack adequate facilities for games, sports and gym for want of space (mostly in metropolitan cities) and funds (particularly in rural based colleges). Even when good sports/gym facilities are available the students need to be motivated and encouraged to utilize them fully. Making provisions for utilization of gym facilities outside the college hours is a challenge.

5. Special Care of Girl Students

These days in any co-education college often the number of girl students exceeds that of the boys. More and more girl students are now in the streams of higher education. They indeed require special facilities. Therefore, colleges should pay special attention to providing sufficient all round facilities to girl students. For instance, the institution should provide big cosy hall, nicely painted, with the help of an interior decorator and with facilities for privacy, relaxation and resting, clean toilets, provision of some indoor games, and women's magazines for reading. The Ladies room should have Wi-Fi, computers, facility for dining, clean drinking water, sanitary napkin vending machine, disposal of sanitary napkins, mats for Yoga and Meditation etc. The overall ambience should be congenial and cosy with descent furniture. Display of portraits of *women achievers* in various fields of science, literature, sports, social work and so on will enhance the ambience and inspire the girl students. A small collection of selected books along with women related magazines may be worth placing in ladies room. They can be changed each month.

6. Commanding Confidence of Stakeholders

The main stakeholders are the students, faculty members, parents or wards and the supporting staff. Principals who are not academically or administratively strong often command less respect from the stakeholders. They need to have sound knowledge of civil service rules and code of conduct. This knowledge gives them enormous power in administration besides commanding respect from the employees. They need to be well read persons and academically far ahead of their junior colleagues in order to command good respect. Person who can command respect in both academic and administrative matters only can contribute effectively to the development of the college. Therefore, appointment of a Principal should not be based merely on seniority. It should go by the competence of the incumbent person and his / her commitment for the all round development of the college.

Every institution will have problems related to infrastructure, academic, and administrative matters, student amenities and so forth. Salvaging these issues requires skill, concern and commitment. The head of the institution must take the teaching/non-teaching staff in to confidence and try to find solutions collectively through periodic interactions. A suggestion box placed near the library or other convenient place can greatly help in getting feedbacks. The grievances, complaints and suggestions should be taken very seriously. The suggestions / complaints received should be resolved at the earliest by discussing with the concerned and taking needed action and thereby avoid magnification of the problem with time.

7. Liaison with Higher Authorities

Principals of Government colleges need to deal with the State Government officials like the Regional Joint Director and Director/ Commissioner of Collegiate Education. Those working in private colleges need to deal with their own managements as well as authorities of the State Government. Often these can be frustrating due to delayed responses, sanctions, nepotism, corruption and apathy towards the colleges. Yet, the Principals have to skilfully establish a smooth relationship with the concerned authorities so that the college can get needed approvals, and grants without much delay.

The concerned State governments, on their part, should streamline the processes of approvals, release of grants in a most transparent ways in the Department of Collegiate /Higher Education. Some kind of delegation of powers at all levels is needed to various officials to ensure quick disposal of files.

8. Utilizing Funds

Timely and judicious utilization of funds is important for smooth conduct of the college activities. Unutilized recurring grants often lapse. It is sad that most Principals especially those near retirement age often exhibit aversion to utilization of funds sanctioned by the State Governments and R and D agencies as they fear audit objections and possible delay in fixation of their retirement benefits and pension. Hence, they leave the funds unutilized. This is very unfortunate as the benefits do not percolate down to the college and stakeholders. It is also true that many auditors find faults unnecessarily and demand money to make harmless remarks. The real culprits often escape but honest and naive ones suffer.

All State Governments need to make the audit process user-friendly. Nevertheless, persons who are thorough with the finance codes, and rules governing the utilization of funds have little to fear. Also, they can give befitting answers to audit observations raised, if any. Let me give an example from my own experience. When I was the Chairman of the PG department an auditor raised objections for purchasing office stationary in the Janata Bazaar housed on the university campus. My office superintendent informed me that the auditor wants to raise objections for purchases made in Janata Bazaar. I knew very well that items purchased in such shops do not require calling for comparative quotations within prescribed limit of expenditure. So I sent a message that the auditor may record his objections and that I will appropriately answer. However, he could not record objections. He however opined informally that goods in Janata Bazaar often cost more than in the open market. And, the matter ended. Another time, an auditor asked me to produce warranty card (hoping to find fault) for the camera purchased in my DST research project. I thought this was silly. Anyway, I had preserved the warranty card and as such he lost the chance of harassing me. Then he found a novel way of bothering me. He still made a remark that there is no mention about the submission of progress reports. I replied saying that the progress is monitored by the funding agency and that it does not come under the purview of the finance auditors who are not experts in academic matters. I also, asked for the provision under which the auditor can ask for the research progress reports. The matter was closed by dropping the audit objections. Evidently, some auditors can unnecessarily trouble the officials even when everything is fine; enlightened auditors are rare. It is desirable that the Principals, personnel working in finance section and investigators who operate research grants are thorough with the rules governing utilization of funds and follow prescribed procedures (e.g. inviting comparative quotations or Tenders as per the Transparency Act 2000, maintaining the Stock / Issue / Day books, and payment related documents and Register books).

It is heartening to note that the Central Government has recently opened Government e-Market (GeM) portal similar to Amazon and Flipkart. Purchases can be made directly from the Government sponsored e-portals like the GeM without inviting comparative quotations / Tenders. Further, goods here seem to be cheaper than in the open market! It is desirable that principals and office staff study such government sponsored portals for purchases ranging from broom stick to furniture without hassle.

9. Autonomous Colleges

The problems and issues listed above for affiliated colleges are equally applicable to autonomous colleges. At the same time, people expect more from autonomous colleges as far as academic programs, curriculum and implementation of various new programs are concerned since these colleges enjoy freedom and opportunity to frame their own curriculum unlike the affiliated colleges. Therefore, the major task in autonomous colleges is developing new academic programs; rational subject combinations, providing more open electives and job oriented courses. These colleges are not bound to follow the routine syllabi and programs given by the affiliating university. Therefore, they can revamp and restructure curricula of courses offered in tune with the modern requirements. If the college is offering PG courses it should plan for 5-year UG-PG integrated courses with exit / lateral entry option after graduation.

The subject combinations offered at UG level need retrospection. There are two aspects to this issue: (1) the existing choices of subject combinations have outlived their utility in many cases and require reorganization, (2) the boundaries between allied subjects have more or less disappeared necessitating their integration. The subsidiary subjects offered are meant to assist in mastering the major subject of specialization. For instance, study of Economics needs knowledge of maths and statistics to enable modelling and predicting the future / market trends. Likewise, multidisciplinary subjects like biological sciences require sound knowledge of biochemistry, maths and statistics. When it comes to allied subjects often it is difficult to draw a line between them (e.g. Economics, Commerce, Business Management or say Sociology, Anthropology, Social work). Therefore, integration of subjects and multidisciplinary approaches are needed. Furthermore, several subjects excepting the languages require basic knowledge of maths and statistics that is judiciously tailored to meet the needs of students studying different subjects, say Economics, Physical sciences or Biology. Major challenge of Principals is redesigning curriculum of various courses offered by the autonomous colleges.

Despite the compelling needs it is unfortunate that our universities and their Boards of Studies are reluctant to change from the existing traditions. Any change invites resistance and opposition first from the faculty members and then from the students due to the fixity of mindset. For any evolving society, change is needed for survival and progress while unwillingness to change leads to extinction. Autonomous colleges being smaller units, it is relatively easier to bring in changes and set model example to other higher education institutions in the country. Therefore, it is imperative that the Principals of autonomous colleges strive hard to bring in progressive changes in the curricula and restructure their UG/PG programs in tune with the contemporary requirements and globalization.

Providing Leadership

In the foregoing passages I have made an attempt to broadly identify major issues to illustrate the nature of problems one is likely to encounter. It is impossible to anticipate all problems. The Principal has to be a visionary, hard working and a well read person with concern and commitments. Honesty and integrity play a vital role in earning respect of the stakeholders. Once these qualities are recognized by the stakeholders, they cooperate and help. It is then that the things start falling in their places. Sincere efforts and sound strategies are needed to remodel colleges. It is in this process, the leadership matters. Leadership essentially involves identifying the challenges and issues, specific to a given college, and finding ways of tackling them. Thinking out of box, generating novel ideas and solving the problems with ease through good governance and, taking stakeholders into confidence are essential attributes of a leader. The Principal's chair by itself does not confer qualities of a leader. On the other hand, a good leader brings credibility and respectability to the chair. Unfortunately, many depend on the 'Chair' for their respectability.

Beyond doubt, a Head of the institution is a 'facilitator' and not the ruler. Once this idea sinks deep in the mind many things happen in a right way. Recall challenges listed earlier in this Chapter. Are challenges the unwanted hurdles? Obviously they are not. In fact, they are needed because they provide opportunity to bring out one's hidden potential and to prove a person's capabilities. Success builds confidence in oneself and in the minds of others who matter.

In steering diverse activities of the colleges in most efficient manner, the following five strategies can help:

(a) First, the Principals should define themselves as the 'facilitators' rather than as the chief executive officers. This will set tone for right functioning.

(b) A Principal should be thorough with the Civil service and Conduct rules as well as accounting procedures.

(c) List out all issues/tasks and classify them as *important* or *trivial*. Then prioritize items from the list of important issues that require immediate attention and initiate actions. The trivial issues can wait. Preparing a 'to do' list and updating it each day will not only ensure attending to all tasks systematically but also generate enormous amount of time.

Soon one will discover that of the numerous issues, there would be trivial many and vital few!

(d) Streamline the administration by 'delegating' responsibilities among the teaching and supporting staff. Taking everyone into confidence ensures sharing of the work as well as transparency. Besides, a larger participation in the general cause of the college will promote a sense of belongingness among the employees of the institution.

(e) In the absence of any hidden agenda, fear vanishes. It is good to keep the administration as transparent as possible with no hidden agenda.

Let us now turn our attention to opportunities of a Principal. Following are some of the many opportunities that a principal can seize for overall development of his college.

1. Setting Goals

First and foremost, it is necessary that each college develops specific goals for the institution following in depth discussion with stakeholders and experts. Once the goals are set and crystallized, they should be made known to all stakeholders. Colleges should develop institution specific 'Vision and Mission' statements that are dynamic and not static so that they can be revised periodically. Every effort must be made to realize the set goals without giving scope for procrastination. Setting new goals can be a regular (say once in 5 years) exercise to ensure a steady and sustained progress for the college over the years. The achievements can be published in the college magazine for a wider reach, accountability and transparency.

2. Adoption of ICT

The next step is to fully computerize all aspects of administration making it virtually paperless (e-Governance). This includes, general administration, finance section, admission processes, students attendances, biometry of employees, library functioning, college website and various documents prepared by the Internal Quality Assurance Cell (IQAC) to name a few. Any information of interest pertaining to the stakeholders should be readily available. The college could also make use of emails, various Apps like, Face book, WhatsApp and so on to encourage paperless communications, group discussions, and monitoring home assignments of students, accessing books and references from the library. In short, use of ICT extensively is the order of the day. It should be fully utilized in teaching, learning and evaluation processes. Likewise, teachers can liberally use smart boards and internet to show live events like blood circulation, brain functioning, actions of enzymes and hormones etc. that can be beautifully illustrated using smart board facility. This however requires uninterrupted Wi-Fi and, ICT facilities. It is ideal to provide Wi-Fi facilities (24×7) especially in girls' hostels so that they can browse and prepare for their studies, projects, assignments even in the night hours.

3. Open Electives

Colleges should provide as many subject combinations as possible and also introduce more 'Open Electives'. Here, the autonomous colleges have more opportunity than the affiliated colleges. Still the affiliated colleges may arrange some lectures through outsourcing to sensitize students about diverse issues like personality development, time and stress management, Government of India sponsored skill development schemes, entrepreneurship, Yoga and Meditation preferably during holidays or as evening courses. The respective colleges may issue certificates directly, signed by the Principal.

4. Skill Oriented Programs

The colleges can introduce self-financed Certificate or Diploma courses in subjects that are in demand (skill oriented) in a given geographical location. Indeed the colleges should specialize themselves in providing demand based job oriented courses and also avoid isomorphism with neighbouring institutions. Many specialized courses like, stewardess (air hostess), catering, hotel management, bakery, fashion design, care of elderly, nursing, tourism, use of computers, mushroom cultivation, and other such courses could be thought of but purely based on employment / entrepreneurial potential in the region. Even Yoga and Meditation courses can be of great help to students who can become teachers in these areas with the help of certificates given by the colleges. In any case, courses on 'Personality development' and 'Communication skills' are needed for all students.

5. College Magazine

Publishing a college magazine regularly is essential. It gives avenue for talented students, faculty members and also supporting staff to express their skills in creative writing in the form of articles, stories, dramas, poems and so on. If college has discontinued publishing the magazine, it should revive it at once and let students and others to satisfy their aptitude, passion and also sharpen their writing skills. Brief reports on Co-curricular activities like short-term projects (e.g. survey of fauna, flora, mineral sources, regional history, and geography) undertaken by the students and teachers may also be published in the magazine. It will promote writing skills besides generating relevant information about the region. Even alumni could be allowed to write in the college magazine providing information on diverse matters like their own accomplishments, contribution to the college, job opportunities and so on. The college magazine can thus be a vehicle for highlighting its activities and also help the stakeholders in many ways.

6. Sports and Games

There is no dearth of talent among the students in various sports, games and athletics. However they need proper direction, coaching and support. The colleges should identify general aptitude of students in their institutions and promote it with the help of outsourced coaches on contract for fixed number of months. The college can very easily promote say, high jump, long jump, sprint and marathon running etc., keeping in mind the previous records of performances in each event with respect to the affiliating University, zone, inter-zone, and national levels so that the students can be trained to reach or surpass these records. Students can be trained to excel in Kabaddi or Kho-kho or Volley Ball without incurring much expenditure. But all this requires sustained efforts on the part of the college and the trainers appointed. No college can provide training or coaches for all games. It can choose one or more areas where the talent lies and deserves support. This helps in enhancing name and fame of the institution as well.

7. Cultural and Social Activities

Many students are talented in cultural activities and different performing arts. They also need to be encouraged. Incidentally, it also helps the college get a name in the field. Similarly, meaningful participation of college in social activities like NSS, adoption of village or some locality for overall visible improvement, besides the routine annual blood donation and sapling plantation activity can go a long way in making an impact. These activities need to be carried out more scientifically. For instance, list of willing blood donors and their contact details can be displayed on the college website. College can have tie-ups with local hospitals which need blood. Keep record of annual requirement of different types of blood groups, total amount of each type of blood (Group A, B, AB and O; Rh-positive or Rh-negative) donated and so on. Likewise, keep records of plantation activity, survival rates of plants, impact of plantation on environment and so on. All such activities should be done systematically and reported in the college annual report and also in college magazine for dissemination of information among the stakeholders and general public.

8. Books and Stationery Discount Shop

Colleges may think of starting book and stationary stores; buy in bulk at wholesale rates with good discounts and pass on the benefit to students. Such shops can be run by superannuated employees of the college with the help of needy students (earn while you learn scheme) who can work in the shop, keep it clean and assist in other related works. It will be a kind of win-win situation for all those involved in running the shop and the shoppers.

9. Promoting Reading Habit

Importance of reading books hardly needs emphasis. Reading good literature is the only way to acquire knowledge, wisdom and get inspired. Only an inspired teacher can inspire the students. It is a pity that reading habits even among the faculty members is fast declining. Each college should therefore evolve its own innovative method to promote and nourish reading habits in both teachers and students for that matter other employees as well. Some colleges have installed software to record monthly, the time spent by each member of the library. Suitable rewards may be given to those who spend maximum time in the college library. Teachers can have a reader's club where exchange of books and knowledge informally or formally in the form of discussion meetings and so on can be profitably undertaken.

10. Providing Insurance

If a college does not have insurance scheme to cover accidents, hospitalization and death of students, it is high time to initiate such a scheme at least on a modest scale with minimum contribution from the students. The college can collect minimum annual subscription from students say Rs 365/per year (@ Rs 1 per day). If a college has say 1000 students amount collected will be Rs 3,65,000/- per year. The scheme is for all bona fide persons who have paid the subscription amount and other college fee. The scheme should have its own clearly stated rules and regulations regarding the extent of coverage, in case of hospitalization or death. Details of bills to be submitted, name of the certifying authority and other related aspects should also be clearly stated to avoid misuse. The regulations must be evolved after a thorough discussion by the governing body of the institution and stakeholders before notifying on the college website or prospectus. Similarly a kind of group insurance scheme may also be extended to all employees following the same or different subscription tariff, rules and regulations. Any unspent balance in a financial year should be added to the corpus funds of scheme. This way the scheme will remain viable and become robust over the years. Roughly once in five years the regulations can be revised to extend more benefits depending upon the availability of the corpus. Alternatively, colleges can explore group insurance provisions of insurance companies. In any case, extending insurance facilities for the college students as well as its employees is a good idea.

11. Collaborations/Linkages

In view of the information explosion and disappearance of boundaries between subjects in recent times, teaching and research calls for collaborations with experts from other teaching and research institutions / industries. Therefore, the institutions should encourage and facilitate 'collaborations' for teaching, research and innovations among the faculty members. Linking colleges with industries where possible may prove very useful especially in skill development, up gradation of laboratories and enrichment of research. Therefore, each college may consider structuring and nurturing periodic interactions between Heads of the departments and Principals with collaborating institutions, faculty and students.

12. Skill Development and Entrepreneurship Training

It is well known that industries find our graduates unemployable as they are not job ready. Generally these graduates also lack entrepreneurship qualities with few exceptions. Therefore, it is commonly felt that we need to focus our attention to skill development, personality development and communication skills as well as entrepreneurship. Fortunately, the Government of India has floated many schemes like 'Make in India, Start up India, Stand up India' under which financial support is given to those endowed with entrepreneurial qualities (see Chapter 17). It is in the fitness of things that the colleges sensitize the interested students to such opportunities. Training in entrepreneurship besides skill development, personality development, and communication skills, will go a long way in shaping the life of our youth.

13. Stress and Time Management

One of the several requirements in recent times pertains to time and stress management. Students often suffer from depression both in response to genuine and not so genuine causes. For example, in metropolitan cities, a girl student may suffer from depression for not finding a suitable boy friend! This is certainly not a life and death issue. Some students may not be able to cope up with studies or ragging by seniors and so on. Regardless of the cause, students who are under stress often do not know how to manage it. This can lead to unpleasant consequences. Conducting Yoga and Meditation classes can help relieve stress.

Time management is essential for anyone. Proper planning and making a 'to do' list each day and prioritising the tasks can greatly help in getting almost all things done in time. This approach actually generates lot of time. The college may periodically sensitize students on the strategy of time management as a means of achieving success. The importance of counselling in stress management is dealt separately later in this book (see Chapters 19 and 20). Timely help can well shape the life of students who otherwise may go astray.

14. Counselling Centre

In view of the modern day stresses and strains, rural and tribal backgrounds, varying competency of students in coping with the studies clearly there is a need for counselling and mentoring. These aspects are considered in detail in Chapter 20 of this book. The college authorities should not neglect this aspect though it is strictly not a part of the curriculum. Every college must provide counselling facility.

15. Earn while you Learn Scheme

It is a good idea to introduce *earn while you learn* schemes wherever feasible. These can be operative outside the office hours of the college. The students can work in libraries, book / stationary shops, cooperative stores of the college, garden or other places (class room cleaning for instance, whitewashing the buildings etc.) depending upon their wish and capability. The college and the students can together discuss and decide on what is feasible.

16. Cooperative Society

The College can promote forming Cooperative Societies for the welfare of employees (providing loans for building homes or buying automobiles or supporting education of children of the employees etc). Such Societies should be properly registered under suitable Act and housed on the college campus with Principal as the President/ Chairman.

17. Creating Corpus/Endowment Funds

Colleges are meant to cater to the students who are the future of this country. Not all students are economically sound to afford paying fee, procure uniforms as per college dress code if any, books, laptops and sustain themselves during the tenure of a course. This can force them to discontinue their studies. Therefore, each college should strive to create endowment funds through the donors, philanthropists, alumni and so on. This will help in supporting deserving and poor students of all sections/categories. The endowment funds could also be set aside to award and reward the achievers: students getting university ranks, medals in sports and cultural activities or other extracurricular activities (NSS, NCC etc.).

In addition to the above, Principals may also motivate college employees and alumni to adopt one or two students and support their education or in giving incentives like annual awards, books and rewards for deserving students. This will not only enhance the reputation of the college but also provide great satisfaction to the alumni and employees involved in this process of *giving*. There is no dearth of givers but a dynamic leader is needed to harness the potential with missionary zeal.

18. Placement Cell

The colleges on their own or in the form of clusters can provide facilities for placement of students. The placement activities are best manned by competent and committed person whose priority lies in serving the students and helping them find suitable jobs. This will also enable colleges to know about the prospects of their own products. In the process, the experience gained will help in redesigning the curriculum. Good placement records for any college will enhance reputation of the college. A retired person with zeal can be entrusted with such a work of looking after the placement cell with some suitable honorarium and or needed logistic support.

19. Alumni Interactions

With the exception of IITs and IIMs and a few other institutions the alumni associations of particularly the traditional nonprofessional degree colleges are at best namesakes or non-existent. This is really unfortunate because there is an enormous potential to harvest from the properly structured and registered Alumni Associations (AA). Colleges can benefit from their AAs in multiple ways involving improvement in infrastructure, creating endowment funds and academic programs, strengthening placements and linkages (see Chapter 23).

20. Best Practices

Each college must have its own unique and where possible, innovative practices such that they become models for other colleges. A college should be known for one or more special features that distinguishes it from the other colleges through its best practices. Therefore, isomorphism should be avoided. The colleges should endeavour to provide a total campus experience in terms of academics, quality faculty, transparent administration, student support, inculcation of values and other best practices that promote all round development of students and make them feel proud of their Alma Mater throughout their life and fondly cherish their memories.

Note: The various extracurricular activities described above (sports, games, yoga, placement cell, alumni associations, skill development, entrepreneurship training, communication skills etc.) are better managed by outsourcing and taking the help of experts in the region. And, strengthening these activities is in the interest of both colleges and the stakeholders.

21. Promoting Holistic Development

Higher education must ultimately lead to enlightenment. What good higher education will do if it fails to produce virtuous human beings? Therefore, apart from imparting knowledge and training in skills, it is necessary to inculcate ethics, self-esteem and national pride in the minds of students. Exposure to discourses on moral/ethical values, and the basic Indian ethos of spirituality by eminent personalities can inspire students and faculty. My last but most important concern pertains to promoting holistic development and citizenry. Evidently, a focussed attention is needed to inculcate among students, faculty and supporting staff three concepts, *ethics, citizenry* and *giving* to make the higher education a meaningful exercise. These are briefly highlighted below:

(a) ***Ethics*:** Ethical practice is essential in whatever we do - selling tea on the streets or conducting a brain surgery. While unethical practices give quick results, lasting benefits come only from practices followed with due respect to ethics. I am reminded of the book "Winners Never Cheat" by John Huntsman a great business tycoon, a philanthropist, first President of Wharton School of business Management, a billionaire, and advisor to then President Richard Nixon of USA. In fact one should read this book to derive inspiration. The very title of this book has profound message. Also an implied message is that cheaters will never win! Surely, every educational institution must teach the importance of ethics and inculcate ethical practices among the students.

(b) ***Citizenry*:** The aim of good education is production of human resource worthy of managing the country to which it belongs. For this, mere technical knowledge is not enough. Education must provide for holistic development, as an expert, a scholar, a patriot, a nationalist and a person with concern for his/her fellow human beings and the Nature in which one lives. This calls for holistic development. The college management, principal, faculty members and the supporting staff by their exemplary actions and behaviour can imbue the concept of citizenry in the young minds, the students.

(c) ***Giving-back to Society*:** Every human being has an obligation to give back to the society. Giving has many dimensions. It does not necessarily mean giving money. It can be giving things, giving time, giving skills, giving gifts of reconciliation and new beginnings (gifts that keep giving), and giving good ideas. Our ancient scriptures proclaim unmistakably that giving is one thing that gives a person enormous contentment and happiness. Therefore, giving is also in the interest of the giver! Unfortunately one cannot experience this till a person goes through the process of giving. Here, let me quote two examples one from USA and one from India to explain length and breadth of what giving is all about. Besides, these are two highly inspiring examples: (1) Oseola McCarty (Symbol of selfless giving) and (2) Palam Kalyansundaram (Tryst with social service)

Ms Oseola McCarty hails from Mississippi, USA. She had no option but to be a school dropout in order to earn bread and support the family and her. She had a small laundry and worked as the washer women. She never bought anything of significance for herself, a home or car and saved all her earnings. One fine day she decided to donate her savings amounting to US$ 150,000/- to the University of Southern Mississippi to support education of poor black women. Soon matching grants poured in and now it is a very successful welfare program in the cause of women's emancipation, especially the black Americans. Her philanthropic and selfless act was recognized by the then President, Bill Clinton who awarded the prestigious *Presidential Citizens Medal* (1995). Subsequently, she was also decorated with Hon. Doctorate degrees of Harvard University (1996) and University of South Mississippi (1988)! This is not all. She also received Community Hero's Award from National Urban League and Avicenna Award of UNESCO. Ms McCarty has now become a symbol of selfless giving.

Philanthropic social service of Palam Kalyansundaram from the State of Tamil Nadu is equally inspiring. He is a Librarian by profession, a Gold medallist in MA (Literature and History) living in Chennai. As young man in 1960s he was impressed by the call of then Prime Minister

Jawaharlal Nehru who appealed for donation to the defence organization soon after the 1962 war with China. Mr. Kalyansundaram met Mr. Kamaraj Nadar then Chief Minister of Madras State and handed over his gold chain as donation for the Indian defence force. This noble act at that time was regarded by many as just a gimmick done for mere publicity. In reality, ever since Kalyansundaram began earning, he has been donating every rupee earned, to the poor, for over 40 years now. Further, he undertook other odd part time jobs to earn for his own living. He even experienced what poverty means by subjecting himself to the hardships. For instance, in India it is rather common that many poor people sleep on platforms in railway and bus stations even in the biting cold months. Kalyansundaram slept in these places too and he thus literally experienced what poor people experience.

After the retirement as the Librarian, he donated all the pension benefits (>10 Lakh rupees) to charity. His empathy for poor and needy was well recognized by the 'Man of the Millennium' award of UNO. All the 30 Crore rupees that he received from this award, he donated! Such empathy from more and more people is needed. In fact, Kalyansundaram very rightly stated that "We cannot sustain ourselves, unless we contribute to the society in some way or the other. I strongly feel even if one person does his bit towards social good, there will be some change". Such noble ideas need to permeate in the minds of our students on whom country depends for future growth and development.

The above and many other examples should inspire anyone and help inculcate such nobility. As an important component of education, colleges/varsities should sensitize and inspire young minds (our students and faculty) about the importance of *giving*. The concept of giving needs to be internalized by every citizen of this country. It is there in our ancient scriptures but sadly we have forgotten it.

To sum up, I believe that all Principals have a decisive 'Leadership' role to play and at the same time it is an opportunity to realize ones' own capabilities as well. But no one can become a leader without doing more than what she/he is paid for and cannot be successful without developing the art of leadership in the chosen field (in the present context, teaching and administration). Success results in satisfaction. Any accomplishment is a reward in itself. And, a failure is a lesson. Therefore, doing the best should be the motto. Let me recall two inspiring quotes from the book 'The Alchemist' by Paul Coelho: (1) "...And, when you want something, all the universe conspires in helping you to achieve it, and (2) "...There is only one thing that makes a dream impossible to achieve: that is the fear of failure". Thus, a positive outlook is needed to fully utilize opportunities that knock the door. A pessimistic view is a trap. People who entertain pessimism are rarely successful in administration or in providing leadership. Heads of the institution need to function fearlessly. He who has no hidden agenda has nothing to fear. Actually fear vanishes in the absence of any hidden agenda. A key aspect to remember is that satisfaction is the measure of one's success and not the position held or the payment received. Being successful is not difficult; it is indeed simple. All you need to do is, *know what you are doing, love what you are doing,* and *believe in what you are doing*. This is very important because people who do not know where they want to go, more often than not, end up going nowhere!

CHAPTER - 9

IMPERATIVES OF GOOD GOVERNANCE

— *S. S. PATAGUNDI*

Undergraduate education is a link between school and university education systems. The successive five year plans have been prioritising expansion, equity and excellence as significant goals of Indian higher education and all of these are equally important. Lord Bhiku Parekh, Emeritus Professor of Political Philosophy, University of Hull, in his convocation address at Nirma University, Ahmadabad on October 21, 2016 said "Expansion, equity and excellence, the three widely canvassed goals of IHE, are closely related and none can be attained at the expense of the other two. Such an expansion has no meaning and even becomes a fraud if it perpetuates poor quality education unworthy of being called 'higher' or university education." Good governance of colleges is therefore important for ensuring quality education. Governance means the capacity to steer the economy and society towards collective goals (IEPS, 2011). Often lack of seriousness is a problem confronting the governance of the colleges possibly due to a poor quality of teachers and the learners. In addition, a crisis of professional ethics, shortage of teachers, inadequate concern and commitment of teachers and inadequate infrastructure are commonly encountered in most of the colleges.

Teachers are central actors in promoting and nurturing higher education. As per Yash Pal Committee report "It should be mandatory for all universities to have a rich undergraduate programme and undergraduate students must get opportunities to interact with the best faculty." Therefore the colleges need to overhaul undergraduate (UG) education. It is in this context and falling standards of higher education, basic understanding of the principles of governance in the working of colleges become imperative for enabling managers of higher education to address diverse issues effectively. The quality of UG education certainly affects the quality of postgraduate (PG) education and research. This Chapter attempts to focus on the concept and importance of good governance of colleges.

It was Harlan Cleveland who first used the word 'governance' as an alternative to the phrase 'public administration' in 1970s. It began to get attention when it was used by the World Bank in the 1980s. The World Bank published a report entitled, "Governance and Development" in 1992 and it was redefined as 'good governance' in the year 1997. The report outlined the concept of governance and its application. The study of good governance or quality of government is a fairly new and rapidly growing field of research (IEPS, 2011). Lynn, Heinrich, and Hill defined 'governance' as "regimes, laws, rules, judicial decisions, and administrative practices that constrain, prescribe, and enable the provision of publicly supported goals and services" holds strong interest for public administration scholars. Governance relates to the processes of interaction and decision-making among the actors involved in a collective problem solving process. It is a theoretical concept referring to the actions and the style of functioning of the institution. Such actions have specific long-term and short-term objectives which may be considered as perspective plans. From this viewpoint, governance is also applicable to profit making organisations; the corporate governance. Besides, we come across multi level governances such as the local, state, national and global, all of which fall under public governance.

In the Indian context, governance is not a new concept. During the ancient period, in the most categorical pronouncement of the principles of good governance Kautilya opined that in the happiness of people lies the happiness of a good ruler; in their welfare his welfare; whatever pleases himself he shall not consider as good, but whatever pleases his people he shall consider it as good. Thus, representing public aspirations for promoting the wellbeing of people is a central concern of good governance. In this regard, the ruling class is expected to formulate people-oriented policies. It also implies that the way or the manner of exercising political power determines the extent of effective governance to serve the popular aspirations and expectations of the society as a whole. Evidently, structure and process of public policy decision-making constitute an important part of governance. Quite commonly, good governance is defined in terms of its antonyms by referring to phenomena that indicate its absence, such as corruption, nepotism, favouritism, particularism, or patrimonialism (IEPS, 2011). Rule of law, transparency, responsiveness, consensus-oriented, equity and inclusiveness, effectiveness and efficiency, accountability and participation are regarded as elements of good governance.

The functions of governance were originally defined in Dr. Lynda Bourne's article 'The Six Functions of Governance' and they are as follows:

Determining Objectives

A major function of governance of colleges is to determine its both short and long term objectives that will reflect in the formulation of a perspective plans. These are based on the 'vision and mission' statements of the institution. A major objective of the colleges is to impart quality education that has relevance to employability, serving the interest of society and contributing to the process of creating knowledge. Ensuring student centric education is essential. The academic leadership (the Principal), management and the State / Central Governments play a vital role in formulating appropriate strategies for achieving the set goals. Furthermore, it is quite necessary that the objectives are precise and unambiguous.

Determining Ethics

All employees, including the Principal, faculty members and the supporting staff are expected to follow the institutional conduct rules and guidelines in their day-to-day working. Yet, following moral and ethical values is also important. The ethical standards of the college significantly influence its overall performance. Undoubtedly, honesty, integrity, competence, benevolence and stewardship play an important role in determining good governance of colleges (www.masaicproject.com.au).

Creating a Culture

The functioning of an institution depicts its culture and thereby the quality of governance. Values such as commitment to the institution, dedication, concern for the students, mutual respect, and a sense of belonging are crucial dimensions of good culture. In this process, the attitudes and outlook of the management and stakeholders play a crucial role.

Designing and Implementing the Governance Framework

The governance framework defines the principles and structure, enabling the factors and interfaces through which the organisation's arrangements will operate, by delegating appropriate levels of authority and responsibility to management and other entities. Delegation of powers and functions is essential to ensure good governance; it ensures transparency and accountability.

Ensuring Accountability by Management

Ethical and cultural environment ensures accountability. Monitoring judicious use of resources to enhance quality of teaching, learning and research will help achieve the stated objectives of the institution.

Ensuring Compliance by the Organisation

Compliance with its regulatory, statutory and legal obligations as well as monitoring and directing the performance of its management and staff, is an integral part of governance. Besides, timely compliances and working within ethical and cultural frameworks contributes to fulfil the obligations of regulatory bodies. Hence, this practice is to ensure good governance of the institution.

Leadership and Governance

Harold D, Lasswell says that influence is unequal and the most influential are the elites. Generally, we regard elites as leaders. Leaders deal with complex problems of human relations. A leader is supposed to understand people and get along with them. A leader's words of appreciation and encouragement will enable him/her to address complex problems of human relations effectively. Such gestures are essential attributes of good governance.

The governance of colleges presupposes to provide adequate facilities including support services for teaching and learning through mobilisation of financial resources. The UGC provides some financial assistance subject to the fulfilment of certain conditions under various provisions. Good colleges develop best and most innovative practices for mobilisation of resources. In this process, the Principals play a significant role both as an academic leader and as a facilitator. It is noteworthy that in the past colleges were identified by the credibility or personality of the Principals and teachers. Unfortunately, in recent times their credibility has declined greatly. Attributes of a good leader are that She/he (1) is ready to give to others rather than expect to receive from others, (2) is equipped to manage change, (3) has nobility of heart, (4) has vision, clear thinking, and capacity to be a facilitator, and (5) has honesty and integrity (Kalam, 2014).

Governance

What constitutes quality teaching from the viewpoint of students? How can students be encouraged to become more engaged and, active learners? Obviously, diverse aspects associated with good quality teaching need to be fostered (www.oecd.org|edu|imhe; see other chapters for detailed consideration on this issue). According to the 12th five-year plan, the governance of HEIs is expected to achieve expansion, equity and excellence, and ultimately, imparting education is to ensure the development of the country. Therefore, leadership provided by the Principal and quality of teaching-learning becomes crucial (see also Chapter 8).

There has been tremendous growth in higher education since independence. In our country, there were 20 universities and 500 UG Colleges at the time of independence. Now there are nearly 864 universities and 40,026 colleges. Majority of the colleges (59.34%) are located in rural area. The national gross enrolment ratio (GER) of higher education is ~ 25 percent as per the recent 'All India Survey on Higher Education' Report (2016-17). Assessment and accreditation (AA) by NAAC has considerably contributed to improvements in the overall performance of HEIs. It is generally observed that around 25% of HEIs might have undergone NAAC accreditation so far though the AA is mandatory (Hegde, 2017).

Role of Regulatory Bodies

Governance of colleges plays a vital role in imparting quality and relevant education from the perspective of employability and service to the society. Various regulatory bodies such as the UGC, AICTE, NAAC, DST, NCTE, State Higher Education Council, Universities established under specific Acts play a crucial role in monitoring governance of colleges. They form the mechanisms for providing funds, guidelines and regulations for maintaining standards in teaching and/ or research. They also provide guidelines and regulations pertaining to appointment, workload and promotion of teachers, introduction of new courses to name a few; these help the HEIs to maintain and improve standards of education. Furthermore, development needs of colleges are carefully identified by the UGC. Accordingly, it provides 'development' grants to institutions recognized under 2(f) and 12(b) of UGC Act of 1956 to augment infrastructure, introduction of new courses and other activities aimed at improving overall performance of the institution. The eligibility conditions differ with the nature of colleges and therefore one should consult UGC guidelines before applying for such grants. The basic concern of UGC in stipulating certain conditions for getting funds is to ensure the quality of education, regulation and promoting overall interests of the colleges.

College Development Council

The College Development Council (CDC) facilitates colleges to get recognition under 2(f) and 12(b) of UGC Act. It also plays an intermediary role between colleges and regulatory bodies for availing financial assistance under various provisions for creating facilities required for teaching and learning. The CDC is also supposed to guide and motivate colleges to make use of several provisions of the granting agencies and procure funds. The colleges can obtain information about various provisions/schemes of the regulatory bodies through the CDC or browsing the websites of UGC or other R and D agencies. Proper utilisation of funds received from UGC by a college is monitored by the CDC.

Most Colleges are affiliated to Universities which provide curriculum, conduct examinations and award degrees. Therefore, the universities send their Local Inquiry Committees (LIC) to visit colleges and make needed recommendations for granting or renewing affiliations. Implementation of recommendations of the LIC is mandatory.

Framing rules governing the colleges will be in conformity with the guidelines of the UGC and other relevant regulatory bodies. In addition, taking inputs from stakeholders like alumni, parents and faculty in making rules or taking decisions democratises the working of colleges and is equally important. Besides, it also helps to ensure transparency and accountability of colleges. Transparency in the admission, internal assessment and conducting examinations as per stipulated norms is absolutely necessary.

Role of Stakeholders in Governance

The stakeholders of colleges are students, alumni, parents, government / management and teachers. The governance of a college is significantly influenced by stakeholders' concern, commitment and sense of belongingness. Clearly, the responsiveness, accountability, transparency, consensus and participation in the process of implementing guidelines and regulations of regulatory bodies of the State/central governments, will determine the effectiveness of governance of colleges. In this respect, the major stakeholders have a significant role to play. Participation of stakeholders in the decision making from the viewpoint of promoting academic excellence is an important part of good governance of colleges. Thus, administrative and academic leadership of Principals, the Governing Bodies, competency and concern of the faculty members, involvement of stakeholders matter a lot in the successful governance of the colleges. Challenges, opportunities and role of Principals are dealt at length in Chapter 8 of this book.

In my view, the academic governance should include nurturing the following:

Creation of Knowledge

Knowledge is power. Hence, high priority should be given for generating new knowledge in a globalised world. Our former President A. P. J. Abdul Kalam said "Whether any nation qualifies as a knowledge society or not is judged by how effectively it deals with knowledge creation and knowledge deployment". From this viewpoint, contribution to the creation of knowledge through effective teaching learning and research is a major challenge to the governance of colleges in the age of globalisation. Deployment of knowledge involves using research findings as inputs in policy decision-making and providing consultancy services by the faculty. This is a big challenge for almost all HEIs. Likewise, making students the lifelong learners is extremely pertinent and important. In the entire process of knowledge and capacity building the attitude of the faculty needs to be positive. Changing the attitude of the faculty is however a challenging task.

Adoption of ICT

This is significant because technological solutions may help the governance of colleges addressing many issues for smooth functioning. Promoting ICT based teaching and learning is imperative for raising standards in conventional HEIs. But the adoption of ICT in HEIs is slow since by and large people are sluggish in accepting change. Hence, adopting rapidly changing ICT in teaching-learning and administration is one of the major challenges to the governance of colleges (see Chapter 17).

Producing Employable Graduates

Developing skills in addition to knowledge is important for ensuring employability. The slow pace of colleges in inculcating the development of life skills is a great threat to the employment opportunities of the main stakeholders, the students. Unless the colleges regard developing pertinent skills is an integral part of the course or introducing add-on courses, it is not possible to address the problems of employability. Hence, the Principals / Management / varsities should think deeply in evolving measures to ensure employability of our youth. Skills are to be developed according to demand of the job market. In India, traditionally our priority has not been to produce skilled workers. Therefore, compared to other countries, our position in producing skilled workers is dismal hovering at 02% compared to Republic of Korea (96%), Japan (80%), Germany (75%), UK (68%), and USA (52%) (Dhawan, 2016).

The important life skills identified by the World Health Organization (WHO) pertain to: 'Self Awareness, Empathy, Interpersonal Relationship, Effective Communication, Critical Thinking, Creative Making, Decision Making, Problem Solving, Coping with Emotions and Stress'.

The Educational Skills fall under 12 Domains classified as under: (1) Self Development Skills, (2) Social Skills: Interpersonal and Collaborative Skills, Communication Skills, Resilience Skills, Social Responsibility Skills, Human Relations Skills, Emotional Skills, Adjustment Skills, Human Development Skills, Citizenship Skills, Accountability and Adaptability Skills, (3) Life Skills (4) Critical Thinking and Training Thinking Skills, (5) Research Skills, (6) Constructive and Connectionist Skills, (7) Systems Thinking Skills, (8) Information Age Skills: Info-Savvy Skills, Techno-pedagogic Skills, Digital Age Skills, Open Education, Resourcing Skills, (9) Leadership, Administration and Management Skills: Creative Leadership Skills, Administration Skills, Time Management Skills, Key Skills for Every Manager, (10) Spiritual Development Skills, (11) Yoga Skills and (12) Holistic Development Skill. (Chhaya Goel and Devaraj Goel, 2015)

In India there exists a national policy for promotion of skill development with a number of good initiatives. HEIs should grab such initiatives as soon as possible and evolve various skill development programmes and make students employable. This calls for a change in the mindsets of all stakeholders, eliminating bureaucratic norms, and easing the implementation processes.

Recruitment of teachers must be based on merit, competency, objectivity and transparency. Inbreeding should be avoided. In this regard, granting autonomy to the colleges is also important. One of the recommendations of the National Knowledge Commission is that colleges are to be encouraged to become autonomous. Good governance can ensure the recruitment of competent, dedicated and committed teachers who can address the problems of quality and relevance with respect to UG education in India. In short, good governance is imperative for meaningful education and production of good human resource.

[Caveat: As per the present media reports (July-August 2018) the MHRD is contemplating repeal of the UGC Act of 1956 and create two new bodies: The Higher Education Council of India (HECI) and Higher Education Financing Agency (HEFA). Therefore, the colleges/ varsities may wait until the constitution of these new bodies, and their specific roles are made clear.]

References Cited

1. Bade, B., Berg-Schlosser, D., and Morlino, L. (Eds.) *International Encyclopaedia of Political Science* (IEPS), Vol.4, Los Angeles, Sage, 2011.
2. Dhawan, S. 2016. *University News* 54(39) 26 Sep. and 2 Oct.
3. *Fostering Quality teaching in Higher Education: Policies and Practices*, An IMHE Guide for Higher Education Institutions, September 2012, www.oecd.org|edu|imhe
4. Frederickson H.G, 2007. In *The Oxford Handbook of Public Management*, Lynn, F. E. and Politt, C. (Eds.), Oxford University Press.
5. Goel, C. and Goel, D. 2015. *University News*, 53(48), Nov. 30 and Dec. 6.
6. Hegde, G. 2017. *University News, 55(28),* July 10-16.
7. http//www.masaicprojects.com.au/white papers.html
8. Kalam, APJ. 2014. Governance for Growth in India. Rupa, New Delhi.
9. Lasswell, H. D, 1965. In *World Revolutionary Elites*, (Lasswell, H.D. and Learner, D. (Eds.), MIT Press, Cambridge.
10. Parekh, B. 2016. *University News* 54(45), Nov. 7-13.

Suggested Reading

1. *Defining Quality in Education, Working Paper Series*, Education Section Program Division, United Nations Children's Fund, New York, 2000.
2. *Internationalization of Indian Higher Education* (Papers presented at the Roundtable on January 26-28, 2001), AIU, New Delhi, 2001.
3. *Indian Higher Education: Envisioning the Future*, Agarwal P. 2009. Sage, New Delhi, 2009.
4. *Higher Education Today and Tomorrow*, Chaudhari U. S. 2009. Gyan Publishing House, New Delhi.
5. *Learning, Teaching and Education Research in the 21st Century: An evolutionary analysis of the role of teachers*, Swann J. 2012. Continuum International Publishing Group, London.
6. *Higher Education in India: In Search of Equality, Quality and Quantity*, Tilak J. B.G. (Ed.). Orient Black Swan, New Delhi, 2015
7. *University News Special Issue* on Higher Education towards Skill Development and Entrepreneurship , 53(48), 2015
8. Globalization: Culture and Education in the New Millennium, Suarez-Orozco, M. M. and Qin Hilliard, D. B. (Eds.), Rawat Publications, Jaipur, 2016.
9. Teaching in Higher Education: is there a need for training in pedagogy in graduate degree programs? *Research in Higher Education Journal*, Robinson, T. E. and Warren C. H. *http://www.aabri.com/copyright.html.*
10. *University News Special Issue* on Contribution of Universities to Skilling, Innovation and Entrepreneurship, 54(39), 2016.

11. *University News Special Issue* on Role of Higher Education in Transforming India, 54(5), February 1-7, 2016.
12. *University News Special Issue* on Designing Higher Education Institutions: Role of Digital Initiatives, 55(51), 2017.
13. *University News Special Issue* on Leadership excellence in Higher Education and Research, 55(49), 2017.
14. *University News Special Issue* on Opportunities and Challenges towards Transforming Indian Universities into Global Premier Universities by 2020, 55(50), 2017.

CHAPTER - 10

FULFILLING THE OBJECTIVES OF 'RIGHT TO INFORMATION ACT'

— *C. S. PATIL*

Democracy must be built through open societies that share information. When there is information, there is enlightenment. When there is debate, there are solutions. When there is no sharing of power, no rule of law, no accountability, there is abuse, corruption, subjugation and indignation. — ATIFETE JAHJAGA

An informed person is an empowered person. Information adds to quality of life. That is the reason for which it is considered as one of the basic rights. In a democratic country, the right to information is akin to the freedom of speech and expression. Thus the right to information becomes the hall mark of a democratic government providing a market place for ideas. It is stated, information is power. By experience everyone knows this. Thus right to information is right to power or right to power sharing. For this reason, it is a right about which the power holders feel inconvenient. However, in a democracy, which is based on the principle of sovereignty of people, right to information is a must. Every citizen has a right to know what happens in the government or other related organizations. On the contrary, secrecy has its own dangers. If allowed to function in secrecy, government may abuse power. Corruption thrives in secret places. This will invite inequality between government and citizens and citizens inter se. Without information public debate over public issues gets undermined. Main objectives of seeking information are the following.

Evaluation of Government

A government working under a controlling welfare Constitution like ours should adhere to the primordial principles enshrined in the Constitution. The Constitution has set the goals which the governments should strive to achieve while respecting the charter of liberty that is carved out in favour of the citizens. The social revolution that is contemplated in Part III and Part-IV of the Constitution should be realized. The performance of every government is to be evaluated. That is the ballot revolution contemplated in the Constitution. The following invaluable words of Dr. Babu Rajendra Prasad, the first President of free India, made in the concluding session of the Constituent Assembly should be remembered here. He said, "Whatever the Constitution may or may not provide, the welfare of the country will depend upon the way in which the country is administered. That will depend upon the men who administer it. It is a trite saying that a country can have only the government it deserves." If the country wants a responsive and responsible government, the citizenry should be alert and should be constantly observing the power holders. The power holders should feel that, the power addressees i.e., citizenry has a right to wrestle information which can be used to saddle them with liability. This will compel them to be fair in the discharge of their functions which is demanded by the transparency and accountability dimensions which the right to information ushers in. Evaluation of the government becomes possible only when adequate information is available.

Participation in Government

Informed citizenry is a *sine qua non* of a democratic government. Periodically the government invites the public opinion on the proposed policy decisions. In a democracy, despite the fact that the people's representatives make legislations, the draft legislations and policies are open for public debate. The opinion of the public will go in moulding the legislation or the policy. The effective expression of public opinion will depend upon availability of the information to the affected interests about the implications of the provisions of the proposed policy and the laws.

Individual Self Fulfilment

The information sought under Right to Information Act is not necessarily meant for use against the government or to find fault with the government. A welfare state may often confer myriad benefits on the individuals not only through laws but also through various schemes. An individual may therefore be interested in knowing them. A differently enabled person, a below poverty line person, an elderly person, a widow, etc should know their entitlements to attain self fulfilment. There should be channels of information available to them.

Finding Truth

Every citizen in a democratic system is entitled to know the truth. By every act unauthorized by law, the society gets disturbed. The society would be interested in knowing why the things have happened the way they have happened. Let it be a killing of innocent individuals, attacks on elderly persons or scams involving finance and other companies. The society expects to know truth so that it can form an opinion and decide either to reconcile with it or otherwise.

Checks Abuse of Authority

It is stated 'sunlight is the best disinfectant'. Transparency arrests abuse of power because, the officers will be exposed. In fact Right to Information Act has come as a boon to law abiding officers and a bane to those who circumvent the established norms. In the present day regime of information revelation the black sheep can be identified. This has become a good tool for subordinate officers to resist the pressure by the superiors and politicians to take actions not sanctioned by law.

Enables Gain Control Over Others

A person possessing crucial information is an empowered person and hence gains control over other persons. An ill informed person renders himself subservient to an informed person. If there is dissemination of information, the dependency will be reduced and each person will be in a position to make his plans for life. A responsible government should not create an environment wherein the citizens are treated like subjects under an alien government totally at the mercy of them. It should open up channels to inform every individual so that she/he can live an independent informed life.

Commensurate with the purposes information serves, we have different types of information seekers. These are described below:

Information Seeker as a Public Citizen

This person is motivated with the higher values the information has to serve in a democratic society. He wants to evaluate the performance of the government, he wants to participate in the government and for that he wants information. Prof. Amarthya Sen in his book, 'Argumentative Indian' observes that 'silence is the enemy of social justice.' One has to speak. To speak one needs information.

Information seeker as a Private person

This person is concerned with fulfilling his needs and desires in lawful manner. He wants to have information required for this. A student is interested in knowing about the courses, hostel facilities, fees concessions, reservations, etc. A householder will be more interested in knowing about the power cuts, supply of water, etc., a poor family may have more interest in a ration card than in passport or electoral identity card.

Information seeker as a Surrogate

Here we have the good Samaritans, those who help others in trouble. Some public spirited individuals always take cudgels on behalf of those who cannot espouse their own cause and fight public injustice. They also will be seeking information for this purpose.

Man has throughout the ages tried different doctrines, principles and methods to control power. The hitherto used mechanisms like administrative supervision, audit, vigilance, etc. have not ushered in the era of administrative legality and administrative liability. In the quest to infuse transparency and accountability in governance, the judiciary took initiative and read right to information into freedom of speech and expression. Under the *Right to Information Act, 2005* we find the right being elevated to the level of a statutory right. The Act came into force on 12th October 2005. The right should surge forward and get entrenched into the Constitution as a fundamental right in due course. All this is the result of information chariot rolling and gaining momentum. Following are the salient attributes of the Right to Information Act.

(a) What is Information?

Under this Act 'information' means any material in any form, including records, documents, memos, e-mails, opinions, advises, press releases, circulars, orders, logbooks, contracts, reports, papers, samples, models, data material held in any form including electronic form and information relating to any private body which can be accessed by a public authority under any other law for the time being in force.

(b) What is Right to Information?

Under this Act all citizens have right to information. This right includes right to have information held by or under the control of any public authority and includes the right to inspection of work, documents, records; taking notes, extracts or certified copies or documents or records; taking certified samples of material; obtaining information in the form of diskettes, floppies, tapes, video cassettes or in any other electronic mode or through printouts where such information is stored in a computer or any other devise.

(c) What is a Record?

For the purposes of the Act, a 'record' includes any document, manuscript and file; any microfilm, microfiche and facsimile copy of a document; any reproduction of image or images embodied in such microfilm and any other material produced by a computer or any other device.

(d) From whom Information can be sought

Information under this Act can be obtained from any 'public authority'. Under this Act public authority means any authority or body or institution of self-government established or constituted by or under the Constitution; by any law made by the parliament; by any law made by the state legislature; by notification issued or order made by the appropriate government. A body owned, controlled or substantially financed directly or indirectly by funds provided by the appropriate government is a public authority for the purpose of this Act. Further a non-government organization substantially financed directly or indirectly by funds provided by the appropriate government is also included.

(e) Voluntary disclosure of information by the Public Authority

All the public authorities are required by the Act to maintain records duly classified and indexed in such a manner as to facilitate the exercise of right to information under this Act. All appropriate records are to be computerized and connected through a network all over the country. The public authority should voluntarily publish the particulars of its organization, functions, duties; the powers and duties of its officers and employees; the procedure followed in decision making process, including channels of supervision and accountability; the norms followed in discharge of its functions; rules, regulations, instructions, manuals and records used for discharge of functions, categories of documents under its control, details of arrangements that exist for consulting members of the public or representatives in formulation of the policy of the authority and its implementation.

Further, the public authority has to publish information about the advisory boards, councils, committees and other bodies constituted and if their meetings are open to the public or if the minutes of such meetings are accessible to public. A directory of its officers and employees along with their salaries and other allowances is to be published. The budget allocated, particulars of all plans, proposed expenditures and reports of disbursements made; the manner of execution of subsidy programs including the amounts allocated and the details of beneficiaries of such programs; particulars of recipients of concessions, permits or authorizations granted by it; details of information available in electronic form; particulars of facilities available to citizens for obtaining information; names and designations of Public Information Officers are all to be published.

(f) Information exempted from disclosure

Certain type of information need not be furnished to the information seeker, the citizen. This category of information is known as 'information exempted' from disclosure. These are listed below:

(i) Information, the disclosure of which would prejudicially affect the sovereignty and integrity of India, the security, strategic, scientific or economic interests of the state, relation with foreign state or lead to incitement of an offence

(ii) Information which has been expressly forbidden to be published by any court of law or tribunal or the disclosure of which may constitute contempt of court

(iii) Information the disclosure of which would cause a breach of privilege of Parliament or the State Legislature

(iv) Information including commercial confidence, trade secrets or intellectual property

(v) Information received by a person in his fiduciary relationship such as doctor-patient relationship, advocate-client relationship, etc.

(vi) Information received in confidence from foreign government

(vii) Information, the disclosure of which would endanger the life or physical safety of any person or identify the source of information or assistance given in confidence for law enforcement or security purposes

(viii) Information which would impede the process of investigation or apprehension or prosecution of offenders

(ix) Cabinet papers including records of deliberations of Council of Ministers, Secretaries and other officers.

(g) Third Party Information

If the application for information relates to the information available with the public authority which relates to a third party and has been treated confidential by that third party, the information officer has to give a notice to such third party about the application within five days and invite the third party to make a submission in writing or orally, regarding whether the information could be disclosed, and such submission of the third party shall be kept in view while taking a decision about disclosure of information. The third party has to be given an opportunity to make representation against the proposed disclosure within ten days. The information may be disclosed if the public interest in disclosure outweighs in importance than any possible harm or injury to the interest of such third party.

(h) Procedure for obtaining Information

A person desirous of obtaining information under this Act has to make a request to the Public Information Officer (PIO) along with prescribed fee. At present the fee prescribed is Rs.10. For obtaining photocopies of information the fee is Rs.2/- per page. If the information is published information, the fee is Rs.1/- per page. In any other case the PIO will fix the fee depending upon the cost of labour and material required to supply the information. For inspection of records, no fee is charged for the first hour. For every subsequent half an hour Rs.10/- will be charged. If the applicant is a Below Poverty Line (BPL) card holder, no fee is charged if the information requested is less than 100 pages; if it is more than one 100 pages a fee of Rs.1/- per page is collected. For providing information in diskette or floppy or C.D. or in any other electronic mode the fee is Rs.50/-

If the request is oral, it is desirable that the PIO provides reasonable assistance so as to avoid seeking information in writing. The applicant need not give any reasons for requesting information. The information is to be given in the form in which it is requested as far as possible unless it disproportionately diverts the resources of the public authority or would be detrimental to the safety or preservation of the records in question. The PIO should give the information within 30 days on payment of prescribed fees or reject the application on the ground that the information requested is exempted from disclosure. If the information sought relates to life or liberty of a person, it has to be given within forty-eight hours. If the application is received by a public authority and the application relates to information held by another public authority, it has to transfer the application to such other authority within five days. In such cases such other authority has to furnish information within 30 days from the receipt of that application. If the information is not supplied within the stipulated time, it shall be deemed that the PIO has rejected the request. The Act provides that if the information is not provided within the time stipulated, it shall be given free of cost. If the PIO has rejected the request for information, he shall inform the applicant the reasons for such rejection, the period within which an appeal against such rejection may be made, and the address of the appellate authority.

Application Format for seeking Information

There is no prescribed format of application for seeking information. It can be made on plain paper. The applicant should mention the address at which the information required is to be sent. The applicant need not give reasons for seeking information. However, the *Karnataka Right to Information Rules, 2005* provide the following format for the convenience of the information seekers.

Form A
(Sections 6(1) and 7(1) of the RTI Act, 2005)

1. Full name of the applicant:
2. Address:
3. Details of document/ inspection/samples required:
4. Year to which the above pertains:
5. Designation and address of the Public Information Officer from whom the information is required:

Place:

Date: Signature of the applicant

(i) Appeal

Any person who is aggrieved by the decision of the PIO may appeal to such officer who is senior in rank to the PIO within 30 days. A second appeal against the decision of the first appellate authority is provided to the Central Information Commission or the State Information Commission as the case may be. A second appeal can be made within 90 days. The appeals are to be disposed off within 30 days or within such extended period not exceeding a total of 45 days, for reasons to be recorded, from the date of filing.

(ii) Penalty

The Central Information Commission or the State Information Commission as the case may be, at the time of deciding an appeal forms an opinion that the PIO has, without any reasonable cause, refused to receive an application for information or has not furnished information within the time specified or with mala fide intention denied the request for information or knowingly has given incorrect, incomplete or misleading information or destroyed information which was the subject of the request or obstructed in any manner in furnishing the information, it shall impose a penalty of Rs.250/- per day till the application is received or information is provided. The total penalty imposed, however, should not exceed Rs. 25000/-. The appellate authority may recommend even disciplinary action against the PIO. However, before imposing penalty, the concerned PIO should be given an opportunity to explain as to why penalty should not be imposed on him.

The enactment of 'Right to Information Act' has indeed created ripples in public life. It has added new dimensions to definitions of 'accountability' and 'transparency'. The shield of information opacity that guarded the vested interests till such enactment has disappeared. Some Governmental authorities / officials may not welcome these developments. They may regard this as an invasion of their 'functional space'. They feel often irritated by the provisions like low fees prescribed for information, no requirement of reason for seeking information etc.

Asking questions under the Right to Information Act

The working of the Act over a period of 10 years has yielded, different interpretations and sometimes even colossal loss of office time in disposing off the information application. The right to information came to be perceived by a section of people as right to ask questions, clarifications, reasons, etc. The response to such applications varied from compliance to rejection. Appreciating the need to clarify some misconceptions the Supreme Court has in the case of *Central Board of Secondary Education v. Aditya Bandopadhyay* (Civil Appeal No.6454 of 2011 decided on 9th August 2011) observed as under:

> "If a public authority has any information in the form of data or analysed data, or abstracts, or statistics, an applicant may access such information, subject to the exemptions in section 8 of the Act. But where the information sought is not a part of the record of a public authority, and where such information is not required to be maintained under any law or the rules or regulations of the public authority, the Act does not cast an obligation upon the public authority, to collect or collate such non-available information and then furnish it to an applicant. A public authority is also not required to furnish information which require drawing of inferences and/or making of assumptions. It is also not required to provide 'advise' or 'opinion, to an applicant, nor required to obtain and furnish any 'opinion' or 'advise' from an applicant. The reference to 'opinion' or 'advise' in the definition of 'information' in section 2(f) of the Act only refers to such material available in the records of the public authority. Many public authorities have, as a public relation exercise, provide advice, guidance and opinion to citizens. But

that is purely voluntary and should not be confused with any obligation under the Act."

In the same manner the Ministry of Personnel, Public Grievances and Pensions, Department of Personnel and Training, Government of India, clarifies the issue, through its Guide to Right to Information, (published vide Office Memorandum no.1/32/2013-IR dated 28th November 2013) Act , 2005) as follows:

> "...It is important to note that only such information can be supplied under the Act that is available and existing and is held under the control of the public authority. The public information officer is not supposed to create information that is not a part of the record of public authority. The public information officer is also not required to furnish information which require drawing of inferences and/or making of assumptions; or to interpret information; or to solve the problems raised by the applicants; or to furnish replies to hypothetical questions".

In some cases, the applicants expect the PIO to give information in some particular format devised by them on the plea that they have a right to get information in the form in which it is sought. It need be noted that the provision in the Act simply means that if the information is sought in the form of photocopy, it has to be provided in the form of photocopy, or if it is sought in the form of a floppy or in any other electronic mode, it shall be provided in that form, subject to the conditions given in the Act. It does not mean that the PIO shall re-shape the information.

Some information seekers request the PIOs to cull out information from some document(s) and give such extracted information. A citizen has a right to get 'material' from a public authority which is held by or under the control of that public authority. The Act, however, does not require the PIO to deduce some information from the 'material' and supply the 'conclusion' so deduced to the applicant. In short, the PIO is only required to supply the 'material' in the form as held by the public authority, but not to do research on behalf of the citizen to deduce anything from the material and then supply it to him.

The applicant should not list out his grievances in the RTI application but should clearly mention which information or record he would like to seek. Further, if the drafting of the application is such that it pin points towards the specific documents required in relation to the information sought, there would be less scope of ambiguity, thereby resulting in less chances of denial of information by the PIO. For example instead of simply asking why my area is not being cleaned, cleaning schedule for the area should be asked. Similarly, instead of asking when we will get water supply, water supply planning of the area should be asked. It may be noted that when the answer to the questions raised is available in the form of information held by the authority, the authority should not reject the application.

Purposive Approach to RTI Act

A. The RTI Act is open for legal and administrative interpretations

While interpreting the provisions, the purpose of the Act is to be borne in mind. The interpretations adopted should advance the remedy which the Act has contemplated in favour of individuals. For example, under the Act only a citizen has right to information. The interpretation of this provision to include an association of citizens also will add to the effectiveness of the Act. In the immediate aftermath of the implementation of the Act, there was a big controversy about notes on the files. Under Sec.2 (i) "record" includes "file". File consists of a "note" portion and a "correspondence" portion. "Note" portion consists of chain of 'notes and orders' relating to papers under consideration. "Correspondence" portion consists of papers under consideration serially filed. There was a fear that exposing note portion would inhibit executive- both permanent and political from discharging their functions objectively. The fear is uncalled for because it will disclose who is an honest officer and who is not. If note remains secret, honest officers also will have to take blame. Note provides an information chain that connects the final decision to its cause, its disclosure will help to fix accountability. Requirement of disclosure would infuse objectivity in discharge of functions.

A. Every Act of Parliament is Open for Easy Amendments

An unscrupulous government with the majority in the parliament may amend the Act to denude it of its effectiveness. Therefore the country should aim at a constitutionally entrenched fundamental right to information which is beyond the pale of legislative and executive encroachment.

B. Right to be Informed and Right to Information Components of the Act

The real information stake holders, the deprived masses are engrossed in their basic fight for survival, how the benefits of RTI Act can be made to reach them. Government should inform to such an extent that recourse to RTI Act should be of last resort. The information voluntarily made available by the public authority should be of such a nature that, there should be no need to file an application for information. That would save so much of precious time for discharging office duties than grappling with RTI application.

C. Two Pronged Approaches to Realise RTI Act

First, a civil society has to gear up in real earnest and propagate the message that frivolous and unnecessary applications would defeat the intent and ultimate purpose of the Act. Right to inspect work and documents, low cost coupled with non requirement of disclosure of purpose for seeking information may lead to harassment. Effective mechanism to keep out busy bodies should be worked out. The amendment to the *Karnataka Right to Information Rules, 2005* notified on 17thMarch 2008 makes us imagine the types of applications the authorities should have received. The amendment adds a new rule, rule 14, which reads as under: 14. Request to relate only to single subject matter: A request in writing for information under section 6 of the Act shall relate to one subject matter and it shall not ordinarily exceed one hundred and fifty words. If an applicant wishes to seek information on more than one subject matter, he shall make separate applications. Provided that in case, the request made relates to more than one subject matter, the Public Information Officer may respond to the request relating to the first subject matter only and may advise the applicant to make separate application for each of the other subjects. Second, concerted effort on the part of government to respect the right of the citizen, by planned investment in information communication technology and a well defined information policy so that the information applications will be reduced to minimum substantive issues.

D. Attitudinal Change on the Part of Authorities and Personnel in Public Life:

The public officials should not feel inconvenienced by the applications seeking information. Instead they should develop a feeling of helping their fellow citizens in their endeavours. They should also be convinced that that it is a right in favour of the honest and upright officers.

E. Assistance to Commoner

Common man will face the problem of sifting the information voluntarily disclosed by the authorities. He needs some assistance in locating the information he wants. For this purpose in each office an officer may be designated as an Information Advocate, whose primary responsibility will be to help those who are in need of information.

In summary, the purpose with which the Act is enacted is to help guide all the activities to ensure smooth and easy access to information. The very spirit of democracy is that the citizen is sovereign. Whether a person is sovereign or not, he is definitely not a slave in a free country. This should be clearly known to and etched in the hearts of all public servants and citizens. Empowering common man with right to information is a step which adds a paradigm shift to our democracy and administration. It adds quality dimensions to the life of the common man. This is a very precious right that the citizen has won 55 years after the country got its own Constitution. It is essential that this right is judiciously used and only in appropriate circumstances. If used indiscriminately, instead of ushering in efficiency in administration it may act to the contrary. The gift of information movement is to be jealously guarded against the temptation of using it as an instrument of exploitation.

Chapter - 11

Fostering Quality

— *S. Sivasubramanian*

Quality is never an accident; it is the result of high intention, sincere effort, intelligent decision and skilful execution. Quality in any institution is everybody's responsibility.

What is meant by quality in higher education? In the context of higher education institutions it stands for preparing the graduates to be the real contributors to the Society. The higher education institutions must prepare the graduates with both "primary greatness" (character and contribution) and "secondary greatness" (achievement in terms of power, position, money etc.). The three main aims of quality in higher education are: (1) preparing the children to face the challenges in life with confidence, ethics, values, citizenry; (2) to impart necessary knowledge and skills so that they become employable or entrepreneurs and lead a comfortable life and, (3) generate desire in the pursuit of truth. Some of these issues are described earlier in the book (Chapter (1). With the changing times, our universities need to redefine teaching methodology to make learning more effective, curricula up-dated regularly with an inter-disciplinary approach and reformation of evaluation mechanisms. It is well known that many higher education institutions in the country do not match global standards and no Indian university featured in the top-200 list. A total revamping may be needed to resurrect the higher education scenario; appointment of quality teachers, providing good governance, enhancing research output. Education institutions must be free of political interferences, nepotism, favouritism and corruption. Our entire system may not be bad as there are pockets of excellence and stories of innovation flourishing within the country, but a lot more is desired. Here I will highlight the major issues and possible remedial measures for fostering quality in higher education institutions, the colleges and varsities.

The challenges faced by our higher education system are the dismal quality of faculty, academic programs, research output, administration / leadership, infrastructure, technology usage, paucity of collaborations, poor relationship with the stakeholders, unethical practices and, privatization. To ensure quality in education teachers matter most as intellectual enquiry, original thinking and, creativity must be inculcated among the students. It is imperative that the teachers possess these attributes. Unfortunately, colleges / varsities throughout the country face acute shortage of faculty; both in quality and number. The faculty often lacks competency, basic knowledge of the pedagogy and commitments. Apparently, the absence of competent, confident and congruent teachers makes the system weak. Recruitment of right kind of faculty with right frame of mind can help recharge the quality in higher education. What we need is a strong, vibrant and sustainable system with highly dedicated and qualified faculty who can impart knowledge, skill and also inspire the students. To an extent this may be possible by providing needed training and motivation especially to new recruits as well as other young teachers. Along with content and methodology, there is a need to integrate emotional competencies, such as, self-management, social sensitivity and social management. There is a need to integrate life skills, such as, self-awareness, empathy, interpersonal relationship, effective communication, critical thinking, creative thinking, decision making, problem solving, and coping up with emotions and stress. There is also a need to integrate info-savvy skills like asking, accessing, analyzing, applying and assessing. There is a need to integrate human development climate through trust, risk taking, openness, reward, responsibilities, top support, feedback, team spirit and collaboration. In addition, there is a need to infuse spiritual ideals in them.

Use of Technology

We are late in fully exploiting the potential of technology in teaching, learning and evaluation. Indeed there is a need for an explosive technological revolution in higher education involving a shift from teaching to learning and, finally to e-learning. This involves a shift from e-learning 1.0 (Online learning) to 2.0 (Twitters, Face-book) and to 3.0 (Semantic Web) formats, that is, from content to community to artificial intelligence. Smart Classrooms have emerged which encompasses e-learning and e-testing. Terms like Wi-Fi, i-pad, i-pod. e-Book, e-Reader, e-News Letters, Webinar are widely used. Digital Lesson designs and e-Portfolios have become common features. There are compendiums of e-Abstracts and e-Journals, Surveys of engineering research in India on the World Wide Web. The UGC, AICTE, NCTE and other related organizations are also expediting higher education on e-Technologies through MOUs with Intel and other e-learning platform providers. Therefore college/varsities may encourage use of ICT enabled technologies for the teaching-learning process and provide access to lectures / power-point presentations by providing such facilities over the departmental or central computer facilities (Drop-Boxes, Websites and e-platforms). The absentees and slow learners can benefit from these to a great extent. In addition, students and teachers (institutions) can effectively utilize the social media like Face book, Twitter, You Tube, what's App and encourage student-centric teaching-learning processes. Using technology for curriculum delivery including LMS, student's innovation including Knowledge Management System (KMS), Environmental Management System (EMS) and Management Information Service (MIS) is a real challenge. Let us remember that majority of students are technology savvy and the teachers cannot afford to lag behind. Therefore, colleges must have smart class rooms with interactive white boards, video conferencing facilities, web based services including e-learning, e-Libraries, e-content creating facilities, Wi-Fi campus with high speed network, facilitating open source usage of all facilities (e.g. CAL; MIS, ERP and institutional HR systems). Facilities for on-line student evaluation of teachers and user-friendly institutional website need to be in place. Creating facilities are important but it is the effective utility of these by both students and teachers is the real challenge and is more important which will enhance the quality in higher education. In short, there is a wide scope for transformation of higher education through technology and make the education system vibrant in order to foster quality of education.

Faculty

In order to promote learning, the teachers ought to motivate the students to inculcate the habit of questioning, develop independent opinions and ability to think (lateral or out of box) in a constructive manner such that a class room becomes the centre of creativity. The students need encouragement to think critically and creatively, and focus on active learning rather than on passive learning or learning by rote. This can help our students develop cognitive intelligence and original thinking. Therefore, teachers should strive to adopt innovative teaching methods whereby every student participates in the learning process. Ideally, a teacher should relate his teaching to real time situations so that the students can understand even the difficult concepts easily. This calls for trying out new things, doing things in an unorthodox manner whenever and wherever possible and question the conventional methods of teaching. It may be noted that non-verbal communications are much more important than the verbal communications. Smile is an inexpensive material that adds beauty to a woman and handsomeness to a man. The teachers should behave like a mentor to his pupil. While teaching is important, reaching is more important. More so, inspiring teachers are the need of the hour. A teacher is always a teacher, that is 24x7 and 365 days a year. Verbal communications become important when it is done properly. Let us keep in mind that the 'Distance mode' education is often very much diluted; e-mode is at its infancy and the face to face mode is static. Can we not make face to face mode an enjoyable one perhaps by blended learning, interactive learning etc.? It is desirable that the teachers adopt innovative teaching methods like Flipped Classroom ambience whereby every student participates in the learning process. Therefore, it is necessary to motivate our teachers to try out new things - doing things in an unorthodox manner whenever and wherever possible and question the conventional methods so that they love teaching and do it as if it is a performing art. I am of the firm opinion that good teaching is one fourth of preparation and three fourth of pure theatre. Every student has positives and negatives. A Teacher's task is to see positives in the Students and give them a direction. The teacher should be like a parent who does not differentiate between kids.

Shift from Teaching to Learning

Teaching must be replaced by the Learning. The students must be taught how to learn, how to relearn, how to unlearn, learn to know, learn to do, learn to achieve and learn to live together. Independent learning, interactive learning and collaborative learning must be the order of the day which will foster innovation and creativity among the students. Every class room must be a centre of creativity. The teachers must provoke the students with some wrong statements which will make the intelligent students to point out the same. The teachers need to encourage students to ask questions. Fear of not knowing the correct answer should not deter them from allowing students to freely ask questions and clarify their doubts. Teachers can answer the difficult questions in their next class. The traditional method of Chalk and Talk has more or less given way to blended learning wherein the video lectures are supplemented by face to face mode which will make the students listen to best of the brains in the area apart from making the whole process of learning interesting and involving. If possible, the teachers should practice Flipped learning in the classrooms which ensures independent and interactive learning leading to creativity.

Academic Programs

With regard to the academic programs, the theory based Curricula with hardly any emphasis on application or technology fails to meet the intellectual aspirations of the students. The pedagogy does not encourage creativity and problem solving ability; hence becomes a challenge. Courses are not relevant to the contemporary situations. Innovative and new courses in emerging areas are infrequent. In some Universities, it takes more than five to ten years to update the Curricula. Accreditation and Academic Audit (AAA) of the courses are often absent in most Universities and hence, the affiliated colleges suffer. There is a total disconnect between academia and industry requirements. Large number of open electives, participatory learning, creative environment, regular academic audits, feedback from students and industries/employers should become integral parts of the academic structure of the curriculum. Independent learning and interactive learning must be inculcated among the students to be innovative and creative. Buddy system of Collaborative Learning must be encouraged to grow further. Imparting knowledge and skills must go hand in hand.

Research

With regard to Research, most colleges (especially engineering and medical) do not take research seriously except a few. Even the projects at postgraduate levels are not taken seriously and taken to logical ends. In most of these Institutions, cut and paste is considered as a research project. The colleges and varsities should ideally have a network of individuals who are trying to create and spread new knowledge and the teachers should constantly challenge the boundaries of knowledge. They must remember that all the cutting edge technologies like IT, BT, and NT are all born out of the interface of different disciplines. Research should be the way of life, i.e. thinking logically and rationally. In fact, doing research is the best way to acquire new knowledge and think critically. Original, innovative, quality research as reflected by publications in impact factor Journals (SCOPUS data base journals), patents, extramural funding, research collaborations (Institution-Institution or Institution-Industry) and Consultancy are the order of the day. Research alone brings global recognition. Hence, creating the right ambience for research both in terms of facilities and teaching work-load, recognizing the research contributions by suitable means and emphasizing the quality work in emerging and multidisciplinary areas must be the role of the Head of the Institution.

Administration

Undoubtedly, it is the Head of the College / University who builds its credibility. Hence, an effective leadership and implementation of the vision and mission of the institution involving all the stakeholders and creating a sense of belongingness to the institution will be a true leader. It is good to create a core group of teachers who understand the unique characteristics of the institution and its best practices. Adopting best practices of global standards and instilling values of excellence and success must be the leader's priority. Earning the trust and confidence of faculty, administrative staff, students, management and the public at large is a must. In every aspect of college/varsity functioning, quality must be kept in mind. Apparently, vision, honesty, integrity and effectiveness of the Head of the Institution are ultimately responsible for the prestige of the institution. It is not the position that matters most but it is the leadership that stems from moral authority matters.

Infrastructure

With regard to Infrastructure, it must be stated that poor academic infrastructure and lack of suitable intellectual capital has had its impact on the type of Scientists / Engineers / Doctors produced in the country. Infrastructure is not just brick and the mortar. Aesthetically designed campus can change the way the people perceive about an Institution. Again here, building green and energy efficient campuses with all latest technologies without compromising Indian traditions is really a challenge (see the Chapter 21 for more details). Student activity centres, meditation/yoga hall, a good auditorium apart from an excellent user friendly library will promote furtherance of higher education.

Collaboration

With regard to collaboration, it must be pointed out that a right kind of collaboration between institutions and industries will give an edge to any educational institution. Building up such collaborations is really a challenge. Besides, collaborations should be truly functional. It should not be merely on the paper to boast. Collaborations succeed when there is equal commitment on both sides. Collaborate to grow and achieve. Collaborations facilitate faculty and student exchanges and broaden their horizon. Working on joint research programs are often very rewarding. Collaborations can also help in course design, materials exchange, transferable credits, dual degree / twinning programs and so on. Thus, collaborative arrangements can help all round development of the institution.

Stakeholder Relations

Building up a strong and vibrant relationship with the stakeholders and more so sustaining it, is a real challenge. The primary stakeholders are students, faculty, and the parents. The Management, alumni, and the society at large are the other stakeholders. Creating the sense of belongingness to the institution is a real challenge. Creating a sense of togetherness is a must. Sustainable development of the institution is a joint responsibility of all stakeholders and not just the Government or one individual (Principal / Vice-Chancellor / Chairman of a Private University etc.).

Changing mindset

I wish to urge our faculty and students to have the right kind of mind-set as I believe that the single biggest challenge facing our countrymen is changing their mindsets from negative to positive and contribute their might to the institution achieving all round growth is certain. The mindset should be: if we Indians cannot do something, nobody else can do. If others cannot do something, we Indians can do. Let our Teachers exhibit this mind set and let that it be imbibed by our Students. Let us try to make the Indian Higher Education System fully quality oriented and our institutional rankings are elevated to the respectable positions.

Avoiding ETC

First, let me consider the factor 'E'. The present day education is plagued by exam centric approaches wherein the teachers prepare the students towards the examinations by rote learning methodology. The question paper setters also follow the method of using the questions often from the earlier year question papers. Hence, the coaching centres are able to train the students and make them succeed in the examinations. There is no room for thinking in this kind of exam centric approach, leave alone creativity. Hence, it is high time that the stakeholders in higher education for that matter even in School education should avoid exam centric approaches and the whole lot of examination process has to be modified where there is no room for rote learning except testing the understanding. Today's education is miffed with '3T's: Text, Teaching and Tradition. We prescribe texts for each subject and force the students to go through only that text. If students walk an extra mile to go through other books/ journals/ MOOC courses and give right answers, they are often punished or failed because the teachers are themselves text centric and not aware of other sources. The curricula and syllabi must be fixed with a number of relevant books / journals / MOOC platforms so that more than one source can be taken up by the students. With regard to the other two 'T's as already seen, the Teaching has to give way to Learning and the Traditional way of 'Chalk and Talk' need to give way to Blended or Flipped learning. Coming to the 'C', we have to shed off 'Corruption and Compromise' which ruin the whole process of education leading to low quality. Corruption in the appointment of Vice-Chancellors, Principals, Faculty or other important administrative positions is sure to degrade the institutions. Deliberate compromises based on considerations in terms of religion, region, caste, community, gender and so on only lead to deterioration in the quality of education.

Amalgamation of 4Cs

In my opinion remedy for most of the ills of the higher education institutions can be overcome by adopting four parameters which I call 4Cs. These are: Competence, Confidence, Congruence and Creativity. Competent teachers with his/her sound domain knowledge and evincing inclination to be a mentor can be a perfect counsellor and also a skill imparter. I want the teacher himself to be not only the facilitator for the learning process, but also must be a blend of skilling and counselling. He/ she must conduct himself /herself as a role model in all respects that include following ethics and values of this great country. Confidence comes with competence and both virtues are based on one's hard work, attitude and concern for the jobs undertaken. The teacher ought to excel in whatever job he or she does, thereby earning the respect as a 'true teacher' of all the times. For a teacher to be successful one needs congruency so that he or she can adapt to changing situations; say teaching UG as well as PG courses simultaneously with distinction. The teachers need to be creative not only in ideas but also in all respects and all situations. In a way, this calls for being creative continuously. The 4Cs described above should be integral part of the teacher and then transmitted to the students. With these qualities students can gain confidence and enhance their career prospects and success in life.

Privatization

As far as privatization of higher education is concerned, it is not clear whether it is a boon or bane. Those Institutions which care for quality and vouch by ethics and values are a boon, but others whose interests are commercial and hence resort to several unethical practices are a bane (especially the institutions offering professional courses). The agencies like UGC, AICTE, MCI, PCI, NCTE etc., have become somewhat ineffective in monitoring and maintaining high standards. Majority of the private sector institutions are headed by promoters rather than the academics. The academic communities in such organizations have often little say! The Public-Private Partnership (PPP) model may provide solution to the problem.

Lastly, the recharging of higher education is possible by explicitly spelling out the vision of the institution and working towards it. Increasing the funds for the educational institutions, creating an enabling human and physical environment to encourage interactions, empowerment of individuals to deliver results, building linkages with various components of the society are some of the urgent needs. Encouraging research and innovation, internationalization of research and entrepreneurship, translation of the outcome of researches into a business venture or a transfer technology must be undertaken on priority. We need to protect the Institution's autonomy and we need to globalize not only the curriculum but also the students and faculty. Performance linked promotions and incentives for the faculty need to be in place.

With appropriate student feedback mechanisms, placement and grievance redress cells, counselling and mentoring systems in place and properly functional many things fall in place. Transformational academic leaders with the futuristic approach and understanding the higher education eco system must alone be allowed to occupy the leadership position. If the performance is not satisfactory he or she must be made to demit the office after fallowing the process of natural justice. The leader (head of the institution) must be a role model in all respects and strive to imbue importance of fostering quality among the students, teachers and employees to bring in attitudinal changes in them.

CHAPTER - 12

QUALITY ASSURANCE SYSTEM: CHALLENGES, CONCERNS AND THE WAY FORWARD

— *H. A. RANGANATH*

Quality assurance in higher education has to involve an integrated and holistic approach embracing different dimensions of the system. The major facets of an institution which contribute to the overall 'Quality' are: Academic ambience, Governance ambience and Moral ambience. The 'academic ambience' encompasses (a) human resource - staff and students, (b) Building and Infrastructure, (c) academic programs, (d) technology usage in teaching and learning, e) research and collaborations, etc. The 'governance ambience' includes (a) Transparency, (b) managing finances (receipts and expenditure), (c) accountability and, (d) stake holder participation. The third component moral ambience focuses on providing the much needed moral ambience in terms of (a) value System, (b) discipline etc.

Time and again, over the years, a few issues such as, how to increase the gross enrolment ratio (GER), why higher educational institutions have become centres to produce unemployable graduates, why none of our institutions figure in the first 100 of the global rankings, are discussed on different platforms by administrators, policy makers and academicians. Therefore, 5Es, namely (1) Expansion, (2) Equity and Access, (3) Excellence and Quality, (4) Empowerment of students and stake holders, and (5) Evolution to respond to the newer challenges, have become focal points in discussions and dialogues on higher education. Also there are strong indications and trends of paradigm shift in higher education from (a) national education to global education,

(b) one time education for a few to lifelong education/learners for all, and (c) teacher centric education to student centric education.

Diversity of Institutions

The Ecosystem of Indian Higher Education scenario is extremely heterogeneous. An increase in the demand for higher education has resulted in the rapid expansion and the establishment of new institutions of varied types. There are about 700+ university level institutions and about 40,000+ colleges. Let us take a look at the diversity of institutions of higher education:

State Universities (Public and Private)

Cluster of Colleges to form a University, Autonomous colleges elevated to University status; Deemed Universities (Public and Private); Central Universities; IITs; IIMs; Institutions of National Importance like IISc; IISERs, NISER; CSIR Academy, International Universities (Nalanda, South Asian University SAARC) etc.,

Affiliated Colleges

Constituent colleges, Government colleges, Government aided Private colleges, Aided colleges with unaided courses, Unaided colleges / Self financing; Autonomous colleges etc.

Over and above these, Rural Vs Urban, Professional Vs Non-Professional, Digital Vs Non-digital divide among institutions as well as multi-faculty v/s mono-faculty institutions also exist in the educational ecosystem. This diversity is not merely limited to names of the institutions. There exists considerable diversity as far as 'inputs received, processes in place, output, outcome and impact and practices followed' under the overall gambit of 'Quality Ambience' dimensions.

Now, the challenge is how to develop, evaluate, monitor and sustain 'quality culture' in institutions that are mosaic in nature with highly diversified features spread all over the geographical terrains of the country. The challenge becomes more complex with the involvement of over 10 different 'Regulatory Bodies' (such as UGC, AICTE, MCI, DCI, BCI, NCI, PCI etc.,) in vogue for providing guidance and stipulating standards for the higher education institutions (HEI).

Quality Assurance Cycles

Maintaining a good and robust health is vital in a person's life. It is a fact that as a person puts on age, he/she might become a victim of ailments unless or until the person undertakes interventional strategies like maintaining a strict fitness regime through clinical processes to monitor bodily functions and seek appropriate remedy. Likewise, maintenance of quality standards of an institution assumes greater significance as deterioration of the same could have adverse affect on a variety of stake-holders like students, society and finally the Nation as a whole. Understandably the deterioration of standards or quality could be checked to great extent if an institution at a nascent stage undertakes quality health checkups at regular intervals of time. Quality Assurance Cycle with reference to HEIs involves; Genesis of new institutions / programs, Affiliation Processes, Assessment and Accreditation by NAAC, Internal Quality Assurance Cells (IQAC), and Academic and Administrative Audit (AAA).

(1) *Genesis*: Most of the problems dogging the higher education scenario in the country particularly with respect to quality concerns have their roots deeply entrenched in the elementary stages of conceptualization of an institution/new programme. As institutions mushroom with no basic prenatal research, they take birth with congenital disorders and defects. Such a predicament can have cascading effect leading to evolutionary problems in quality assurance and maintenance of standards. Ultimately the products churned out from such institutions would be mediocre in nature. Therefore, the onus is on the Central/State policy makers as well as Regulatory Agencies to undertake prenatal research with appropriate groundwork before starting new institutions/programs.

(2) *Affiliation process*: Colleges are the 'backbone' of our higher education sector. With the exception of couple of Central universities, public funded State Universities across the country are the ones which have taken the burden of guiding and monitoring the colleges through 'Affiliation system'. In the beginning, 'University as a Big Brother' model worked well for many reasons. The universities had the moral authority to exercise powers such as to grant, regulate and even withdraw affiliation to any college / course, number of admissions, fee structure, make sure the adequacy of infrastructure and quality of

staff etc. The type of education was general with greater emphasis on literacy and basic studies rather than technology and commercialization that we witness today. Birth of institutions with market-oriented courses and self financing courses create new power centres in the University structure. Entry of business and political groups into education stream makes inroads into the authority of the University. The number of colleges/courses/students could be both a boon as well as a curse to a University: Colleges are a source of certain income to the University. From this angle number of affiliated colleges add to the comfort zone of the university especially the financial position. Alternatively, the number factor could strangulate a university by affecting standards and achievement of excellence.

Reforms in the affiliation system are the need of the hour. There is a need to change from ritual redundant procedures to facilitating developments. We also need to focus on liberating the universities from the economic overdependence on the affiliated colleges and institutions. The final aim should be to strengthen the 'backbone', that is the 'college sector' of higher education.

(3) *Assessment and Accreditation by NAAC*: Since 1994, the National Assessment and Accreditation Council (NAAC) has promoted the concept and process of assessment and accreditation of institutions. The accreditation was voluntary but now it is mandatory for all institutions. It is felt that 'Accreditation' is equivalent to 'health check-up' of institutions. The role of NAAC is that of a 'diagnostic centre'. The NAAC has evolved a set of parameters over the years to assess and accredit institutions on a set of criteria like (i) Curricular aspects, (ii) Teaching-Learning and Evaluation, (iii) Research, Consultancy and Extension, (iv) Student Support and Progression, (v) Governance, Leadership and Management, and (vi) Innovations and Best Practices (Ref. NAAC Manuals). In a way, this is comparable to clinical and pharmacological parameters of diagnostic centres for testing patients. The NAAC has continuously revised and upgraded its instruments, manuals, protocols to accommodate the new dimensions of higher education as expected by internationalization and globalization. The NAAC through its 'experts' only takes a diagnostic approach - assesses the performance of the institutions besides exploring the reasons for their accomplishments and limitations. The experts, by adopting time-tested parameters, analyze the strengths, weaknesses, opportunities,

challenges and threats, and it is for the institution to respond and to comply with the recommendations of the expert committee. Just as human being is afflicted with age-related ailments, so are the institutions. Therefore, once in 5 years or as prescribed by NAAC, institutions may opt for 'Reaccreditation' and avail the advice of experts. With new challenges, the institutions have to evolve and innovate by having systemic check on their policies, courses, and schemes to keep in synch with the dynamic and evolving higher education sector. Gearing up for assessment and accreditation processes by NAAC are described in Chapter 14 of this book.

(4) *Internal Quality Assurance Cells* (IQAC): NAAC was born with a vision "to make quality the defining element of higher education through a combination of self and external quality evaluation, promotion and sustenance activities". The important words of this statement are 'self evaluation' and 'sustenance' activities. In addition to the preparation of self-study report (SSR-self-evaluation) by the HEI for the peer team to review and validate, NAAC is expected to undertake steps to bring in the concept of continuous self-auditing by the institution itself with regard to the processes concerned with quality assurance (QA), quality sustenance (QS) and quality enhancement (QE). Hence, NAAC propagated the concept of IQAC as a post-accreditation activity of the institution. This is expected to take care of QS and QE of the institution.

The idea of IQAC was envisioned to operate as an internal organ of the institution which would work 24X7X365 for qualitative improvement in all its activities. The NAAC has also clearly laid out the functions, strategies to be employed and the potential benefits of IQAC (see Chapter 11 for more details). As per the requirement, the IQAC of institutions need to submit (on line) the Annual Report to NAAC and seek its advice for future course of action. The NAAC provides funds to IQACs of accredited institutions to organize workshops/seminars.

Time and again, NAAC has advocated the concept of 'home-grown' quality consciousness, which alone can keep the journey towards quality achievement. Thus, it is clear that 'quality of HEIs is the responsibility and task of each institution itself'. Human health science is moving towards 'personalized medicine' specific to each individual to meet his/her requirements. On a similar line, every HEI is confronted with problems and issues of diverse nature, which are variable both in space (location) and time (aging). Therefore, one size fit all prescription for QA, QS and QE is virtually impossible. Therefore, IQAC has to undertake routine health checkups of the institution to develop its own remedial measures and, integrate the same in the functioning of the organization so as to institutionalize measures for assurance, sustenance and improvement of quality. This strategy emphasizes the idea that quality is a journey without destination. Therefore, there is a need to impress the institutions that quality is just not responding to the standards only at the time of accreditation/audit process. Instead of a periodic response to the assessment by the visiting peer teams, the quality has to be looked upon as a continuous and ongoing process and it should be integrated in the quality culture of the institution.

Taking cue from the efforts of NAAC in sustaining quality culture amongst institutions, now UGC is funding institutions to establish and run IQAC institutionally. After the success of IQACs, the idea of State Level Quality Assurance Cell (SLQAC) was floated by NAAC with a view to support and coordinate IQAC activities in a given State. At present, many States have established SLQACs, and NAAC periodically organizes SLQAC Coordinators' interaction programs. In view of the importance of IQACs' activities, time has come to empower it. The IQAC deserves the status of a 'statutory body' in the organizational structure of an institution.

(5) *Academic Administrative Audit* (AAA): The University Grants Commission (UGC) introduced the concept of AAA during its 10th Plan (2002-2007) for universities and colleges to create a mechanism for monitoring their activities. The objective is to review the academic and administrative discipline of the institution which is comparable to financial auditing. The UGC has also provided guidelines for constituting the committee as well as a broad frame work for its functioning. The AAA is supposed to be undertaken annually.

Finally, why this 'Quality Assurance Cycle (QAC)' with five different steps to be repeated at different intervals? It is because of the following reasons: It has been felt that (a) there is strong symptom of inertia among the institutions, (b) compliance indifference, (c) it is extremely individual centric than institutional centric, (d) it has become a ritualistic and a mundane process, and (e) no space for dynamism and quality process etc. The QAC is meant to address these unhealthy trends and keep the institutions in a state of 'alertness'.

In view of these, I envisioned five existing practices; Genesis of new institutions/programs, affiliation process (for colleges-Annual), assessment and accreditation by NAAC, the IQACs and AAA as an integral part of QAS of institutions. With the periodical iterative implementation of these, it is possible to 'institutionalize' the processes and protocols which are required to take care of QA, QS and QE all of which have to be on an evolutionary mode of 'Dissent with Modifications' cycle after cycle of assessments. Institutions will have scope for introspection, improvement and innovation. This will be the remedy to address the quality journey as a perpetual mission and thereby the institution will be a learning organisation with quality culture embedded in its DNA. Finally, views expressed here are based on my experiences as the coordinator of IQAC and AAA committees at Mysore University, Vice Chancellor of Bangalore University, Chairman NAAC Peer Team and Director NAAC, Bangalore.

Suggested Reading

1. Harvey L. and J. Williams 2010, Quality in Higher Education 16: (1) 3-36; and16: (2) 81-113
2. Hegde G.A, 2011, University News, AIU 49: (44)1-6; NAAC Publications 2003-2004, Guidelines for the creation of the IQAC in Accredited institutions; Revised version of 2007 by G.A Hegde.
3. Ranganath H.A. 2012. NAAC NEWS: Editorials: Vol XI (Issue 1 and 2) 2011; Vol XII (Issue 1) 2012.
4. Sanyal B.C and M. Martin 2006, Quality assurance and the role of accreditation: An overview. GUNI Series on the Social Commitment of Universities, Palgrave Macmillan.

Chapter - 13

Internal Quality Assurance Cell and its Functions

— *H. M. Kasinath*

The University Grants Commission (UGC) established in the year 1956 as a Statutory body of the Government of India through an Act of Parliament is the only grant releasing body which has been vested with the responsibilities of providing funds and coordinating maintenance of good standards in Higher Education Institutions (HEIs), the degree colleges and varsities. To monitor standards the UGC has established the National Assessment and Accreditation Council (NAAC) as an autonomous body, under Section 12(c) of its Act in September, 1994. Since then it has been instilling a quality consciousness among the institutions coming under its purview and ensure continuous improvements. However, soon it was felt that lasting improvements do not come only by accreditation from outside once in five years. Therefore, an internal mechanism for sustenance, assurance and enhancement of the quality culture in imparting education became essential. Accordingly, many HEIs have now established the Internal Quality Assurance Cells (IQAC) as a post-accreditation quality sustenance measure since the UGC XII plan period. Further, the UGC also provided seed financial assistance for establishing IQACs.

All educational institutions typically comprise of several sub-systems like the infrastructure, instructional systems, linkages and interfaces, management and administration and so on. Therefore a basic approach to quality enhancement is identifying and understanding the various sub-systems and their interrelationships / interdependences. The following figure shows subsystems of an education institute as per Mukhopadhyay (2010).

The various subareas and their major functions are described below:

Vision, Mission and Goals

Vision provides the direction of movement to an Institution. It is painting the picture of an institution as it will be accomplished in years to come. Mission is the transformation of vision into a plan of action. Goals are the milestones on the way to vision through missions.

Academic Management

It comprises of planning and management of admission processes, design of curriculum, preparing academic calendars, examination related works, and co-curricular activities.

Personal Management

It comprises of recruitment of personnel and their induction, staff development, maintenance of personnel records, management of staff associations, conducting staff meetings, staff welfare, job allocation etc.

Financial Management

This includes preparation of annual budgets, resource mobilization and optimization, accounting and auditing.

Infrastructure Management

It revolves around construction and extension of buildings, utilization and maintenance of infrastructure, improvement of library and laboratory facilities, procurement of audio-visual aids, looking after the hostels, sports and games facilities and total sanitation of the campus facilities.

Linkage and Interface

This involves establishing linkages and communication with the parents, the alumni, the community, local bodies like Panchayats, Municipal Corporations, authorities at higher levels, non-educational authorities like PWD, transport, health, etc., educational institutions at the local, regional, national and international levels, employers and so on. In addition, it involves developing inter institution and industry level linkages for teaching and research activities.

Student Services

It includes creation and management of student information systems as well as the student amenities, providing incentives, scholarships, guidance and counselling facilities. In this process involvement of students in decision-making process will go a long way.

Rules and Regulations

Institutional management needs to be familiar with dynamic affiliating University's Act, Statutes, Ordinances, Regulations, Rules, Minutes of the meetings of the relevant statutory bodies, Likewise, the institution should be fully acquainted with all administrative procedures (e.g. admission of students, procurements appointment and promotion of teaching and supporting staff, writing off unserviceable equipments, reviewing the performance appraisals, handling grievance of stakeholders and so on.

Institutional development

It comprises several aspects like institutional evaluation, planning and organizational development.

Managerial excellence

This component comprises understanding the self, communication, leadership, group dynamics, team building, decision-making, motivation, and overall management of issues arising from time to time.

Each of the above areas comprises of several activities and components. Therefore, it is important for IQAC to identify the various components and their functioning so as to undertake annual evaluation and documentation of all the achievements and prepare Annual Quality Assurance Report (AQAR) to be submitted to NAAC annually. These reports are generally uploaded on the college website. The NAAC has identified 07 important criteria to enable its assessment and accreditation of colleges/varsities (for details see Chapter 14).

At the instance of NAAC many HEIs have established IQACs as a post-accreditation quality sustenance activity. The experience of NAAC reveals that the IQAC in these Institutions are proactive and functioning in a healthy way. Based on this success story, since April, 2007 NAAC has been propagating establishment of IQACs even prior to the first accreditation thereby promote quality culture in the higher education institutions. The UGC has recognized this initiative and it has taken a policy decision to direct all HEIs to establish IQACs for which it also provides seed financial assistance.

Objectives of IQAC

Principally, the IQAC aims to (1) to develop a system for conscious, consistent and catalytic actions to improve the academic and administrative performance of the institution and, (2) to promote measures for institutional functioning towards quality enhancement through internalization of quality culture and institutionalization of best practices. Hence, the IQAC need to function rather effectively in the interest of the institution.

Strategies

A good IQAC is supposed to evolve diverse mechanisms and procedures for accomplishing the following and many more benefits:

1. Ensuring timely, efficient and progressive performance of academic, administrative and financial tasks.
2. Maintenance of relevance and quality in academic and research programmes.
3. Creating equitable access to and affordable academic programmes to various sections of the society.
4. Innovative methods in teaching, learning and evaluation.

5. Ensuring the adequacy, maintenance and proper allocation of support services.
6. Sharing of research findings and networking with other Institutions in India and Abroad.

Main Functions of IQAC

Following may be considered as the some major functions of the IQAC. However, the managements and IQAC itself can add more to the list for meaningful functioning of the colleges.

1. Development and application of quality benchmarks/ parameters for the various academic and administrative activities.
2. Facilitating creation of a learner-centred environment conducive for quality education, participatory teaching-learning process, adoption of new knowledge and technology, and faculty improvement.
3. Arrangement for feedback responses from students, parents and other stakeholders on institutional quality related issues regularly.
4. Dissemination of relevant information.
5. Acting as a nodal agency for coordinating all quality-related activities, and best practices.
6. Organization of inter and intra-institutional workshops, seminars on quality related themes.
7. Development and maintenance of institutional database through MIS. This is one important task of the IQAC.
8. Documentation of all important activities and accomplishments of the institution and preparing Annual Quality Assurance Report (AQAR) as per the format given by the NAAC.
9. Bi-annual development of Quality Radars (QRs) and Ranking of Integral Units of Colleges based on the AQAR.

Composition of the IQAC

As per the UGC/NAAC guidelines IQAC is constituted under the Chairmanship of Head of the Institution with Heads of academic and administrative units, few teachers, distinguished educationists, representatives of local management and stakeholders. The suggested composition of IQAC is as shown below.

1. Principal (Chairperson)
2. Three to eight teachers
3. One member of the Management
4. One or two nominees from Local Community, Students and Alumni
5. One or two nominees from a Industry/Quality Management / Stakeholders
6. One Senior Administrative Officer
7. Director/Coordinator of IQAC (Member Secretary)

The membership shall be for a period of two years. The IQAC shall meet at least once in four months. In order to ensure validity of the meeting, two-thirds of the total members need to be present to make up for the quorum. The agenda, minutes and action taken reports are to be properly documented.

The Director / Coordinator of IQAC may be generally a senior person with expertise in quality aspects. However, even a junior but dynamic, competent and a computer savvy person can also be appointed as the Coordinator. He/she may be a full-time functionary or may be a senior academic/ administrator entrusted with an additional responsibility. The coordinator may be provided the secretarial assistance to help him submit AQARs approved by the Management authorities of the college to various monitoring bodies like the affiliating university, State Quality Assurance Cell (SQAC), and the NAAC regularly as per the regulations. The Colleges shall also submit AQARs and/or Quality Radars (QRs) and follow up reports to the UGC as and when called for. Functioning of the IQAC of the universities is monitored by the NAAC. The SQAC and Affiliating Universities shall monitor the functioning of IQACs in the Colleges coming under their jurisdiction. The AQARs shall be approved by the Statutory Bodies of the HEIs like Syndicate, Governing Council/Board for follow up of quality enhancement measures. The AQAR may be part of the Annual Report as well. Timely submission of AQARs is essential for 2nd, 3rd or subsequent cycles of accreditation. The IQAC must create its exclusive window on the institutional website to depict its updated information (all aspects) and activities undertaken or completed. During the visit of the NAAC peer teams the members will interact scrupulously with the IQACs to know the progress, functioning as well as quality sustenance initiatives undertaken by them.

Financial Assistance for Establishing IQAC

The colleges covered under Section 2(f) and 12(B) of the UGC Act, are eligible to receive the financial support for establishing and strengthening IQACs to the tune of Rs 3.0 Lakhs to be utilized for a 5 year period for following purposes.

1. Honorarium to the Director /Coordinator @ Rs 1000 per month for 5 years (Rs 60.000)
2. Office Equipments (Rs 60.000)
3. Hiring Secretarial /Technical Assistants (Rs 60.000)
4. ICT Communication Expenses (Rs 70.000)
5. Contingencies (Rs 50.000)

It is mandatory for every college to get accredited by NAAC after passing out of two batches or six years whichever is earlier. Moreover, IQAC helps ensure heightened level of clarity and focus in institutional functioning towards quality enhancement, internalization of the quality culture, and coordination of institutional activities, and institutionalization of best practices. It also provides a sound basis for decision-making to improve institutional functioning. It can act as a dynamic system for overall quality changes in the Colleges besides building a systematic documentation methodology over the years. Therefore it is in the interest of the institution to keep the IQAC in an active and dynamic state, revive and rejuvenate if needed. Managements should also give them enough freedom. Indeed IQAC has a great role to play in overall elevation of the quality concerns of the institution and interests of the stakeholders by carefully attending to all areas and subareas, vision and mission identified for all round development of the institution. Involving the various stakeholders in this process will go a long way in building the institution.

Suggested Reading

1. Mukhopadhyay, M. (2010) Total Quality Management in Education, (2nd Ed.), New Delhi: Sage Publication.
2. Kurup, M. R. (2016) Role of State in Improving Higher Education Institutions, Curriculum and Teachers' Quality, University News, Vol. 54, (36), Sep. 5-11.
3. NAAC (2013) Guidelines for the Creation of the Internal Quality Assurance Cell (IQAC) and Submission of Annual Quality Assurance Report (AQAR) in Accredited Institutions.
4. NAAC (2007) Guidelines for the Creation of the Internal Quality Assurance Cell (IQAC) in Accredited Institutions.
5. Sternberg, R. J. (2015) A Model of Institutional Creative Change for Assessing Universities as Learning Organizations. Creativity Research Journal, 27(3), 254-261.
5. UGC (2012) XII Plan Guidelines for Establishment and Monitoring of the Internal Quality Assurance Cells (IQACs) in Colleges (2012-2017). University Grants Commission, New Delhi (www.ugc.ac.in)
6. UGC (2007) XI Plan Guidelines for Establishment and Monitoring of the Internal Quality Assurance Cells (IQACs) in Higher Educational Institutions (HEIs) (2007-2012). University Grants Commission, New Delhi (www.ugc.ac.in).

Chapter - 14

Aligning Colleges for Assessment and Accreditation

— *S. K. Saidapur*

Quality is never accidental; it is the result of careful planning. And, quality does not cost money; it is the attitude of mind.

The assessment and accreditation (A&A) of higher education institutions (HEIs; 1st Grade or Degree Colleges and Universities) was initiated by the Ministry of Human Resource Development (MHRD) by establishing 'National Assessment and Accreditation Council' popularly known as NAAC at Bangalore in the year 1994. Likewise, National Board of Accreditation (NBA) was established by All India Council of Technical Education (AICTE) in the same year for accreditation of engineering colleges. Later, Indian Council of Agricultural Research (ICAR) established Accreditation Board (AB) to accredit agricultural colleges in the year 1996. This chapter focuses mainly on the NAAC which has developed its own methodology for of HEIs using certain criteria that are more or less on par with international standards. The methodology of assessment and grading are revised from time to time based on the experiences and inputs from the peer team members as well as the institutions that have gone the process of A&A. The methodology of A&A was revised in July 2017. The new methodology has both quantitative and qualitative parameters and only 30% weight-age is given for report of the Peer Team. This ensures more transparency and objectivity. Subjective assessment is thus drastically reduced. The NAAC grading, called Cumulative Grade Point Average (CGPA) indicates the overall status of the institution. This reflects in a way the overall quality of the institution: governance, infrastructure, various facilities, faculty strength, performance of students in examinations and their progression, and so on.

Any institution that has undergone A&A proccss, its website will display the Grade obtained. In all probability, a college with good grade attracts good students, more funds from Research and Development Agencies (UGC, DST, CSIR etc.) and enjoy great reputation. Once the details of the courses offered, facilities available (library, sports, gym, cultural activities etc), the demand ratio, performance of students in curricular, sports and extracurricular events, and other features of the institution are made known along with the grades awarded by the accrediting organization, the stakeholders can decide to opt or not to opt taking admission in a given college. In any case, A&A of colleges / universities is mandatory. Therefore, many educational institutions are undergoing A&A process for their own good. As a matter of fact, periodic assessments (normally once in 5 or more years) by external experts gives an opportunity to introspect and know institution's strengths, weaknesses, opportunities, and challenges (SWOC). In turn, the assessment process provides directions to the institution for future qualitative and quantitative improvements by fixing the weak points and areas. Consequently, several colleges and universities have already undergone three or more cycles of A&A.

Many institutions decide to undergo A&A under some or the other pressure and therefore face challenges in organizing everything in a short time. This results in stress and strain to a few persons who are involved in preparing the 'Self Study Report' (SSR); they have to do everything from collecting and compiling the data, writing the report and so on. Added to it often colleagues do not cooperate with enthusiasm and involvement thereby contributing to a conundrum. Finding accurate and authentic data for preparing the report is not easy. Naturally, all this affects the outcome, the quality of SSR and its authenticity. A badly drafted SSR adversely affects the judgement of the NAAC Peer Team members about the institution even before their actual visit to the institution. Therefore, ideally, preparation for A&A should begin with 5 years in hand, by carefully documenting all needed data.

In this Chapter, I wish to highlight key issues that need to be carefully and systematically internalized by the institutions so that they can be in an ever ready state for A&A sans anxiety and stress. Besides, the suggestions and ideas given here are meant to help the colleges in streamlining administration as well as curricular and co-curricular activities and maintaining their records. As far A&A process is concerned, seven Criteria identified by the NAAC are important. Keeping this in mind, I have tried to explain the seven criteria points and associated key aspects wherever necessary. However, my suggestions are not merely to facilitate the institutions in the A&A process but also for an overall improvement and effective management of colleges. Every institution aspires for a highest possible grade. In any case, gaining decent Grade from NAAC should be a consequence of overall good governance of higher education institutions rather than the end in itself. The quality of education provided and the eminence of citizens produced are truly the hallmarks of higher education institutions and not the NAAC grades *per se*.

In my opinion most important tasks before a college pertain to the accomplishment of the following before proceeding for A&A:

1. Dynamic Website

First and foremost any college should have is a website depicting everything about the college. In this modern ICT ridden world, it is expected that each HEI systematically documents details of its infrastructure, facilities available, and achievements of the college in curricular and extracurricular domains. All this information should be depicted on the college website. This helps in projecting the true image of the institution to the stakeholders who have every right to know the standing of a given institution. Sitting at home the parents and students can access all needed information about the institution through the website. Therefore all educational institutions must have a dynamic website that is updated on day-to-day basis and provides for feedbacks from the users. In any case, all important information pertaining to the college will have to be in the public domain. It is a good idea to outsource maintenance of the website rather than entrust to one of the faculty members.

2. Dynamic Principal

Every college needs a dynamic principal who is not only well versed in Civil Service Rules and Code of Conduct Rules and, Finance

Codes, in addition to being a good academician superior to all her/ his colleagues. He should be computer savvy as well. More than anything, he should have concerns and commitments to produce worthy citizens through quality education. Therefore, the Government/Private College managements should appoint a worthy Principal who is capable of steering the college to greater heights. In my opinion, leadership qualities do not come automatically based on number of years of service or seniority. Therefore, a person with leadership qualities should head the institution.

3. Faculty

As the primary aim of any college is to provide good education, competent persons need to be on the faculty, preferably drawn from all over India. Consideration of cast, creed, nepotism, favouritism and other criteria in the appointment of faculty have caused decline in the quality of education imparted in most institutions. Unfortunately, many State Governments have shown scant regard in identifying and appointing right persons as the Principal or faculty. Many positions remain vacant for years and teaching is managed by the part time or guest faculty. Most state-run degree colleges are managed by the senior most faculty member as in-charge principal. Such personnel merely mark their time and do not contribute effectively to the development of colleges. Furthermore, the colleges in rural and tribal area are often in a pathetic state and principals work under fear. Actually, these days there are not many takers for the position of Principals. Consequently, Principal-ship is forced upon someone who is disinterested and unwilling. All State governments and private managements should realize that no ship can reach its destination without a competent Captain. Also, it is not enough to appoint merely qualified personnel as faculty / principal but we need competent and committed persons to occupy these positions. Faculty also needs hybrid vigour *vis-a-vis* appointment on all India level that brings in cross culture hybridization.

4. Maintenance of Records

A main activity of any institution is often properly documenting all relevant past and present information about the institution and its activities. These can then be publicised on the institutional website. As far as the colleges are concerned, information starting from the establishment to current day must be properly documented and revealed. It may include qualifications and profile of all faculty members including the Principal, their achievements (books and research papers published, grants received etc.) if any, details of the supporting staff, infrastructure and facilities available (e.g. coaching facility for slow/advanced learners, scholarships/endowment programs, promotion of skill development, personality development, entrepreneurship training provided if any, placement promotion, achievements in social and cultural activities, sports and so on). The college can also project its 'vision and mission' as well as plans for the next 5 years. Funds received from the various agencies (planned and unplanned) and amount spent can be publicised on the website. In short, excepting the confidential matters all information related to the college must be promptly documented and updated on the website. Activities of the Internal Quality Assurance Cell (IQAC) and its composition may also be depicted on the website. Once documentation is in place generating annual or self study reports becomes very easy.

5. Internal Quality Assurance Cells (IQAC)

The importance of IQAC is described in the previous Chapter. Here I wish to briefly touch upon the functioning of IQAC. First, the IQAC is a think-tank and therefore, its members should be eminent personalities from different walks of life who are capable of contributing substantially to an all round growth of the institution. In reality this is generally not a case. IQACs are constituted merely to fulfil the requirement. The members are for namesake. This does not help the institution. Institution must make efforts to invite persons who are brilliant and thinkers so that they can provide ideas and solutions for improvement of the institution in academic, administrative and other matters. A poor quality IQAC is a futile exercise. In a way IQAC reflects the quality of the institution, its concerns and commitments. Therefore, composition and functioning of IQAC should be taken very seriously since future growth of the college depends on it. If the college ceases to grow, it begins to die.

6. Collaboration and Linkages

No institution can have all facilities and competency for teaching and research in the era of knowledge explosion and globalization. Besides, the boundaries between different subjects have disappeared and integration is order of the day. Hence, collaboration within and between departments to strengthen academic programs is needed. In order to enhance quality of teaching and research collaboration with other institutions and industries is imperative. Good collaborations provide access to facilities, resources and reinforce academic activities. Likewise, collaborations with industries, forest departments, hospitals, non-governmental organizations can help in many co-curricular and extracurricular activities of the college. No institution can work in isolation anymore.

7. Vibrancy

How to make a college campus a vibrant place? It is not easy. Ideally, the campus needs to be a vibrant place even after the college hours. It should bubble with activities like sports and games, cultural programs, NCC/NSS activities, cleaning drives, alumni meets, placement related activities and so on. Evening lectures by eminent visiting faculty or personnel from industries and other organizations, on skill and personality development, value of Indian ancient scriptures, various schemes of State / Central governments for encouraging entrepreneurship, concept of nationalism / patriotism, Indian ethos and value systems can go a long way in shaping the career of students. Such activities undertaken periodically keep the campus in a state of vibrancy, inspire the students and mould their personalities.

8. Value Addition

In addition to the regular courses there is an urgent need to provide training that contributes to value addition: counselling on time / stress management, mushroom cultivation, yoga / meditation, entrepreneurship related aspects and soon. For these activities experts can be outsourced for short terms. Likewise, coaching for Basket ball / Athletics, Entrepreneurship, maintenance of College Campus could be outsourced. Depending upon the specific needs of the college experts can be outsourced for brief periods to train the students with minimum exchequer. This will go a long way in getting appreciation of the stakeholders and earn their trust in the institution.

9. Feedback System

A properly structured feedback system between college authorities and stakeholders is necessary for incremental and sustained growth of the institution and timely resolution of difficulties, if any, faced by the students and others. The college website can have a provision for stakeholders to write their suggestions, comments and feedbacks concerning any aspect of the college with a choice to be anonymous. The will enable the college authorities to initiate corrective actions quickly.

10. Green Campus

Maintenance of campus, the buildings and open spaces, garden etc., spick and span year round is essential. Likewise, waste management, rain water harvesting, generating solar energy need to be in place. Good ambience provides congenial atmosphere for teaching and learning processes. It may be a good idea to involve students, teachers and supporting staff in campus maintenance drive on weekly basis to ensure their indulgence in the maintenance of the campus facilities. In many instances, the college buildings are painted and campus is tidied just before the NAAC Peer Team visit. This is not enough. Campus should look the same year round. For more on the concept of green campus reader may consult the Chapter 22 of this book.

11. Alumni Association (AA)

It is a pity that historically colleges and universities in India have ignored the importance of their own alumni excepting few exceptions like the IITs, IIMs, and a few other premier institutions. Involving the Alumni in the development of HEIs is a very useful venture. Unfortunately, AAs are often floated just before the NAAC per team visit. They are not even registered and no office bearers elected. This does no good to anyone. The AA must be registered under suitable legal frame and follow all procedures. It is a great source for getting feedbacks, financial and many logistical supports for the institution. An active AA is a boon. For more detailed consideration reader may consult Chapter 23 of this book.

The above factors constitute the basic requirements of any college. Hence, every college should have these in place firmly and held in dynamic state. Having detailed the basic requirements let me now share my views on preparing for A&A of the institution. Before going into the details, I must make it clear that the suggestions do not guarantee high grades. They will however assist colleges in preparing well before subjecting a HEI for A&A process. Therefore, the colleges may carefully and judiciously take those suggestions that may be relevant, useful or convincing. Good performance of the concerned institution alone helps in securing high grades.

In A&A process, performance of the institutions (colleges and universities) in the 7 defined Criteria is used to judge and grade them. Therefore, the institutions must keep in mind these criteria while planning their academic and administrative strategies. As a matter of fact, the 7 Criteria identified by NAAC are helpful in ensuring planned growth of HEIs.

The 7 Criteria identified by NAAC are as follows:

Criteria 1: Curricular Aspects

Criteria 2: Teaching, Learning and Evaluation

Criteria 3: Research, Innovation and Extension

Criteria 4: Infrastructure and Learning Resources

Criteria 5: Student Support and Progression

Criteria 6: Governance, Leadership and Management

Criteria 7: Institutional Values and Best Practices

Here I will briefly deal with each of the above seven Criteria and the associated key aspects to enable preparing a good 'Self Study Report' (SSR). The first Criterion, which pertains to 'Curricular Aspects' (Design and Development) has 4 key aspects: Curricular Planning and Implementation, Academic Flexibility, Curriculum Enrichment, and Feedback System. The Universities and autonomous colleges have a significant role in curriculum design and development. As far as the affiliated and constituent colleges are concerned, they have no role in the curriculum design and development. Therefore, their role is limited to planning the implementation of the prescribed curriculum. The college should reveal the steps taken to ensure that the prescribed syllabus is properly covered. Here one could also mention the names of teachers who may be on the Board of Studies (BOS) of the University, frequency of syllabus revision and feedbacks given to BOS by the college from time to time and supported by documentary evidences. Meaning of academic flexibility is often not clear to many colleges. It basically means whether students have flexible options in terms of choice of programs / subject combinations, number of open electives, credit transfer provisions, change of subjects/courses, supplementary enrichment programs if any, number of years to complete the course, re-entry of dropouts and, girl students who discontinue education following their marriage, pregnancy and maternal care etc. All available provisions in such situations may be highlighted. The curriculum enrichment refers to provisions of add on courses like personality development, skill development (value added) courses, holding cultural programs, promoting ethical practices, endowment lectures instituted by the college and so on. The last key aspect pertains to collecting feedback from students, parents and alumni with regard to relevance and appropriateness of courses in catering to the requirements of the society, economy and environment. Further, it also involves systematic analysis of the feedbacks and appropriate follow up actions and improvements.

The Criterion 2 pertains to 'Teaching-Learning and Evaluation' processes. There are seven key aspects. The first key aspect concerns with student enrolment and their profile. This requires providing category wise details of students admitted from the State and outside the State (different geographical locations), demand ratio for different courses, socio-economical, cultural and educational backgrounds of students. The second key aspect, 'Catering to student diversity' is meant to know the provisions made by the college in relation to gender needs, slow and advanced learners, hostel facility, ramps, brail facility for visually challenged, scholarships to poor and deserving students, promotion of sports and cultural activities and so forth. The third aspect pertains to 'Teaching-Learning Process' focussing on the methodologies used in imparting education in the institution. For example, teachers may be using predominantly chalk and talk method, and at times make use of OHP, LCDs, smart boards, seminars, group discussions etc. Teaching methods used, including teacher's familiarity with Learning Management Systems (LMSs) need to be depicted here. The fourth key aspect pertains to the 'Teacher's Profile and Quality'. This essentially means qualifications of the teachers: NET/SLET qualification, possession of research degrees, recruitment methods, number of permanent teachers and vacancies, part time teachers, guest faculty and their qualifications. The fifth key aspect concerns evaluation process and reforms. The process of evaluation as followed by the affiliating university or the autonomous college is to be specified. Affiliated and constituent colleges however follow what is prescribed by the affiliating university. In case the university has made any reforms with respect to examinations in the recent past, the same could be made explicit. The sixth key aspect pertains to the 'Students' Performance and Learning Outcomes'. It refers to pass percentages, ranks secured by the students at the university level examinations and dropout rates: performance of the students in varsity examinations is an ultimate parameter to judge a college. A newly introduced key aspect is 'Student Satisfaction Survey'. This survey is considered as the direct indictor of the effectiveness of the teaching-learning processes in the institution. The survey is based on a sample of students and not the entire college.

The 3rd Criterion deals with 'Research, Innovations and Extension' activities. The 1st key aspect of this Criterion seeks information on how the institution promotes research by its faculty. Hence, it is more pertinent to universities and autonomous colleges. It does not apply to affiliated and constituent colleges. Providing seed money, granting leave for those who wish to pursue research degrees, financial support to participate and/or organize seminars/conferences/symposia indicate promotion of activities under the said key aspect. Providing basic physical facilities (e.g. library, journals, laboratories, computers, dark rooms, animal house and so on) by the institution is critical for carrying out research. The 2nd key aspect is meant to reveal how and how much funds are mobilized by the faculty members for research through R and D agencies and industries etc. The 3rd key aspect pertains to developing innovation ecosystem that includes features like incubation centres, means of transfer of knowledge, patents obtained, dissemination of Intellectual Property Rights (IPR), Academia-Industry innovative practices and, recognitions received if any for these activities. The 4th key aspect is straight forward requiring cataloguing books and research papers published, and awards/recognitions received by the faculty. Some Peer Team members distinguish between the research publications made before and after joining the institution as they believe that work done elsewhere need not go to the credit of the institution under assessment. They do however go to the credit of the concerned faculty member. This key aspect is more important for Universities than for the colleges. The key aspect dealing with 'consultancy' is not much of relevance to affiliated /constituent colleges. But, it is very pertinent to universities and autonomous colleges. The consultancy work done should be properly documented along with revenue generated. The 6th key aspect pertains to extension activities undertaken by the institution. In most colleges mainly the NSS and NCC volunteers are involved in the extension works that routinely include blood donation and plantation of trees. Much more could be done under extension activities and institutional responsibility towards the society (e.g. community services). The last key aspect pertains to collaborations in teaching and research activities if any. If yes, the same could be highlighted.

The Criterion 4 has four key aspects designed to assess the adequacy of 'Infrastructure and Learning Resources' and their maintenance; this includes the level of physical facilities like, class rooms, library, laboratories, sports, gym, ladies room, faculty rooms and so on. A key aspect on library deals with the various library facilities, qualifications of librarian, mode of issuing books (open access etc.), facilities for browsing (accessing journals through INFLIBNET, N-LIST), photocopying, and number of books issued per day and visits of students and faculty per day, adequacy of library space and other related aspects. The 3rd key aspect deals with the 'IT Infrastructure'. Here facilities like computers, LCD projectors, smart boards, and so on are to be catalogued. Furthermore, the visiting NAAC Peer Committee will try to ascertain how much of these are really utilized. Use of IT in administration, teaching, learning and evaluation form the focal points. Finally, 'Maintenance of Campus Infrastructure' is assessed. The committee invariably visits all important facilities including rest rooms, and facilities for girl students. It is absolutely essential that campus facilities are well maintained year round and proper mechanisms exist for the same. Remember, there are always people in the college who will usher in the ears of the committee members that most of the up keeping works are done just a day or two ago and that the whole year the toilets stink horrendously. So it is in the interest of the college to maintain its facility in best possible way year round.

The Criterion 5 concerns 'Student Support and Progression' which has 4 key aspects. The first concerns facilities like career guidance cell, placement cell, provision of bridge and value added courses, counselling facility, scholarships, grievance redress cell, feedback system, and the like. Mentoring activity should be properly institutionalized by a formal mechanism. Mentoring may involve, taking care of slow and advanced learners, counselling, helping resolution of personal and official problems of students to the extent possible and so on. Pertinent records should be maintained. The key aspect pertaining to student progression is a measure of how the students are progressing from lower to higher classes and their performance in the university examinations. Student's progression from UG to PG courses must be revealed through proper documentation. The third key aspect is concerned with the participation of students in sports, cultural activities, NCC and NSS. The awards received in any of these activities at the State or National level competitions could be highlighted. Likewise, NCC students participating in Republic Day parade and joining the defence services is a good point to highlight.

The Criterion 6 dealing with 'Governance, Leadership and Management' of the colleges has 5 key aspects. The first pertains to the very 'vision and leadership' of the Principal and the management. Progresses and accomplishments of the college have to be in tune with the set vision and mission statements. Introduction of new courses, add on courses, a rise in demand ratio, good mentoring and counselling facilities, proactive support to sports and cultural activities, a proper documentation of all claims and, overall appreciation of the institution by the stakeholders reflect good governance and leadership of the administrators. The 2nd key aspect is intended to know the various steps taken in respect of developmental activities and their implementation. The 3rd key aspect concerns faculty empowerment strategies of the institution. These include encouraging academic pursuits of faculty members (e.g. pursuing research degrees, participation in conferences/ symposia and organizing such events and attracting research grants etc.). The 4th key aspect relates to financial management, resource mobilization and their utilization. Non-utilization of sanctioned funds is inexcusable. Likewise, if the funds are not utilized as per norms and if there are adverse audit observations, it is bad for the institution. Under this key aspect, mobilization of funds is equally important. The last key aspect is of great significance. It pertains to the very functioning of the Internal Quality Assurance Systems (IQAS). Ideally, institutions must constitute the IQAC with very eminent experts with freedom to debate discuss and give important suggestions. The decisions taken in the IQAC after in depth deliberation should be implemented without delay. Namesake IQACs serve no purpose. The NAAC peer team gives considerable importance to the functioning of the IQAC.

The 7th and the last Criterion focuses on 'Institutional Values and Best Practices'. It has three broad key aspects namely *Institutional Values and Social Responsibilities, Best Practices* and *Institutional Distinctiveness.* The first concerns with aspects like gender equity promotion, sensitivity to environmental issues, adoption of environment friendly practices, like harvesting solar power and rainwater, waste recycling, solid waste and e-waste management, maintaining a green campus. Other social responsibilities include diverse aspects like: Divyangan friendliness, concern for human values and professional ethics. The 3rd key aspect concerns best practices of the institution. Each institution has to envisage its own best practices for which it should be known and would have made an impact on the society. Best practices can be thought of in academic, administrative and other matters. Every institution should earn a name for some kind of distinctiveness through some innovative practices that help in enhancing the quality of education and comfort of students. Further, the institution also needs to highlight the actual outcome of the efforts made by the institution in respect of the three key aspects.

Preparing Self Study Report (SSR)

The Self Study Report (SSR) needs to be prepared very carefully as it creates the first impression about the institution in the minds of the readers, the NAAC Peer Team members. I have seen SSRs of many institutions that are poorly prepared and fail to project achievements of the institution properly. In some rare cases, SSRs are written excellently but the ground situation belies it. False claims usually get noticed and they lower the image of the institution. Therefore, care should be taken to be realistic and transparent. All claims made in the SSR need to be validated through documentary evidences.

Some of my specific suggestions for preparing the SSR are as follows:

1. The SSR should be brief and crisp
2. Avoid repetitions and jargon

3. As far as possible restrict the size of SSR to 125 pages or so
4. SSR should clearly highlight major points
5. Use bullet points wherever possible and avoid long descriptive paragraphs
6. Ensure that all claims are supported by the documentary evidences
7. The 'Executive Summary' should highlight all important accomplishments

SSR for Subsequent Cycles

As far as SSR for subsequent cycles (say 2nd/3rd etc) of A&A is concerned, the institution should mainly highlight the achievements of the past 5 years. The accomplishments of the period before the last 5 years are not under consideration during the subsequent cycles. However, a few very noteworthy features of great importance though already written in the first SSR may be briefly mentioned without spending too many pages on them. It is very useful to provide a comparative picture of accomplishments of the past 5 years in relation to the earlier 5 years for which NAAC has already graded and given suggestions. This could be done criteria wise using tables and figures. A 'compliance report' with reference to the suggestions of the previous NAAC Peer Team is a must.

New Methodology

The NAAC has revised its methodology of assessment since July 2017. Now the assessment parameters include quantification of several parameters that ensure more objective assessment. For instance, students admitted to degree courses, certificate/diploma courses, number of students undertaking field projects and internships, number of students from other States, average enrolment percentage in last 5 years, actual number of students admitted from reserved categories, number of differently abled (Divyangan) students enrolled, new courses introduced, number of programs with CBCS, number of students passing NET/SLET/GATE/GMAT/CAT/GRE/TOEFL and, Civil Services and State Government examinations, part time/full time teachers, teachers with research degrees, number of teachers using ICT, pass percentages, number of research guides, number of research projects, number of Ph. D degrees produced, number of publications in UGC notified journals / proceedings, number of students participating in extracurricular / extension activities, number of class rooms and seminar halls with ICT facilities, budget allocation for infrastructure augmentation (excluding salary component), annual expenditure on books and journals, number of teachers and students using library per day, expenditures on campus maintenance, number of students benefitted by scholarships/free-ships (Government and other), number of students benefitted by guidance for competitive examinations, number of students attending vocation education training, number of outgoing students progressing towards higher education or placed with jobs, number of sports and cultural activities, competitions organised by the institution in sports and culture, funds generated from Alumni, number of teachers provided financial assistance to attend conferences/ workshops, membership fee provided, number of professional development programs organized for teaching and supporting staff, number of teachers participated in Orientation/Refresher/Short term courses for faculty development, power generated using renewable energy sources, power met through LED bulbs, and expenditure on green initiatives and waste management (excluding salary component) and so on. Data pertaining to all these aspects are to be first computed for each year and then used to get averages for 5 year period preceding the assessment. Therefore, a systematic documentation of data is very crucial. I suggest that all HEIs should first become familiar with the new methodology prescribed by NAAC by carefully studying the Manuals for assessment of affiliated, constituent, autonomous colleges and varsities as the case may be. In the new methodology, 70% weightage is given for the data provided online. The remaining 30% is based on the Peer Team assessment following its visit to the institution undergoing A&A.

The grading system has also changed from July 2017. The grades are given in the form of letters 'A to D' where D denotes for 'Not Accredited' when the CGPA <1.50. All other grades A-C are considered 'Accredited'. The Grades are further classified based on the CGPA scores: A^{++} (3.76-4.00), A^{+} (3.51-3.75), and A (3.01-3.50), B^{++} (2.76-3.00), B^{+} (2.51-2.75), B (2.01-2.50) and C (1.51-2.00).

Lastly, I wish to comment on (1) the importance of A&A process and (2) significance of Grade points. First, subjecting an institution for A&A is like availing opportunity to know the institution's strengths, weaknesses, opportunities and future challenges (SWOC). It is therefore helpful in initiating corrective and progressive measures for the betterment of the institutions. In addition, it helps the stakeholders to know all about the institution; the infrastructure, quality of faculty, facilities available and academic standing. Thus, there are many benefits of subjecting HEIs to A&A process periodically. Furthermore the new methodology with qualitative and quantitative matrices has become more objective, more transparent and less subjective. However, the new methodology calls for preparations for A&A from Day 1 meaning 5 years in advance by carefully documenting everything as per the NAAC manuals. My second comment pertains to the significance of Grades and CGPAs. I had the fortune of interacting with hundreds of peer team members who worked with me and many who have not worked with me. Therefore, I believe in having accumulated enough experience to generalize my observations. The perception of the peer team members varies greatly depending upon their own backgrounds, academic standing, philosophy and personal accomplishments. Some members are quite serious and meticulous while others are rather casual in their approach to the assessment process. Such a scenario is unlikely to change in the near future. Therefore, let me emphasize that no one needs to be excessively elated or desolate after the announcement of grades and scores by the NAAC. The Grades broadly indicate the position of the institution. While lower grades will compel the institutions to make further improvements and progresses, the higher grades may sometimes lead to self-satisfaction and arrest further growth. Hence, HEIs should not get carried away by grades and CGPAs they receive. HEIs must continuously strive to accomplish all round improvement of the institution for which the sky is the limit.

Library Resources and Digital Literacy

CHAPTER - 15

FROM CLAY TABLET TO DIGITAL TABLET: TOWARDS IDEAL LIBRARY

— *N. V. SATHYANARAYANA*

A library is the delivery room for the birth of ideas, a place where history comes to life. — NORMAN COUSINS

The library is perceived with a divine feeling in India as a temple of knowledge. It evokes a feeling of mystical silence. The book as an embodiment of recorded human knowledge enjoys the status of an immortalised holy object in the hands of the Goddess Saraswathi. While this is an idealised image of libraries, an ideal library of today symbolizes as an embodiment of knowledge curates, disseminated and used through several media, driven by technology.

Libraries in the Ancient World

From the tablets of Mesopotamian civilization found in Iraq and Syria (2600-1900 BC) to the Papyrus in the Takshasila (600-500 BC) (now in Pakistan) and Royal Alexandria Library in Egypt (295 BC), and the palm leaves in the Library of Nalanda (427-1193 AD), libraries have illustrious recorded history of serving the promotion of knowledge and scholarship in the ancient world. Invention of paper in 2nd Century AD (China) and Guttenberg's printing technology almost thousand years later (1140 AD) changed the face and growth of the libraries completely to what we see today. This technological revolution is primarily responsible for the wider penetration and the democratization of access to knowledge which is further catalysed by the Internet of today. It is a lexical irony that this history started with the tablets (clay) is now being lead again by tablets (digital), besides several other electronic media.

Academic Libraries in the Recent Past

Historically, academic libraries have derived value as an essential campus infrastructure from the research support they gave to scholars by providing content (books, journals, research papers etc.) and tools (abstracting and indexing products like Chemical Abstracts, Biological Abstracts, Sociological Abstracts) for literature survey. Going back to fifty years, literature search in those days was an arduous and time consuming task. When a user found a few relevant documents through literature search he expected the library to provide them quickly. Users perceived the library's value and quality of service by how quickly the library could make available those documents. The exponential growth of information, it's ever increasing costs, particularly for research journals, and declining budgets of libraries created a situation of poverty amidst plenty even for users in the countries with developed economies. Things were unimaginably worse for Indian researchers and their libraries. During the 60s and 70s of the last century many established premier institutions and universities in India could still subscribe to around 1,000 international journals while their counterpart like Harvard and Stanford were subscribing to 10-15 times more. The gap widened further over the years reaching a point when most universities in India were found it difficult to sustain subscribing to even 200-300 international journals. At one time, there were close to hundred subscriptions from India for the print version of Chemical Abstracts, one of the most expensive but indispensable search tools for chemical researchers. This dropped to less than 25 over the years. The situation was far from anything like an ideal library dream in the last century. It was also the time when technologies were evolving to take us closer to an ideal library of a different world.

Universal Access to Knowledge

It is important to understand a little bit about how libraries evolved and function in the modern world of today beginning last century. Libraries operate on a fundamental principle of providing universal access to knowledge, for all their user communities. This principle is in fact the ultimate goal for an ideal library system. However, with the exception of National Libraries, no single library in the world, however rich, can afford to buy more than 10-15% of all that is published every year in the globe. Even the best of Indian Libraries can hardly afford to buy 2-3% of what is published. Knowledge needs of the users being global, more particularly in the sphere of science and technology, users will require access to all that is published, with choice of what to select and read left to their local needs and context. Libraries have two on-going challenges in evolving their systems towards achieving the goal of universal access.

1. Creating and providing a discovery (search) infrastructure for all that is published in the world. This would help the user to find what is available within the scope of what he/ she is looking for.
2. Facilitating access to the material that is beyond the reach of one's own library. To address these challenges effectively, libraries around the world consciously evolved mechanisms to network themselves as a collaborative system at local, national and global levels. They have developed the following two sets of tools and a mechanism for resource sharing.
    (a) A local catalogue for all the reading materials a library acquires. The map of a library is its catalogue. It is popularly known as OPAC (Online Public Access Catalogue) in the language of Librarians ever since the card catalogues in the library went online several years ago. In a way, libraries were one of the earliest institutions to go online with their OPAC long before the Internet.
    (b) A Union Catalogue of libraries through a collaborative model: the union catalogue is a merger of the catalogues (OPACs) of several libraries in a defined region or nation, volunteering to participate and collaborate for sharing the content resources among themselves through a set of rules operating within, what is called, fair-use provisions of the copyright laws. Many nations have union catalogue of libraries. USA leads this initiative with a Global Union Catalogue called WorldCat (www.worldcat.org) which is a Union Catalogue of around 18,000 libraries in the world which includes most of the National Libraries. WorldCat

has a list of close to 200 million books in all media and all languages of the world, including over a million books published in Indian languages. The impact value of a Union Catalogue like 'WorldCat' is in the indication of the libraries having every book in the Union Catalogue. It is a pity that India is not an active part of such global initiatives and the country does not have a national union catalogue of its major libraries.

Resource Sharing

The OPAC acts as the local discovery (search) tool for the content held by the library. The Union Catalogue acts as a global discovery tool for the content beyond one's own library holdings. Libraries around the world have developed a system called Inter-Library Loan (ILL) to facilitate sharing of their collection with other libraries if the user of a library doesn't find what he is looking for in his own library.

Libraries largely catalogued books and other material they procured including the journals. But they rarely indexed every article in a journal they subscribed which is a massive activity beyond the domain of libraries. Hence, this task was taken up by a specialized group in the publishing industry called database publishers who compiled and indexed articles in different disciplines and made them available as commercial database products to the libraries. But these databases did not indicate the library location of a journal which was shown in the Union Catalogue. Thus if a user found an article from Biological Abstract Database, the Union Catalogue would tell him which library closer to him would have that journal if his own library did not have. Libraries facilitate the fulfilment of such needs through ILL or photocopy delivery service.

Resource sharing through ILL service is largely voluntary. Even if a library in the networked system of resource-sharing does not agree to lend a material to other library, the user has an option to at least locate and visit the library for consulting the material if in need. The University Grants Commission (UGC) through e-ShodhSindhu program of its INFLIBNET has mandated resource sharing among 150 university libraries for journal literature. The service uses an indigenously developed discovery platform called J-Gate (www.jgateplus.in) which indexes all the journals subscribed by Shodhsindhu, a consortium of

E-Journals funded by UGC and journals subscribed independently by 150 university libraries, IITs, IIMs and NITs. J-Gate also acts as the union catalogue of journals subscribed by the libraries of these institutions, both in print and e-version to facilitate resource sharing.

Libraries in the Post-Internet Era

The Library today is born digital. Its content, books and journals etc., are all digital. The print edition of a book is the by-product of a digital master copy. Several thousand peer-reviewed journals like PLOS Biology don't even have print edition today. Access to e-Journals is predominantly digital. There is evidence to show that in many of the national research libraries in India the back-volume section of print journals is rarely visited by the users. A new concept in publishing called print-on-demand has emerged to deliver print as custom copy only on request. This is largely to meet the demands of the users of previous generations who are not comfortable with the digital media and screens. The library usage habits of current generation of users, particularly the millennial is shifting significantly to digital medium. While journal access and usage has gone completely digital, the same is not the story for books. E-books are comparatively slow to catch up with user acceptance.

E-Resources: Closer to an Ideal Library Scenario?

Libraries going digital has a definite advantage of instant and round-the-clock access to library's collection of e-books and e-journals from anywhere if the user has access to Internet from his desktop PC or laptop or an e-book reader (like Kindle) or mobile devices such as tablets (like iPad) or smart phones. While access is instant how easy is the navigation process? Let us understand this from the imaginary experience of a university researcher in a university, which has a hybrid library of digital and print collection.

A Library has its catalogue available as OPAC, cataloguing its book collection. The Library lists its journal collection in a separate webpage as A-Z listings with links to journal site for e-versions. The library has recently set up a browsing centre, which is a parallel reading hall with PC screens connected to the Internet on every reading desk, named as E-Resource Centre. The library also provides off-campus access to its collection for searching for the benefit of its faculty and students who can access library from their homes and hostels. It is indeed a modern library system offering convenient access.

The primary function of the library is to provide access to recorded knowledge, largely in publications. For a researcher, knowledge needs are global in nature. Therefore, library facilitates use of access gateway to whatever the world has published and helps the users in deriving needed information out of the global pool of knowledge resources. In the library's browsing centre, our user, typical of her search habits, goes to Google to discover something she is looking for, as she perhaps doesn't know that her library has its own set of Google-kind of search tools, even better than Google. After a long and exhausting Google search session she finds four publications of her interest, a book and three journal articles. Google takes her to the sites of those publications where she finds she will have to pay for three of them and one of them, a journal article, is available free as it is an open access journal. She emails the free article to her personal email address for browsing at home. She lists the details of the remaining three publications and goes to the library catalogue (OPAC) to find whether her library has it. She is happy to find that the library's OPAC shows the book as available in the library but on circulation. She makes a reservation for that book which she can borrow when it is returned by the current borrower. The other two being journal articles are not shown in the OPAC. To find whether the library subscribes to those two journals she goes to A-Z Listing of the Journal in her Library's web page. She is happy to find one of them subscribed by her library as e-Journal. She clicks on the link provided which takes her to the journal site again, which she had visited earlier through Google search. She is excited that she is so much closer to the paper she is looking for. She searches for the paper in the journal site and finds the abstract with a link to full-text. A click on the full-text says she will have to buy that article. Perplexed, she goes to the Librarian only to find that the library's subscription is limited to recent year's content and what she is looking for is in an older volume. Using a tool called Union Catalogue of Periodicals subscribed by a group of Universities, the librarian finds that this journal is subscribed in another library and helps her separately to get that article through an inter-library loan system.

As she is with the Librarian, she asks the Librarian for help to find the second paper published in another journal that her library does not subscribe. The Librarian does a bit of research and finds that the publisher of that journal is an enlisted publisher of e- Shodhsindhu a Consortium for Higher Education Electronic Resources set up by UGC/ INFLIBNET. His library being a member of e-ShodhSindhu, he advises her to go back to the browsing centre and browse in e-ShodhSindhu pages for the journal under its publisher. Back to the Library's browsing centre, she is able to find the article with a bit of laborious navigation through a few more pages.

While on the e-ShodhSindhu page she also discovers certain search tools that are better tailored to her literature search needs such as - J-Gate (www.jgateplus.com) SciFinder (www.scifinder.cas.org), Web of Science (www.webofknowledge.com) JSTOR (www.jstor.org), etc. As she gains some knowledge about this set of e-resources through a few training programs provided by the library, she realizes that her library offers better tools for her research than Google, though still not as simple as Google! She also discovers that J-Gate, which is an e-Journal Gateway, could have helped her in completing all her journal search in one place including locating the library in which one of the journals she was looking for was not subscribed by her library and to send an online request to that library. Google has an appeal to the user as a universal search system although it is not as universal as the library is from the user's real need, which is exemplified by this story. If not an ideal library for all purposes of what a library is meant for, e-ShodhSindhu is a service in the direction of making a college/ university library an ideal library.

Open Access (OA)

The power and reach of Google as a search engine has created a myth that information is free. What Google does is a machine cataloguing/indexing of content available in public domain on websites which have unrestricted access to all without requiring any identification and authentication. To this extent millions of website content are available for Open Access (free) to the world through Google, Bing and similar search engines.

The concept of open access in the scholarly world has a different meaning. It is about removing the pay-wall barrio created by subscription model to scholarly journals which have become prohibitively expensive over the years. The average annual subscription cost of an international scientific journal today, whether in print or online is more than US$3,000. As the authors assign exclusive copyright to the publishers for publishing their research papers, publishers have developed the journal market as a proprietary product market enjoying monopoly in pricing. Authors publish their papers without any royalty expectation from journal publishers for wider global dissemination and recognition of their work through citations. This very purpose and the social good behind the intention of publishing without royalty expectation are being defeated by the high subscription charges. The Open Access movement started about twenty years ago as a strong resistance to journal publishers' high-pricing trends and monopolistic practices. The movement has gained ground over the years by the Governments of several nations recognizing the movement and its public good particularly since research in academic institutions are extensively funded by the Governments. The movement has resulted in agencies like NIH (National Institute of Health), USA and many such research funding agencies in the world mandating that the research papers published as by-product of their funded research should be available to public domain either immediately or within a period of one year. US Government has also issued a policy directive that research papers resulting out of substantially funded research projects should be made available to public domain. Driven by strong support from the scholarly community across the world and the Government initiative, new models of open access publishing have evolved. Two major models in practice are: 'OA Green Publishing Model' and 'OA Gold Publishing Model'.

The Green model is an extension of traditional publishing through subscription fee based model where the publisher opens up the journal for OA after one year of embargo. Several professional societies like Oxford University Press, Cambridge University Press, Journal of Biological Chemistry, Institute of Physics, UK, etc. have favoured this model.

The Gold model is an independent publishing model based on author fee. For the accepted article through a peer-review mechanism, the author or his institution is expected to pay page charges. Beginning with PLOS (Public Library of Science) founded in 2001, which is the earliest and one of the largest publishers of OA content by number of articles, today there are several OA publishers publishing a few thousand journals under Gold model.

A few commercial and professional society publishers like Elsevier and Springer have also started hybrid models of OA publishing where in a subscription journal, authors can publish their article for free global access by all. While the entire journal will be available on subscription model, articles where authors have opted for OA model are made available globally for open access.

There is a wider misuse and abuse of OA publishing model (Gold) in countries like India and China largely due to policy constraints and general disregard to quality in research and publishing. The situation is alarming enough to lead to major scam in science journal publishing and research quality unless this is addressed on priority by the policy makers in higher education and research.

Currently there are more than 20,000 OA journals published in the world in English language contributing almost 20% of the total number of research papers published every year. The trend is likely to accelerate with more than half of the research papers of the world likely to be opened up for OA in the near future. OA movement has taken strong roots in the journal publishing world and is very likely to change the future of journal publishing. Will this have an impact on scholarly book publishing is a still a matter of mute debate. In any case, OA is certainly driving the world in the direction of achieving universal access to knowledge, a primary goal of an ideal library.

Ideal Library

An ideal library is much more than facilitating universal access to knowledge. An ideal library can be perceived from two angles, user perspectives, and the provider's vision. The perspective keeps changing from generation to generation of users and even within a generation which is largely driven by the technology and ever increasing user expectations. The latter too is driven by technology. As users get used to one type of convenience provided by the technology they start expecting more of it. This changing user expectations and the emergence of many disruptive digital technologies that control the creation of, access to and delivery of content (books and journals) set the bench mark for what an 'ideal library' of the day should be. If the library is perceived to be just a source of information that a user wants, Google kind of services may set the bench-mark although it will not have all the information the user would need. If the library is perceived as a knowledge support for learning and research, besides the cultural value of the library as protector of the intellectual heritage of the civilization for posterity and re-use, an entirely different set of bench mark may decide an ideal library. While library standards and best practices have evolved over the years, the idea of an ideal library has still remains a perception in widely varying degrees, particularly from the user's view which is very kaleidoscopic.

Users' Perception of an Ideal Library

Alberto Manguel's essay on "Notes towards a definition of the ideal library" in his book "A Reader on Reading" is a serious scholarly effort to define an ideal library from a user perspective. In this essay Manguel leans towards an ideal library being personal in a public place. He says, "The ideal library is meant for one particular reader. Every reader must feel that he or she is the chosen one". Interestingly, the evolving Digital Library systems of the day meet this ideal by providing for every user to create his/her own personal library space within a Digital Library System. Following are a few ideas and observations selected from various websites of what users think and feel of what an ideal library should be:

(a) A place to date with books where you ask for any book of your choice, you will not be disappointed. A utopian thought indeed, but not any longer. Conceiving such a library is not impossible today.

(b) Personal and private, yet public. Personal to every reader in a community setting.

(c) Connects content and community (users) facilitating conversation (exchange of knowledge). (The expectation here is similar to user experience with Face book, LinkedIn and YouTube)

(d) Both virtual and physical. It allows for every technology, every container, and every manifestation of the text.

(e) An inspiring place for reading and learning

(f) Has no closing hours (a virtual library is open round-the-clock)

(g) Fireplace, comfy chairs, study area. Without unscientific health advice books. Tours and talks about the books in the historical section.

(h) More group rooms.

(i) Has a coffee and fast computer at big desk with comfortable chairs! Lots of lights for reading.

(j) Would have a coffee bar, soft music and a reflecting pool with oversized chairs to sit in and relax while reading/studying.

(k) Free access to software used in research methodology.

(l) Movie rooms and gaming rooms

(m) Lots of toys and game boards.

(n) Allows users to have the book out for as long as he/she needs it. So of course there are no late fines. And the library hours, open whenever the user has the time or inclination to walk through its doors. (Technology of the day makes this possible)

(o) Symbolises everything a society stands for

(p) Ergonomically designed for user's comfort for long sessions of reading and writing

(q) No shelf in the ideal library is higher or lower than the reach of the reader's arm. The ideal library does not require acrobatics.

(r) Cool, clean and calm a place of tranquillity where minds of men and women of all ages are in an intensely heated interaction with their favourite authors.

(s) Beautiful and usable

There is a common thread flowing across these divergent views. Users perceive library as something more than a place to read or borrow books. They feel this to be a community centre for meeting their learning and leisure needs in a cultural setup.

Social Views and Professional Vision

Increasingly libraries are changing from silent zones to happening places and from private study desks to collaborative learning spaces in both academic and public spaces. In the academic space, libraries of the day are showing signs and enthusiasm to become an integral part of the academic eco-systems not by just providing access to knowledge but also by contributing to the creation and management of knowledge as publishing and content management service providers. As early adapter of technologies, libraries are professionally equipped to play the role of campus information mangers and archivists.

At a philosophical level, the society needs libraries to promote and facilitate the utilisation of knowledge. At a cultural level we need them to preserve and protect the knowledge assets as intellectual heritage of the society for future generations. At the institutional level, the library is expected to act as a study and learning centre for its community and facilitate dissemination of information and knowledge to the community. Thus, an ideal library is expected to contribute to all-time educational and cultural development of its community through the preservation and dissemination of the knowledge created by the society, from generation to generation.

Lastly, in the technology driven world of today which can compete with divine miracles in creative power, crystal ball gazers are predicting the disappearance of the printed book that is part of our learning culture for centuries now. Library as we knew until recently is undergoing metamorphosis. But its value perception as the intellectual repository of all the knowledge of our civilisation for everlasting dissemination and usage continues to be valid and strong. Creation of knowledge and its preservation for re-use and posterity will continue to be a technology dependent activity. This dependence is more likely to intensify with progressive civilizations. Library as we see today will continue to evolve with benchmark shifting constantly for creating an ideal library. The ideal library of today in the evolving ecosystem of academic campuses is sure to enjoy a demanding and enviable position in the coming days, competing with rest of the campus infrastructure.

CHAPTER - 16

LIBRARY: A LEARNING RESOURCE CENTRE

— *ANUPAMA N. JOSHI*

Ordinary people have big TVs. Extraordinary people have big libraries.
–ROBIN SHARMA

Academic Libraries are integral part of a college, university or any other institutions importing education. They are considered as the nerve centres of the academic institutions and are meant to support teaching, research and other academic programs. In the changing information environment, libraries are evolving to suit the needs of users. Information and communication technology (ICT) has changed the way in which people interact, communicate, seek and acquire information. Use of ICT in academic environment has helped in enhancing the productivity of researchers. Therefore, the libraries being a central part of the academic environment also need to equip themselves with all necessary ICT based services. Libraries have been serving to the general and academic communities from time immemorial; it ranges from the famous library of Nalanda University to the libraries attached to the most advanced research institutions today. A wide range of specializations are coming up due to research and development has become the prime focus in academic setup. At the same time, Distance Education is growing at a very fast pace. Hence, the information needs of users differ greatly. Therefore, the library collection should have very wide range of materials to meet the generalized or basic needs of users to teaching needs of teachers to very specific needs of researchers.

Earlier the *sine qua non* of academic libraries was the sufficiency of information resources developed in tune with the vision and mission of the parent institutions. But now libraries face a diametrically opposite situation where on one hand information resources are growing and on the other library budgets and space are shrinking. Under such a situation to strike a right balance between the two and also satisfy the user community, many electronic resources have proved to be very helpful.

Electronic Resources

These constitute information resources that can be accessed in an electronic format only. An e-resource may be in the form of e-journal, e-book, e-database, e-thesis, e-newspaper etc. E-resources have taken a firm place in academics and are preferred by teachers and students alike because of the following features.

1. Easy to carry
2. Easily accessible with a click of mouse
3. Contain Multimedia information
4. Multiple accesses
5. Provide links to further searches
6. Information accessibility round the clock (24x7 hours)
7. Alerting services

The numerous advantages of e-resources are often highlighted everywhere. There is also a myth that print collection is redundant. One should not forget that the librarians over a period of time have painstakingly developed huge print collections suiting to the needs of the parent institution. The information contained in print resources is precious and needs to be well preserved and provided access, as all that is available on the net is not authentic information. Hence access to both print and electronic resources is obligatory to the users. This has led to the emergence of hybrid libraries.

Hybrid Library

It is a continuum between the conventional and digital library where electronic and paper based information sources are available to the users under a single roof. Hybrid libraries are needed both in colleges and Universities because of the following reasons:

1. Updated infrastructure to access e-resources is not always available

2. IT and information handling skills of the students are often inadequate
3. Vast knowledge in print resources needs to be made available to the users more easily
4. Power supply and speed of internet are still to be improved in many colleges.

Serial Crisis

Research Journals / Serials are an essential part of information resources required for academic community. They are the most sought after information resource as they carry latest information. Hence, libraries attached to institutes of higher education give great importance to journal subscription. As a result, *serial crisis* has put the libraries in a very difficult position. The term "serials crisis" refers to exponential and continuing increase in subscription cost of scholarly journals. It is a result of the rising cost of journals in much faster rate than the rate of inflation. Rapidly rising journal subscription prices have severely eroded the ability of libraries (both in colleges and universities) to purchase/subscribe scholarly publications. Further, the number of journals has increased due to growth of various specializations and this phenomenon is coupled with the paucity of funds available to the libraries. Nevertheless, libraries are the places which have the responsibility of providing information to support teaching and research activities of the parent institutions. To overcome such a situation, consortiums were set up in India. Consortium is a cooperative arrangement among the institutions to pool their resources for common benefit. In case of libraries 'common benefit' is access to information. INFLIBNET (Information and library network) centre, an autonomous inter-University unit of University Grants Commission (UGC) took a leading step in this direction and started UGC-INFONET Digital Library Consortia to help universities to access e-journals. Some of the various consortia established related to academic libraries are:

1. Indian National Digital Library in Engineering Sciences and Technology Consortia (INDEST)
2. N-List
3. Council of Scientific and Industrial Research (CSIR e-journal consortium)

4. Health Services Library and Information Network (HELNET)
5. IIM Consortium
6. Indian Council of Medical Research (ICMR)

E-ShodhaSindhu is formed by merging the UGC-INFONET Digital Library Consortium, NLIST and INDEST-AICTE Consortium based on recommendation of an Expert Committee, of the MHRD. It is a consortium for e-resources to provide current as well as archival access to over 15,000 core and peer-reviewed journals, number of bibliographic citations, and factual databases in different disciplines from a large number of publishers and aggregators to its member institutions like the centrally-funded technical institutions, universities and colleges that are covered under 12(B) and 2(f) Sections of the UGC Act. Through this consortium, the users can have access to full text subscription of e-journals and e-books. It provides archival access to over 9000 core and peer reviewed journals and databases. E-resources can be reached by subject, publisher, journal name, and database or by collection.

The Project entitled "National Library and Information Services Infrastructure for Scholarly Content" (N-LIST) provides access to e-resources to students, researchers and faculty members of colleges and other beneficiary institutions through server(s) installed at the INFLIBNET Centre.

The users from colleges can access e-resources and download articles required by them directly from the publisher's website once they are duly authenticated as the authorized users through servers deployed at the INFLIBNET Centre. In this way they can have access to contents in journals and books. The students from their 10+2 grade to undergraduate courses may be exposed to using such e-resources.

Shodhaganga

Theses being the rich and unique source of information often remain untapped and underutilized. Apart from this there is duplication of research work due to lack of knowledge regarding research work conducted in various universities which leads to wastage of human and financial resources. To overcome this hindrance, INFLIBNET has started '*Shodhaganga*' which is indeed a boon to research community allowing them access to theses submitted to any Indian University in

India. It has been made mandatory since 2009 to all the researchers to submit an electronic version of their theses. Shodhaganga facilitates searches through subject, Universities, name of researcher/guide/title and keywords. As on today there are 139213 full text theses, 3871 synopsis contributed by 281 Universities. If this facility is fully exploited by the research community, the colleges even in remote villages will never feel the heat of the lack of access to literature, and they can put forth their best in the research work.

Open Access Resources

In spite of the consortiums, the escalating costs of journals have created barrier for researchers to access required literature. Developing countries face even tougher challenges in procuring the latest scholarly research works than their counterparts in the developed world, as they often suffer from scanty library budgets. Limited access to research articles makes them settle for the information that is available rather than that which is required and relevant. Open Access can ensure best possible access to all the literature which is available on public domain so that the researchers are not limited by the selection of journals their campuses are able to provide. Open access (OA) is a generic term used for knowledge resources made available in the public domain for public access or public consumption at large scale, without any hindrance of subscription fee or access charges. OA is facilitated in an internet based online environment. OA provides access to digital literature, free of charge, and free of most copyright and licensing restrictions. In short, OA is a concept, a movement, and an economic model for accessing works that are freely available to user via the internet without financial cost and without economic, legal or technical barriers other than those intrinsic to the internet. Users can thus freely read, download, copy, distribute, print, search or link to the full text of OA works. It is expected that the integrity of authors' work will be respected and that authors' right will be correctly acknowledged and cited.

Major features of OA are, access to freely available publications, freedom of copyright and licensing restrictions, online availability, efficiency of archiving and retrieval, harvesting metadata, guaranteed sustainable storage and accessibility, provision to link publications to any research dataset used in producing the paper, availability of full text, anybody from anywhere can access without any discrimination, can access all formats (e.g. software, audio, video, and multi-media, scholarly articles and their preprints etc.). The OA Journals perform peer review like their conventional counterparts before making them available to the world. Therefore, OA greatly enhances the information available to researchers and significantly improve the quality of work especially in developing nations. Peer reviewed literature which is very essential for research is traditionally stored in journals with heavy subscription costs. Now, this information is also placed in the public domain and hence many journals are accessible as OA literature. Some of the major OA resources are listed below:

1. **Directory of Open Access Journals and Books (DOAJ):** It is the leading open access (OA) directory was launched in 2003 with 300 open access journals. Today it covers various fields of Science and Technology, Social Sciences and Humanities with more than 9000 OA journals. It also has quality control system to guarantee content.
2. **Directory of Open Access Books (DOAB):** It is another source for accessing books and monographs in many disciplines. It provides a searchable index for peer-reviewed monographs and edited volumes published under an OA business model, with links to the full texts of the publications at the publisher's website or repository. Academic publishers are invited to provide the metadata of their OA books to DOAB. The metadata is harvestable in order to maximize dissemination, visibility and impact. Aggregators can integrate the records in their commercial services and libraries can integrate the directory into their online catalogues, thereby helping scholars, students and the general public to discover the books. DOAB is open to all academic publishers:
3. **Directory of Open Access Repositories (DOAR):** It is primarily a service to enhance and support the academic and research activities of the global community. It maintains a comprehensive and authoritative inventory of institutional and subject-based repositories. Users of the service are able to analyze repositories by location, type, the material they hold and other measures. One key point about DOAR is that it

is of use not only to users wishing to find original research papers but also for third-party service providers, like search engines or alert services, who need easy tools for developing tailored search services to suit specific user communities. This service can be linked to the college website.

4. **J-Gate:** It is an electronic gateway to global e-journal literature. Launched in 2001 by Informatics India Limited, it provides seamless access to millions of journal articles offered by as many as 13356 publishers. It is available online. It has a huge database of journal literature with full text lines at publisher's sites for 45910 indexed e-journals.

In short, there are many OA e-resource sites which anyone can make use for furthering their academic and research pursuits and also to quench their thirst on various topics of interest. Some of the important sites are listed below.

In summary, the origin and adoption of ICT has changed the performance and service pattern of every institution and organization; library is no exception. In fact, ICT and Internet have made profound impact on the structure and functioning of libraries though the basic mission remains the same (i.e. preservation and access to documents). Yet, the format of the libraries is changing, with this ever changing technical scenario. With the changing perception about the information system, it is almost obligatory for the libraries to understand the current trends and work proactively to handle them. After all it hardly matters whether it is a hybrid library, a digital library or a virtual library as long as it is a resource centre for learning and dissemination of resources to users.

Suggested Reading

1. www.inflibnet.ac.in
2. shodhgangainflibnet.ac.in
3. Price Kate and Havergal Virgima, E-books in libraries A Practical guide 2011, Facet London.
4. Subbaiah Open access Scholarly Initiations in India: Status Report 2011, Centre for Internet and Society, Bangalore
5. Joshi (A.N) and others Open Access Initiations: A Boon to Academic Libraries. 2012. Library Philosophy and Practice (e-journal) paper 792 http://digiallcommons.un/edu/libphilprac/292.

General Reference Sources

http://bcs.bedfordstmartins.com/resdoc5e/index.htm
http://www.worldstatesmen.org/
http://guides.library.ucla.edu/reference
http://ph.infoplease.com/
http://www.electionresources.org/
http://www.chambersharrap.co.uk/chambers/features/chref/chref.py/main
http://www.ipl.org/div/news/
http://dir.yahoo.com/
http://www.oed.com/
http://www.unep.org/yearbook/2010/
http://www.guinnessworldrecords.com/
http://maps.google.co.in/
http://www.mapsofindia.com/
http://www.hw.ac.uk/libWWW/irn/pinakes/pinakes.html
http://www.censusindia.net/
http://www.worldbank.org.in/india
http://elibrary.worldbank.org/content/subject/
http://lib.unipune.ernet.in/Portal/portal.html

Social Science and Humanities

http://dictionary.reference.com/wordoftheday/
http://www.britannica.com/bps/browse-alpha
http://www.encyclopedia.com/
http://www.encyclopedia.com/
http://en.wiktionary.org/wiki/Wiktionary:Main_Page
http://epw.in/epw/user/userindex.jsp
http://www.ilovelanguages.com/index.php?category=Languages
http://librarysupportstaff.com/librefpg.html
http://www.refdesk.com/
http://www.allwords.com/
http://archaeologydataservice.ac.uk/
http://www.bized.co.uk/
http://bubl.ac.uk/link/linkbrowse.cfm?menuid=2822
http://www.intute.ac.uk/
http://www.psychwww.com/
http://wwar.com/
http://www.openj-gate.com

http://www.censusindia.gov.in/
http://www.vidyanidhi.org.in/
http://www.aber.ac.uk/media/index.html
http://www.rudi.net/
http://www.infolibrarian.com/
http://www.doaj.org/
http://dsal.uchicago.edu/
http://www.ipl.org/

Sciences

http://www.bartleby.com/reference/
http://www.asindexing.org/i4a/pages/index.cfm?pageid=3323
http://www.loc.gov/rr/scitech/
http://www.ucmp.berkeley.edu/glossary/gloss1phylo.html
http://accessscience.com/
http://www.science.dke-encyc.com/search.asp?type=exampleandkeyword=body+systems
http://www.eoearth.org/
http://www.oup.co.uk/oxed/children/oise/
http://www.daviddarling.info/encyclopedia/ETEmain.html
http://www.ipni.org/index.html

CHAPTER - 17

IMPORTANCE OF DIGITAL LITERACY IN THE 21ST CENTURY

— *J. S. BHAT*

In this digital age, we have an opportunity to transform lives of people in ways that was hard to imagine just a couple of decades ago.

— NARENDRA MODI

The above statement of Modi made in his speech delivered in Silicon Valley on 26th September 2015 amply highlights the importance of the digital literacy. The ongoing, very forceful and rapidly progressing fourth industrial revolution is indeed based on the complex digitization and cyber-physical systems. This has already affected the life of practically every one especially the youth. Everyday life now heavily relies on the use of such a technology all over the world. In fact, advances in communication technology have made the entire world a petite village. This chapter is designed to highlight the significance of digital literacy, its ramification in education, and finally inevitability of embracing digital technology fully in all spheres of life and future education systems, teaching, learning and evaluation in meeting the challenges of the current industrial revolution.

Digital Media

In the recent years, technology has changed the way people work, live and treat each other. Knowing the importance of technology, scientists and engineers are constantly inventing and exploring the world of technology to build a better society for everybody. Recent advances in information communication technology (ICT) have made it possible transfer of digital media, the digital version of text, audio, video and image to any terrestrial or extraterrestrial location within fraction of a second. The speed of communication is same as that of light when light wave communication techniques are used for sending information. Traditional telegraphy and telephony (landline phone) are based on wired connectivity, whereas radio, television, Bluetooth and Wi-Fi are based on radio frequency wireless communication technology. Satellite and cellular phone communication are based on radio frequency waves in Giga Hertz frequency for information transmission. Direct to home telecast of hundreds of TV channels was realized with the development of satellite based global telecommunication system. Global Positioning System (GPS) along with mobile communication can give us exactly our location on earth. The networking of continents through optical fibre cables and satellites allow sharing of enormous amount of digital data between the countries. Global networking of servers has given us internet, storage servers and cloud computing. Evidently, information technology plays vital role in the functioning of industries, transportation, financial services, hospitality, automotive, aerospace, core industries (oil, gas, steel, and mining), services (education and healthcare), retail marketing and e-Governance. With the digitization of all public services and facilities, data stored in the servers of internet presently is in the order of several trillion Exabyte. Interestingly, such "big data" can be fetched and utilized by means of simple digital gadgets like desktop computers, laptops, tablets and smart phones.

Education and sound knowledge of scientific principles lead to development of technologies, which in turn spur industrialization. Growth and expansion of industries demand new technologies and innovations on a rather continued basis. Therefore, education and industrialization are interdependent and also impact each other. Furthermore, the industrial revolutions have changed human approach of producing the machinery and materials. Scientific discoveries and innovations during each century have profoundly affected education systems at all levels. The introduction of applied science or engineering education customized the systems for improving performance of industries as well as human life. First industrial revolution (IR.1.0) of 18th century was due to introduction of mechanical production of equipment driven by water and steam. The second industrial revolution (IR 2.0) of 19th century based on division of labour concept and use of electrical energy. Steam based driving systems were replaced with electric motors and, electrical switching mechanisms were introduced to run industrial production lines. Innovations in electronics and computing systems lead to interfacing mechanical systems with microelectronic control systems, and this simplified running production lines. The industrial transformation thus facilitated increase in manufacturing capabilities, and 20th century is marked with third industrial revolution (IR 3.0). The advanced control systems developed based on microelectronics collect data through sensors and dedicated programs logically decide the next course of action in fabricating a product. Production machines embedded with microcontrollers or microcomputer systems have become smart enough to complete the assigned job, against the instructions given only in terms of dimensions and features needed in the finished product, with highest precision. With the advances in the automation, human involvement in modern industries has drastically reduced. Very recently, a new generation of systems realized with the tight integration of computational capabilities, physical systems and internet facilities are referred to as cyber-physical systems (CPS). Examples of CPS include smart grid, autonomous automobile systems, medical monitoring, process control systems, robotics systems, and automatic pilot avionics. Cyber-physical system is the key feature of fourth industrial revolution (IR 4.0) of 21st century. It has dramatically increased the adaptability, autonomy, efficiency, functionality, reliability, and safety of industrial production systems. Thus, the industries have become smarter and the complexity of the production systems has increased with each IR. In addition, the companies are revolutionizing their businesses with the use of artificial intelligence, robotics, cognitive computing and the Industrial Internet of Things (IOT). Apparently, industrial revolutions have their impact on society, living style, global politics and academia. Therefore, invigorating the education system in the 21st century through integration of ICT at all levels of education is need of the time and a challenge. Though, higher education institutes like universities and colleges are using ICT in teaching and administration, there is a pressing need for total changeover to incorporate ICT for modernizing entire academic and administrative processes.

Digital Age Literacy

In the present scenario of globalization of economy, marketing, employment particularly following the fourth IR, conventional style of teaching will not systematize the employability of learners. Generally, education institutions arrange for campus selection of stu dents during the final semester of graduation courses. Now let us ask whether the students after graduation in any field employable? Even though this question deserves extended debate the general answer is no. The institutes and governments (State/Central) have shown little concern to answer this question. The purpose of education is to make them ready for accepting the challenges in any job at the national as well as global level. A recent national survey indicated dismal figures that less than 10% of total engineering graduates are employable for any kind of job. Seemingly, students (at all levels) are not encouraged to learn beyond the scope of the prescribed syllabi. On the other hand, it is imperative that the students are exposed to newer concepts of science, engineering and social science so that innovative ideas burgeon in them based on the knowledge thus gained. Grooming students for their employability during their learning period in colleges/varsities is glaringly dismal. The focussed and well tuned education system is needed to make the students learn skills and become experts in a particular field. In such a system curricular flexibility, in terms of the choice of the course is very much essential.

In workplaces, use of ICT through computers, internet and information technology is becoming universal feature. One of the most commonly cited reasons for using ICTs in classrooms is to better prepare the current generation of students for technological literacy and enable use of ICTs effectively and with ease, in spite of the digital divide that can hamper such an effort. However, technological literacy is not the only skill required for premium jobs in the new global economy. The North Central Regional Educational Laboratory of USA has identified what it calls "21st Century Skills", which includes digital age literacy (consisting of functional literacy, visual literacy, scientific literacy, technological literacy, information literacy, cultural literacy and global awareness), inventive thinking, higher-order thinking, sound reasoning, effective communication and high productivity.

Functional literacy refers to the ability to interpret and express ideas in a range of media, like images, graphics, video, charts and graphs. Understanding of both theoretical and applied aspects of science and mathematics is scientific literacy. Technical literacy is the ability to use information and communication technologies, i.e., the gadgets for ICT. Aptitude to find, evaluate and make appropriate use of information using ICTs is information literacy. Knowledge of interrelation of nations, corporations and communities all over the world is called global awareness. Cultural literacy stands for ability to understand and appreciate diversity in culture. In a classroom the cultural background of students often differs. The teacher is expected to appreciate each one of them and treat all of them with equal respect. According to Prof. Larry Cuban of Stanford University "Technology will not have a significant impact on student learning until teachers change the way they teach". Thus, teachers at all levels of education and training need to be highly competent in the skills for imparting education needs of the present as well as future days.

For many years, teachers taught and students were responsible for learning the material. It was the student's responsibility to acquire the knowledge for success. The primary concern of the teacher was to impart knowledge. This teacher centric approach has to change to learner centric approach. Student learning shall be the primary goal of the teacher. The teacher is expected to motivate the students to learn, participate, critically think and successfully perform in assessments. The process of learning can be through objectives, examples or discovery. The students need motivation; the teacher is the only source of it. The learning by discovery requires inventive thinking, which can be explicated in terms of adaptability, curiosity, creativity and risk taking. Ability to get used to and manage in a complex and interdependent world is adaptability, desire to know is curiosity and ability to use imagination to create new things is creativity. Teacher can only create the suitable environment for such all-round intellectual growth of students.

Communication skill matters a lot in classroom teaching as well as convincing the students. For effective communication, teacher must have the tendency to work in a team. Teamwork by the employees always elevates the status of any organization. Teamwork is possible only if team members accept ideas of others and are ready to implement the approved work plan collectively. Collaboration and interpersonal skills refers to the ability to interact smoothly and work effectively with others. The interactive communication requires competence in accessing the information, understanding and conveying it effectively.

High productivity of any industry/organization is possible only if the person responsible can prioritize, plan, and manage programs and projects to achieve the desired results. Students generally need suggestions for organizing themselves to be successful. In any educational institution high productivity refers to number of high quality students produced who employable for in the field of their specialization. Learning will be easy if students realize that what they learn in the classroom is relevant to real-life context.

ICT enabled learning mobilizes tools for examination, calculation and analysis of information, thus providing a platform for student inquiry, analysis and construction of new information. Students therefore learn whenever appropriate, work on real-life problems in-depth making learning less abstract and more relevant to the real life situation. In this way and in contrast to memorization-based learning, ICT-enhanced learning promotes increased learner engagement. The learner may be connected with the teacher in two ways; either asynchronous or synchronous learning modes. In asynchronous mode, learning is characterized by a time lag between the delivery of instruction and its reception by learners. For example, online course materials accessed 24 hours a day, 7 days a week. In a radio or television broadcast information is dispensed as per the need of all learners while the instructor is in one physical location. In synchronous mode of learning, teacher and learner are in one-to-one link. In teleconferencing technologies, instructions are transmitted to receive them simultaneously by multiple, often geographically dispersed learners. ICT enabled learning encourages interaction and cooperation among students, teachers, and experts regardless of their geographical location. Apart from the modelling real-world interactions, ICT supported learning provides learners the opportunity to work with people from different cultures, thereby helping to enhance learners' teaming and communicative skills as well as their global awareness. It models learning done throughout the learner's lifetime by expanding the learning space to include not just peers but also mentors and experts from different fields.

In the ICT based education system, the teacher's role has transformed from the traditional role of erudite teacher to learning facilitator, collaborator, trainer, advisor, knowledge manager, curriculum designer, instruction designer, team coordinator, co-learner and assessment specialist. The ICT supported teaching renovates learning and helps teachers to be more efficient and effective. It helps in planning the structure of the courses and the course materials. Further, it also provides innovative ways to help students learn basic concepts and skills. The students will be stimulated and motivated by the technology because visualization helps in understanding of difficult concepts and processes, and caters to different learning way. It also gives valuable computer skills that are necessary to interact, collaborate and work in groups. Google Classroom and Microsoft Teams along with One Drive have now become indispensable learning tools in modern schools. These platforms are the digital hubs, which bring conversations, content, assignments, and apps together in one place. They promote equity and student voice with collaborative classrooms, connect in professional learning communities, and communicate with staff. Flipped classrooms will make their worth felt in education, guaranteeing the benefits of collaborative learning. These online learning tools are very significant and pivotal to students to make the most out of the modern educational practices.

The educational technology infrastructure of a country sits on top of its telecommunications and information technology infrastructure. Before launching any ICT based programme there is a need to check the availability of necessary infrastructure with modern facility for installing the ICT equipments and accessories. In this era of fourth IR the digital consumer enjoys more interactive and personalized experiences through social, mobile, analytics and cloud (SMAC) technologies. The digital enterprise leverages on SMAC technologies to optimize the cost of corporate functions and also transform enterprise collaboration for greater productivity. Sometimes, one may wonder how digital facilities are disrupting the normal course of human thinking. In any case, an optimized ICT scheme suitable for a region or society can be accepted and with necessary infrastructure it will be possible for producing the useful and meaningful final product for the society.

For nourishing ICT based education, innovators and practitioners need to become 'facilitators in a disruptive era' through public and private partnerships and assimilate the transformative power of education technology. The Government of India's online programmes like e-Education and e-Pathshala, developed by NCERT, are consequences of such collaboration. These programmes disseminate educational e-resources including textbooks, audio, video, periodicals and a variety of other print and non-print materials through website and mobile applications. Simulation software like Matlab, Simio, Witness, Ansys, AnyLogic, Solidworks, Arena, MedSim, Simtics etc., are used for modelling variety of real phenomenon with a set of mathematical formulas that allow the user to understand a process without actually performing it. These simulation software packages help the students to clearly understand various principles and facts in science, engineering and medical fields. Colleges/varsities should provide necessary infrastructure facilities for students to use such software, which can kindle innovative and realizable ideas.

To initiate ICT in higher education requires clear and specific objectives; time bound goals, guidelines, extensive resource mobilization and political commitment. The first step towards implementing ICT in education is a rigorous analysis of present state of education system. Every institution has its own practices and arrangements, which may become severe obstacle for implementing ICT fully. The common barriers for enabling ICT are the existing curriculum, infrastructure, capacity building, language and content and, financing. Many a time these barriers virtually stop full utilization of ICT in education. It is necessary to specify educational goals at various levels of education and training in order to identify the modalities of use of ICT that are suitable for pursuing the goals. This demands a clear understanding of potentials of different ICTs when applied for different purposes. Further, a clear idea of priority of ICT in education, financial and human resource availability and local constraints are needed before launching a workable model of ICT.

ICT in Administration

A well-managed and performing HEI plays a key role in the overall prosperity of a nation. Some of the major HEIs have implemented ICT that is limited to library and office management and monitoring student progression. However, growth in the higher education sector has made administration of higher education institutions more complex. The administrators of the institutes must have digital literacy for effective and efficient administration. Integration of ICT in administration reduces the complexity and enhances overall efficiency of the institution. Many of the universities and colleges have adopted ICT in areas like fee collection, student data management, examination data processing and declaration of results. One can identify the various functional areas and sections of the institute to which ICT can be deployed with the clarity of extent of usage of ICT in all the functional areas. A good knowledge of statutory provision like the 'Acts, Statutes, Rules and Regulations' governing the institutions (colleges/varsities) are required for logical development of the web portal, app or software. Hierarchy of administrators shall be known for sequencing of decision making. Establishment of policies and continuous monitoring of their proper implementation is part of administration. The organizational structure determines how the roles, powers and responsibilities are assigned, controlled and coordinated, and how information flows between different levels of management. It is apparent that organization structure depends on the organization's objectives and strategy. In a centralized structure, the top layer of management has most of the decision making power and has tight control over various divisions, departments, and sections. On the whole, ICT can be deployed for general administration, examination section, pay roll and financial accounting, maintenance of employees' records, administration of student data, inventory management, library management and general amenities. Each of these areas has many subsystem requirements that require interfacing seamlessly for information exchange between the sections/departments so that authorities can take decisions judiciously. With ICT in place administration is bound to become paperless, effective and also transparent.

Changing to ICT based administration can start with sending e-mail notices and agendas to staff rather than printing and distributing them, submission of lesson plans through e-mail, foster technology growth by asking parents to write e-mail as part of feedback mechanism, insist all teachers to create a class webpage and conduct admissions through web-portal services. In addition there are other communication modes like *Face book, Whatsapp, Instagram and Twitter* etc., which provide cross-platform messaging besides voice and videos over IP service for instant information exchange.

Awareness of ICT practices working successfully in the global level, and methods of adopting such workable models for country's requirements is compelling. The most important fact is the identification of stakeholders and balancing of efforts across different interest groups. This has regional, societal and political context, and policies have to be carefully framed to incorporate individual group's interests. After having understood all that the next step is piloting of a chosen ICT based education model on a small scale to check the feasibility, correct glitches if any in instruction design, effectiveness etc. In addition, the piloting should be useful in estimating the financial requirements for a full-scale implementation of ICT model.

In summary, though many institutions have adopted digital management of information systems (MIS), there is long way to go in accomplishing complete digitization in higher education systems. People tend to oppose introduction of any change in a system that existed for years. When a modification or a revolution is for the good of the generation, better to accept it and bring it in practice as soon as possible. Furthermore, education in the 21st century will drastically change the role of teachers in which they may find a big digital divide between them and the learners. The learners will be as a rule more advanced than the teachers in the use of ICT. Therefore, digital literacy of teachers needs to be continuously updated to be effective in class rooms and, earn respect from the students. In short, the teachers also need to be lifelong learners. Secondly, ICT enabled administration will become streamlined, effective and transparent. This will greatly help in earning high reputation for the institution. In this 21st century, the information age, day today life depends heavily on ICT in one form or the other. Mastering digital literacy is thus imperative, lest we will be regarded as illiterate!

Suggested Reading

1. Brosnan, T. (2001). *Teaching Using ICT.* University of London.
2. Chris, A. (2001). ICT: Changing Education. Taylor and Francis, London.
3. Krishnaveni, R. and Meenakumari, J. (2010). Usage of ICT for Information Administration in Higher education Institutions - A study. Int. J. Env. Sci. and Dev. 1, 282.
4. Mikre, F. (2011) *Roles of Information Communication Technologies in Education*, Ethiopian Journal of Education and Sciences, 6, 109.
5. Samad, T. and Annaswamy, A.M. (eds.), (2011). In: The Impact of Control Technology. www.ieeecss.org.

Student Support Systems

CHAPTER - 18

PROMOTION OF SKILL INDIA INITIATIVES

— *FARZANA M. PATHAN*

The purpose of training is to tighten up the slack, toughen the body, and polish the spirit. – MORIHEI UESHIBA

Skill is an ability and capacity acquired by an individual through deliberate, systematic, and sustained effort to smoothly and adaptively carryout complex activities or job functions involving ideas (cognitive skills), things (technical skills), and/or people (interpersonal skills). It is the science involved in a specific task combined with an art of executing that task. Hence we can say that it is a combination of both science and art. In an educational context, most of the times the word 'skills' is confused to vocational training. But the fact is skill is way beyond acquiring the technical expertise and involves all the behavioural aspects that an employer looks for or an individual himself / herself might need if he / she are starting his / her own business. The skill set includes: problem solving skills, learning skills, hard skills, soft skills and interpersonal skills. The skills can be acquired through training, and therefore it is quite essential for acquiring the needed skills.

Importance of Skill Development

Underlining the importance of skill development and vocational education, the 12th Five Year Plan (FYP) document reveals that while diminishing labour force is a major concern in most industrialised countries including the China, India has the benefit of a demographic dividend because the age structure of the population is such that the labour force will grow rather than decline in the years to come. Therefore, the skill development initiatives of the Government of India

(GOI) have great impact on both employment opportunities and, entrepreneurship. Some of the benefits of skill acquisitions are listed below:

1. It raises confidence, in turn improving the productivity of the individual
2. It will make the youth capable of earning their bread and butter on their own i.e. they could be self-employed
3. In case the youth want to gain job experience, skill development will greatly help them get blue-collar jobs.
4. At an young age (even at the school level) it helps the youth to channelize themselves for proper job opportunities
5. The benefits can reach rural and remote areas and thereby generate employment opportunities for people skilled in specific areas; they could be the trainers as well
6. Corporate educational institutions, non-government organizations, Government, Academic institutions, can participate in providing skill based training to youths so that more number of persons can be trained in the shortest time.
7. India being a developing economy and population being a major problem it's difficult to provide job for all. However, skill development programs can help convert the job seekers into job givers and thus provide a better life and dignity to many. It is with this very idea that the GOI has developed a mega project to Skill India.

Skill India Mission

A. The mission's priority is to generate employment for the youth of the country
B. 65% of the population is below 35 years of age. How will they face the challenges if they are not skilled? If they can't face challenges, they themselves will become a Challenge, India's 1st priority is therefore to generate employment opportunities.
C. Poor do not have high ambitions of buying a house or high-priced cars. They need to be self-dependent. This mission works in a very structured and organized manner, taking States on and along with a new start.

D. To create structures and mechanisms to nurture youngsters, facilitate them to seek out employment

E. Skill India Mission aims to instil self-worth in poor and bring a brand new energy to nation. Talent solely does not bring cash in the pocket; it instils confidence, brings a new strength in life.

F. The project seeks to enhance institutional capability to coach over 40 Crore skilful individuals by the year 2022.

G. To make India the human resource capital of the world

H. The youth of the state doesn't need to live a life of pity; they need to live with self- respect and dignity

I. It is a weapon against poverty and we ought to win it over

J. The Pradhan Mantri Kaushal Vikas Yojana (PMKVY) is indeed a flagship initiative of Ministry of Skill Development and Entrepreneurship

K. An important objective of this mission is also encouraging Entrepreneurship. It intends to incentivise skill training, provide financial rewards to those who successfully complete approved skill training programmes. PMKVY hopes to skill 24 Lakh youth in the next one year investing Rs.1500 Crore and focus on 500 and more skill trades.

L. In a pilot scheme 5000 youth have already been trained and certified with a skill card.

M. Under the 'Skill Loan Scheme' 34 Lakh skill loans are planned for disbursement in the next 5 years.

N. Recognition of Prior Learning (RPL) Scheme: It is a first time initiative for workers from the unorganised sectors, lacking formal certification to be assessed and certified for the skills that they already possess.

Skilling and Education Institutions

From the above it is clear that industry/academia can play an important role in the mission, 'skill India'. Hence, let us try and understand the interface between skilling India and Educational Institutions. Every person today needs specific set of skills to survive in this competitive world. Besides, economic growth country needs skilled and learned people. The one answer to both is Education; which alone has the invincible role in all round development of a country, be it economic or social growth or contributing to human resource needs. Today's competitive world demands trained and skilled manpower to address the challenges of growth and converting them into opportunities. This necessitates production of a highly competent / skilled workforce of global standards.

India is one of the fastest growing economies and populated with large force of English-speaking and young people. Thus, it has the potential to meet the skill needs of other countries as well, in addition to catering to its own demand of skilled manpower. It is further estimated that the average age of the population in India by 2020 will be 29 years, as against 40 years is USA, 46 years in Europe and 47 years in Japan. In fact, in the next twenty years industrialized world will decline by 4% while in India it will increase to 32%. This poses both challenges and opportunities. To reap the demographic dividend which is expected to last next 25 years, India needs to equip its workforce with employable skills and knowledge so that the youth can participate productively to make India a fully developed country. Unfortunately, as a rule, higher education does little to address the skill requirements and encourage the youth to go into the professional world and succeed. It is now imperative that higher education institutions start introspecting their programs and tune to the modern needs.

It is very important that the country produces more of job givers as compared to job seekers. Ironically however majority of the job seekers are way below the employability quotient. Of the 40 million people registered in Employment Exchange offices, only 0.2 million get jobs. Sadly, nearly 75% of job seekers are considered unemployable. This is often attributed to a large extent to the present education system. A rise in unemployment is ascribed to the present education system for the following reasons:

1. Lack of relativity between education and skills, outmoded curricula and a mismatch between aspiration, skills, salary and job
2. Pedagogies and assessment are focused on input and routine learning; students have little opportunity to develop a wider

range of transversal skills, including critical thinking, analytical reasoning, problem-solving and collaborative working.

3. Lack of importance for entrepreneurship at the college level: India has too few entrepreneurs even when compared to countries like Thailand, Brazil and Malaysia. Incorporating entrepreneurship training in the traditional courses may be needed.
4. There are hardly any colleges who focus of developing entrepreneurial skills of the students. They rarely provide incubation to the start-up projects.
5. There is no focus on improving the employability of graduates in Indian Higher Education sector. The sector is broadly classified into "General" and "Professional" streams. However both streams need to provide practical training suitable for job markets or self employment.
6. Higher Education sector concentrates mainly on the basics of reading, writing and arithmetic. But the demand of the hour is that it has to emphasize on the '4C's i.e. Skills such as Critical thinking, Communication, Collaboration and Creativity.
7. The gross enrolment ratio (GER) in Indian higher education is still low in India.
8. There is uneven distribution of Universities. For example there are no universities in Andaman and Nicobar Islands, Dadra and Nagar Haveli, Daman and Diu and Lakshadweep.
9. The Student Teacher Ratio (STR) in higher education (universities and colleges) is 1:23 i.e. there is one teacher for 23 students. The number of permanent teachers in colleges/ varsities is dismally low and often teaching is salvaged with the guest faculty or part time teachers.
10. Inability of the fresh graduates to relate the concepts learnt in the classrooms to the practical world in their professional life is a major area of concern.

11 The Universities show little concern for applied research, patenting, skill development and innovations.

Promoting Skill Development in Colleges

Following are some of my suggestions that the higher education institution can think of adapting teaching to enhance skill development and entrepreneurship among thc students.

Inception of skilling

Skill Development is a continuous process. It involves attitudinal pieces. Skilling is to be incorporated since the childhood, which means it has to be introduced right from the schools. Higher education institutions can undertake more and more research in this direction and contribute to the school curriculum.

Syllabus Revision

The syllabus needs revision at regular intervals or as often as needed s as to effectively inculcate skill based education. The syllabus should be so framed that it encompasses all aspects of skilling be it soft skill or hard skill development and also entrepreneurship related aspects. The students should be given more of practical orientation to the courses and the job markets.

Pedagogy

The institutions should adopt inquiry based learning pedagogy rather than just the classroom teaching of some established facts. Inquiry based learning starts by posing questions, problems or scenarios, rather than simply presenting well-known facts or portraying a smooth path to knowledge. The process is often assisted by a facilitator. It involves more of workshops, practical sessions, industry institute interface etc.

Incubation Centres

An 'incubator' is a collaborative programme designed to help the new start-ups. These incubators help entrepreneurs solve some of the problems commonly associated with running a start up by providing workspace, seed capital, mentoring and training. These incubators are usually established by the non-profit organisation run by both public and private entities. Incubators are most of the times associated with Universities and some business and technical schools. The concept of incubators need not be restricted only to the technical sector. It is applicable to farming, service sector and all other possible areas.

Example: The KLE Technological University, Hubballi, earlier known as B.V. Bhoomaraddi College of Engineering and Technology, is a pioneer in technical Education in Hubballi Dharwad region (Karnataka). The institution came up with a 'Centre for Technical Innovation and Entrepreneurship' (CTIE). The first company to come on campus was the Sankalp Semiconductors. They started connecting with the internship of the students. Interested students with acumen of entrepreneurship were selected, made into teams and trained. Then they introduced the incubation training i.e. summer term courses. They were trained for customer relation, team building, financial viability etc. The institute went a step ahead and helped the students reach the Angel investors, thus nurturing their skill. As a part of special skilling program special skilling programmes like PUPA, entrepreneurial leadership and make in BVB are also organised. Under PUPA, the students are expected to develop their skills in converting their idea into product which is sellable in the market. Students would be given seed funding to develop and manufacture their products.

Today, the CTIE is a MSME recognized incubation centre, currently housing around 38 companies on campus, creating around 230 jobs in the campus itself. The students are trained and they graduate and move to the KLE tech park. Few of the students who have successfully established their start-up are Sarah D'souza and Amith Vernekar who converted their project on anaerobic work station as a product. Now they started a company called Biosyl Technologies Pvt. Ltd.

Vocational education: Vocational Knowledge is basically imparting the procedural knowledge in association with the conceptual knowledge. It is usually used in the context of technical knowledge. Such an education can be introduced at the secondary or post-secondary level. It can be recognised as a partial academic credit towards tertiary education (http: //www.aicte-india.org/vocationaledu.php).

Information Hub

The HEIs should act as information hubs. They should provide all possible information about the various avenues available for the students after their graduation. They should also provide all the necessary information about the various initiatives of the GOI in the direction of skilling India.

Association with industries and government institutions

The institutions should associate with industries and government institutions like the Micro, Small and Medium Enterprises, Development Institute (MSME-DI), District Industries Centre (DIC) etc. for developing new ideas and also provide a platform to trainees to exhibit their skill and ideas. It could also be a very good source of funding some innovative ideas.

Bridging gap between industry and academia

The National Skill Development Corporation (NSDC) has developed a unique model to integrate skill based trainings into the academic cycle of the universities. The key aspects of the model are as follows:

(a) Identification of Sectors and job roles based on state skill gap report-
(b) Development of implementation and integration models in university systems
(c) Training of Trainers by Sector Skill Council
(d) Curriculum alignment and Capacity building workshops
(e) Student orientation sessions for choice of sector/job role based on career aspirations
(f) Standardised Training Delivery by NSDC Training Partners
(g) Internships and On- the - job Training
(h) Assessment and Certification by Sector Skill Council

At present the NSDC is working with a little over 20 Universities, UGC and AICTE catering to more than 1200 colleges, and also 400 community colleges across the country.

Entrepreneurship Development Institute of India

The Entrepreneurship Development Institute of India (EDII), an autonomous body and not-for-profit institution, set up in 1983, is sponsored by apex financial institutions, namely the IDBI Bank Ltd, IFCI Ltd. ICICI Ltd and State Bank of India (SBI). EDII conducts various Entrepreneurship development programmes through for prospective entrepreneurs. The institutions can delegate the aspiring students for weekly or fortnightly training programmes. Certification of candidates undergoing such trainings will be helpful in securing loans for future entrepreneurial undertakings.

Government Initiatives for Skilling the Youth of India

Following are some of the initiatives under taken up by the Indian Government for skill development in India:

1. *National Policy for Skill Development and Entrepreneurship 2015*: Provides policy direction to stakeholders on skill development and entrepreneurship ecosystem.
2. *Pradhan Mantri Kaushal Vikas Yojana* (PMKVY): A flagship scheme for providing reward-based skill training
3. *Recognition of Prior Learning* (RPL): Scheme meant for those who possess skill but have no formal education or certification
4. *Skill loan*: Scheme to facilitate participation in skill development programmes; can avail Rs 0.5- 1.5-lakh loan.
5. *Deen Dayal Upadhyay Gram Kaushal Yojana* (DDU-GKY): This is a placement linked skill development program for the rural youth.
6. *Deendayal Antyodaya Yojana - National Urban Livelihoods Mission* (DAY-NULM): The mission of this program is to curb poverty of urban poor households by providing them access to their skill related employment opportunities in an organized manner.
7. *Director General of Training - Modular Employable Skills* (DGT-MES): Government of India (GOI) and the Ministry of Labour together have launched Modular Employable Skills (MES) under Skill Development Initiative (SDI).
8. *Ministry of Labour and Employment* (MoLE): It is one of the oldest and important Ministries of the GOI meant to protect the interests of workers in rural, urban, poor and, deprived sections of the society.

9. *Ministry of Skill Development and Entrepreneurship* (MSDE): The ministry has aided and supported several other missions like: NSDA, NSDC, NSDF and 33 Sector Skill Councils (SSCs) as well as 187 training partners registered with NSDC. The Ministry also intends to work with the existing chain of skill development training centres, universities and other institutes in the field.
10. *National Skill Development Corporation*: It works with 267 training partners who represent the core ideology of NSDC. Over the past 4 years, NSDC along with its partners have delivered over 2 million skilled people in more than 25 sectors. The NSDC works closely with GOI and facilitate financing the training programs in reaching the target of skilling 400 million people by 2022.
11. *National Skill Development Agency* (NSDA): NSDA is an autonomous body of Ministry of Skill Development and Entrepreneurship, which coordinates the efforts of the GOI with the private sector to achieve the set targets. It works in partnership with several agencies like the NSDC, Central ministry skill programs, ministry of skill development and entrepreneurship, sector skill councils. There are at present 26 different kinds of skill sectors. The NSDA is a major agency for State Skill Development Missions. It also strives to ensure the skilling needs of the disadvantaged and the marginalized groups and minorities, women and differently-abled persons without any bias.
12. *National Rural Livelihood Mission* (NRLM): It is an initiative launched by Ministry of Rural Development (MoRD), GOI. The Aajeevika Skill Development Programme (ASDP) operates under NRLM to know the professional aspirations and interests of youth, and help them increase their daily income.
13. *Pradhan Mantri Kaushal Vikas Yojana* (PMKVY): The PMKVY is a unique initiative by GOI that aims to train as many as 24 Lakh youth to be industry relevant, skill based and compete with the global market. Under this scheme, the

trainees will also be given financial support and a certificate on successful completion of training to help them in securing a job for a better future. The scheme is being implemented successfully with many skill sectors all over the country.

14. *Mahatma Gandhi National Rural Employment Guarantee Act* (MANREGA): The scheme guarantees right to work in rural areas by providing daily wage to unskilled manual workers at least for 100 days to every household member who is willing to work. The scheme has legal clauses and, it is directly implemented by the Gram Panchayats. Apart from providing for economic security and creating rural assets, the scheme endeavours in protecting the environment, empowering rural women, reducing rural-urban migration and fostering social equity, among others.

Finally, the responsibility of the HEIs goes way beyond imparting knowledge. It is their responsibility to equip their students with the skill and make them employable. The GOI is doing everything possible for skill development with an objective to provide employment to the youth. The success of this mission is not possible without the involvement of all stakeholders. Higher education sector being one of the most important components of the country must assume its responsibility. As said in the foregoing sections of this Chapter, the HEIs can contribute in different ways like aligning the curriculum to promote skills, adopting more practical oriented pedagogy, establishing incubation centres, encouraging innovation and start-up ventures. The institutions should also come up with information hubs in their campuses. They should also enter into specific Memorandum of Understanding (MOU) with government organisations, industries and other relevant institutions in India and abroad. HEIs need to promote entrepreneurship; they can depute students and teachers to various EDP conducted by various organisations like EDII, RUDSETI etc. The institutions should facilitate funding the exceptionally good ideas and thereby contribute to their Corporate Social Responsibility (CSR). At the least, the colleges/varsities should sensitize the students on the various skill development and entrepreneurship programs through series of lectures by experts in the field from industries and institutions that have successful and inspiring stories to narrate and inspire our youth who are struggling to find meaning to their life. Recall the Chinese proverb that says: *You give a poor man a fish and you feed him for a day, you teach him to fish and you give him an occupation that will feed him for a lifetime.*

References

1. Entrepreneurial Development by S. S. Khanaka, S. Chand and Company Ltd.
2. http://www.nationalskillsnetwork.in/government-of-india/
3. http://indiatoday.intoday.in/education/story/engineering-employment-Problems/1/713827. html
4. http://www.skilldevelopment.gov.in/higher-education.html
5. https://www.linkedin.com/pulse/skill-development-key-economic-growth-role-higher- india-vijay- vallabh
6. http://www.mapsofindia.com/my-india/society/skill-india-a-new-programme-to-be-launched-in- march-2015
7. http://www.mapsofindia.com/my-india/government/skill-india-campaign-a-step-towards-promoting- entrepreneurship
8. http://www.nationalskillsnetwork.in/government-of-india/
9. http://economictimes.indiatimes.com/topic/Skill-India
10. http://www.indiaeducation.net/universities/
11. http://www.msde.gov.in/higher-education.html

Chapter - 19

Stress Management

— *Manika Ghosh*

It is not the load that breaks you down, it is the way you carry it.
– Lou Holtz

Naveen joined a multinational company with an enviable pay package and soon he reached a position that normally takes several years. It was his sheer hard work, zeal and continued knowledge up-gradation that helped him to soar above his peers. His job gave him riches, prestige and power, all that he ever dreamt albeit at the cost of family time, social life and personal health. He rarely sees his children awake or spends time with his wife. At office, most of his colleagues keep a distance either out of reverence or envy. Of late he finds his job too tedious and less enjoyable, feels tired too soon, is irritated most often, does not sleep well and feels lonely. His recent annual medical report was not very encouraging. His Doctor suggested that he meet the hospital Psychologist. He was diagnosed with stress related symptoms and 'Burn Out' and was advised a holiday and a stress management training.

Naveen is not alone; many people suffer from similar stress syndrome. Stress that seems all-pervasive is perhaps one of the most commonly used terms in modern times. Stress experience knows no age, gender, class, occupation or nationality bar although the reasons and magnitude may differ from person to person and in the same person from time to time. Since long stress has been a subject of discussion and research for psychologists, educationists, medical professionals, various organizations and laymen alike; yet it remains more of an enigma. Hans Selye, the pioneer of stress research opined that "stress, like relativity is a scientific concept which has suffered from the mixed blessings of being too well known and too little understood".

Meaning of Stress

The word Stress derived from the Latin word *strictus* meaning "tightened" is a person's reaction to events that are threatening, challenging or demanding. The reaction depends on two aspects: 1) when the person feels that the resources he possesses in terms of knowledge, skill, time, money, network etc. are insufficient to deal with a situation, 2) when the person thinks that the consequence of not meeting the demands /challenges will be drastic.

Often we blame negative events like death in a family, soured relationships, economic difficulties, unpleasant boss as the cause of stress. Interestingly, even pleasant events like winning a competition, new job, promotion, marriage, birth of a child and so on can cause stress. Almost any change in the environment or personal schedule has the potential to cause stress because it brings with it new demands on the person in terms of responsibility, decision making, dislocation and rescheduling of daily routine. Stress therefore can either be negative stress called distress or positive stress, termed eustress. The consequences of negative stress have attracted the attention of researchers more often because its consequences are more fatal.

Causes of Stress

The causes, intensity and impact of stress may vary with the persons and, even in the same person at different point in time. The magnitude of stress experienced by a person may range from being mild, moderate or extreme depending upon the following (a) Duration of the stress period, (b) Frequency of stress experience and (c) Severity of stress.

Categorization of major stressors and factors that cause stress are categorized below:

1. Daily hassle

Day to day activities like managing household chores, commuting, job specific tasks, meeting deadlines, keeping appointments can cause recurring stress. These routine, unavoidable activities if not managed well can lead to accumulated stress.

2. Uncertainties

Uncertainties are part of life. Yet, they do not stop us from being perturbed. The examples of being unsure include exam results, outcome of a job interview, possible transfer, appreciation of superiors etc. Inability to have little or no control over such matters leads to stress.

3. Relationship

Humans being social in nature, relationships with others around are of prime importance. Hence, when relationships go sore with close associates, family members, friends or colleagues, it gives rise to stress.

4. Decision making

Frequently one is involved in making decisions even for mundane matters like what to eat, what to wear, where to go etc. However, making certain decisions especially those that have long term consequences can be stressful, for example selecting course of study, taking up a job offer, choosing life partner etc. In such cases stress experienced is often high.

5. Financial constraints

Money is needed for meeting our basic needs and lack of it can be very unsettling. Research has shown that money and happiness have curvilinear relationship. Lack of money makes us unhappy at the same time too much of it does not necessarily make us happier. Financial status can also induce stress in a person.

6. Negative life events

Negative life events can leave a person with long term stress. Death of a close relative or friend, divorce, loss of job, property / huge sums of money, accident, and other such occurrences termed negative life events give rise to high stress for a long duration making it difficult to cope.

7. Health concerns

Personal illness or that of a close relative or friend can cause stress, the magnitude of which depends upon the duration of the illness and its seriousness.

8. Occupation

Most part of the adult lives is devoted to earn for a decent livelihood. Student life onwards persons are geared up to get a suitable job. While not having a job is stressful, being in a job is no less stressful. Several stressors like too much work, difficult deadlines, subordination etc. exist in job environments which have negative effects on performance, health and relationships.

Effects of Stress

One of the largest and in-depth research studies undertaken in Psychology in the past few decades has been in the area of stress, its antecedents and ramifications. The data available rings an alarming bell and shows that stress and its consequences have become global phenomena with severe consequences. According to World Health Organization (WHO), the present millennium faces an epidemic of stress and stress related diseases, with only Coronary Heart Disease and ulcers making up for the largest part. Illness and accidents related to stress account for 75% of all the time lost at work. Around 170000 deaths occur due to stress related suicides each year in India alone. Manifold effects of stress can be listed under four main types:

1. Physiological health

Stress can give rise to several lifestyle disorders that can only be managed but not cured (e.g. coronary heart disease, hyper tension, diabetes, asthma, migraine, gastric ulcer, skin disorders, certain types of allergies, cancer, immune deficiency, arthritis, impotency, weight loss or gain etc.). Many other physiological disorders are being increasingly related to stress.

2. Psychological health and wellbeing

The psychological effects are best recognized by persons experiencing stress. These are expressed as tension, pressure, hassle, frustration, irritation, anxiety, worry etc. Stress causes high arousal, irritability, memory loss, depression, burn-out, emotional exhaustion, indecisiveness and so on.

3. Social relationship

Psychological problems caused by stress can affect a person's interpersonal relationships; disruption in existing relationships, inability to make new relationships and inability to network with people. All these can lead to loneliness and anomie.

4. Performance

Mild stress acts as a motivator to perform better but if it becomes acute and lasts for prolonged period it may have a debilitating effect on performance. Too much stress gives rise to panic, indecisiveness and lack of confidence. This can hamper efficiency and ability to perform at optimum levels.

Finding out Stress and Life Satisfaction Level

The following test is useful in providing a preliminary knowledge of one's stress level so that certain needed changes can be made to manage and cope with stress. Answer the following probes with either 'often', 'sometimes' or 'never' depending on your actual experience in the past 30 days.

- Able to achieve your goals
- Engaged in activities that you love to do
- Have been appreciated for your work
- Have been in good health
- Help rendered to someone in need
- Participated in enjoyable occasions
- Received some good news
- Spent good time with your family or friends
- Travelled to your favourite places
- Undertaken something interesting

Note: Assign 3 marks for 'often', 2 marks for 'sometimes' and 1 mark for 'never' and total the marks. High score indicates that currently you are less stressed and have higher life satisfaction and low score indicates that you are at currently more stressed and have low life satisfaction. The scores are only indicative of your current psychological state; they do not reflect on your general behaviour. *Source*: Ghosh, M. (2013)

Management of Stress

It is only when people face prolonged and severe stressful situations that they recognize the distress they are undergoing. It is not often that we can avoid a stressful situation but we can surely learn to react in a manner that keeps stress at a manageable level and prove less harmful.

Today, with increasing awareness about the negative impacts of stress the world over, a large industry dedicated completely towards various aspects of stress management has been growing exponentially. Self-help books, videos, CDs, talks, workshops and training sessions are being accessed by millions of people. Life skill training and stress management sessions are being held at work places, colleges, schools, religious and community gatherings. All of these have been found to have clear health benefits.

One may ask whether stress management techniques should be learnt only by people who have developed stress related ailments, or are at risk of developing them. Research has shown otherwise. The various stress relieving techniques are now known to reduce the severity of many stress related ailments and help in postponing or preventing them. Learning stress management techniques much before the onset of the ailments that act as a Stress boosters is therefore very useful. Thus imparting Life skill education in schools and colleges is gaining importance throughout the world. There are well documented procedures that alleviate stress and associated stress responses. The management of stress focuses mainly on switching from maladaptive behaviour to adaptive behaviour.

Techniques of Stress Management

Stress management is neither a quick fix solution nor a onetime activity. It is aimed at keeping stress at bay on a long term basis. Accordingly, stress management focuses on forming a lifelong habit, bringing about modifications in personality, thoughts, belief systems and lifestyles. The popular techniques in use for stress management can broadly be categorised into two: (1) Behavioural Approach, and (2) Self-Development Approach. These are briefly described below.

Behavioural approach

In the 1960's and 1970's, behaviour modification and behaviour analysis met with stunning successes which paved way for the now well recognized discipline of behavioural medicine. Most noted behavioural approaches to stress management are: *Meditation, Yoga,* and *Progressive Muscular Relaxation.*

Meditation

The ancient Indian methods of meditation practiced and perfected by Yogis for controlling mental and bodily functions have been used by masses from the beginning of history. Since a few decades it has elicited renewed interest and fascinated the scientific fraternity the world over. Meditation involves using a number of awareness techniques that focuses particularly on current sensory experience in order to help quieten the mind and relax the body. The two most common meditation techniques are Transcendental meditation (TM) and Mindfulness Meditation.

The TM established by Maharishi Mahesh Yogi in the 1960's is an adaptation of 'Mantra Yoga' suited to Western sensibilities which today has millions of followers around the world. It is a fairly simple method wherein the person seated in a "lotus position" chants a single word or phrase, called 'mantra' repeatedly allowing other thoughts and feelings to pass. The technique of repeating the 'mantra' continuously needs to be followed for a period of 20-30 minutes twice daily with closed eyes in a quiet place. Research has revealed that TM facilitates reduced oxygen use, marked reduction in blood-lactate levels, increased skin resistance and intensification of alpha waves. All these are marks of deep relaxation and wellbeing. TM seemingly elicits a fourth state of consciousness called "wakeful hypometabolic state" quite different from the other three states of consciousness - waking, sleeping and dreaming.

The Mindfulness practice, another variant of TM, inherited from the Buddhist practice of 'Vipasana' or Insightful Meditation is a form of meditation involving relaxation and deep breathing designed to develop the skill of paying attention to the inner and outer experiences with acceptance, patience, and compassion. In this process, the person does not really think but rather becomes aware of his/her thinking; develops awareness regarding each of the other ways of experiencing the sensory world i.e., seeing, hearing, tasting, smelling, and bodily feelings. Mindfulness is generally employed to alleviate variety of mental and physical health conditions that include stress related physical disorders, obsessive-compulsive disorder, anxiety and in the prevention of relapse of depression and drug addiction. When used in pain control it requires the individual to focus on the pain with "detached observation" making it less emotionally distressing.

Yoga

It is an ancient Indian practice that has a prominent place in the Indian healthcare system. The term yoga means "union", signifying union of the body and mind. It has been defined in the Pathanjali Yoga Suthra 1:2 as "annulling the ripples of the mind". Various stages of yoga help to relax, energize, remodel and strengthen the body and mind. It begins with relaxing parts of the body which eventually positively influences all aspects of the person; mental, emotional, intellectual and spiritual. One of the most systematic collation and compilation is the Raja Yoga practiced thousands of years ago by Rishi Pathanjali. This system has eight limbs of practice called the Ashtanga Yoga.

The 'Asanas' or the Yogic postures are the ones that are popularly identified as 'Yoga' by lay persons, it is but one of the eight limbs of yoga philosophy. Yoga encompasses different types of asanas: physical culturing, balancing, relaxing and meditating. Practicing various yogic postures is found to be very useful in pain control, reconditioning the body, realigning skeletal muscles and for correcting faulty postures. It opens up the vital flow of energy through the body that gives rise to a sense of wellbeing.

The science of Yoga has remained unchanged since the ancient times, but our understanding and realisation of its benefit has undergone a profound change in the last few decades. Several research studies on Yoga suggests that performing this ancient practice regularly is helpful both for physical as well as mental health. Yoga also appears to slow down heart beats and breathing rates and lowers blood pressure thereby blunting the harmful effects of heightened stress and reducing the body's response to stress. Many more benefit of Yoga is emerging through on-going research in the area.

Progressive Muscular Relaxation (PMR)

Relaxation training rests on the basic yet simple premise that one cannot be relaxed and tensed at the same time. Relaxation and tension are functions of two separate parts of the Autonomic Nervous System (ANS) namely the Parasympathetic and the Sympathetic systems respectively. Since the two systems are reciprocally inhibitory in nature they cannot be active simultaneously; when one is aroused, the other is quiet or subordinate. Logically therefore, tension and relaxation cannot take place simultaneously. Scientific world for long believed that ANS being an involuntary system cannot be controlled but the carefully documented method by Edmund Jacobson (1938) proved otherwise. He developed a technique which he called Progressive Muscular Relaxation (PMR) that could control ANS.

Instances of ANS control are not new. It has been in practice in India since ancient times, although the mechanisms were not obvious at that time. Research on Indian Yogis jointly done by Indian and American research teams found that they have remarkable control over their ANS. Through heart and respiratory control the Yogis were found to survive burial for several days, by regulating their body temperature they could live in the freezing snow capped Himalayas with least clothing, and they could enter into a trance state and alter their brain waves on volition.

PMR follows a series of sequenced actions of sixteen muscle groups which are alternately tensed and relaxed. The sequence can be practiced appropriately to suit individual preference; while some prefer head-to- foot relaxation others may prefer foot-to-head relaxation. It needs to be performed with three repetitions for each muscle, 10-15 seconds for tensing muscles and 15-20 seconds for relaxing them. PMR has obvious advantages and one can develop proficiency in it without much training and, at no extra cost. Following prerequisite conditions are important for practicing PMR successfully:

1. A comfortable place and a suitable time free from distraction need to be identified.
2. PMR should be performed at the same place and at the same time as a matter of habit formation at least twice daily.
3. It should be practiced with a right frame of mind, without hurry and with self belief.
4. One should avoid drugs or artificial means of relaxation. If a person is on medication he/she should wait till the course is completed or take medical advice.
5. Persons with physical conditions like backache, injuries, broken bones etc. should exercise caution.

Self Development

Stress is a complex phenomenon requiring multipronged

approaches to control and manage. The approaches to stress management discussed above are largely focused on bringing about physiological changes through various methods of relaxation. In addition, a change within the person that contributes to stress is of utmost importance. For instance, change in the way we think, perceive and react to stress as well as the lifestyle we lead can certainly alter the impact of various stress-causing situations thereby change the stress response. It is said, "tough times do not last, tough people do". The various forms of Self-development include the following 7 major ways:

Developing assertiveness

In regular day-to-day interactions people often experience stress due to their inability to be assertive. For instance, people say 'yes' when they actually want to say 'no', they allow someone to overtake them in a queue, criticize them unduly, or take advantage of their kindness leaving them seething with anger and irritation. All these situations lead to lowered self-esteem and distress. Learning appropriate assertiveness skills can help remove the source of distress.

Time management

Most of the daily hassles that people face is due to the inability of keeping pace with the required time schedules and undue procrastination. An important approach to deal with such situation is firstly organizing one's environment and managing time optimally. Most individuals especially in modern times are steeped with various tasks both at home and at work place. The basic strategy of time management is to plan well and classify the various tasks at hand in the following four categories in order of priority:

(a) Urgent and important
(b) Urgent but not important
(c) Not urgent but important
(d) Not urgent and not important

Based on the above grouping of tasks, one can initiate actions. One has to learn and decide what can wait and what should be done immediately because there is a difference between urgency and importance.

Maintaining physical health

It is a well-known fact that body and mind are interconnected; poor physical health can cause poor mental health and stress. It is important therefore to follow regimens that include:

(a) Daily exercise and walk
(b) Regular sleep
(c) Nutritious and balanced diet
(d) Weight watch
(e) Regular health check

Developing sense of humour

Sense of humour or an ability to laugh even at trivial things, plays a very significant role in human life, especially in maintaining good physical and mental health. Though the exact mechanism is unknown, it is known to help in establishing healthy social relationships. Humour is a wonderful stress-reducer; it allows a person to perceive the event more lightly in a stress free manner.

Garnering social support

People with good social support are known to cope better with stress, since they find more resources to deal with it. Cultivating good interpersonal relationships and establishing a social network with different kinds of people is an effective strategy that one needs to cultivate and nurture to remain stress free. It helps in sharing troubled moments and receiving timely counsel.

Engaging in creative activities

Research has shown that people who have multiple interests and engage in creative activities are able to deal with stress more easily. Therefore, developing interest in preferred hobbies and positive leisure time activities like listening to music, painting, gardening, writing, reading help in combating stress.

Learning to be happy

One of the recent and exciting developments in the field of psychology is the emergence of Positive Psychology first coined by Martin Seligman in 1998. Research in Positive Psychology has found positive relationship between happiness and physical and mental health which in turn help in reducing stress. Seligman identifies five different factors that make us happy. These are:

(a) Pleasure- (tasty food, comfort, sex etc.)
(b) Engagement- (engaged in an enjoyable yet challenging activity)
(c) Relationship- (social bonds)
(d) Meaning- (perceived quest or belonging to something bigger)
(e) Accomplishment - (having realized tangible goal)

Although an ultimate goal of human life is to be happy, very often factors that cause real happiness are ignored and momentary pleasure is given importance. Following Seligman's theory one needs to make conscious efforts towards being happy.

In summary, experiencing stress is a reality of life. Everyone experiences it at some point in time. In fact, stress to an extent keeps us going. However, stress is bad when it is severe, frequent or prolonged. This can lead to many negative consequences. It is beneficial not only to learn the techniques of stress management but also to remember that stress management is an on-going, conscious and deliberate act. It is aimed at forming a habit of keeping stress at bay in order to lead a healthy and fulfilling life. In the modern stressful world many students are affected by stress due to variety of reasons. Therefore, colleges need to ensure that the students learn to cope with it and do not suffer from stress related disorders by initiating appropriate counselling and other needed measures.

Suggested Reading

1. Baumgardner, S. and Cothers, M. (2015). Positive Psychology. Pearson Education
2. Ghosh, M. (2013). Positivity a way of life. Orient Blackswan
3. Ghosh, M. (2014). Health Psychology, concepts in health and Wellbeing. Pearson Education
4. Seligman, M.E.P. (2002). Authentic Happiness: Using the new positive psychology to realise your potential for lasting happiness, New York: Free Press.

Chapter - 20

Counselling Students

— *Manika Ghosh*

If you can't fly then run, if you can't run then walk, if you can't walk then crawl, but whatever you do you have to keep moving forward.
— **Martin Luther King Jr.**

Lately, Shanti has been found looking pale, sitting quietly in a corner of the class looking distracted and gloomy and is often seen wiping her tears. She barely talks and hardly ever responds or goes out with her friends. Although a bright student her grades have started falling since last semester. Mrs. Dixit, her class teacher noticing this change in Shanti referred her to the college counsellor. A few counselling sessions with Dr. Sheela the counsellor revealed that she was suffering from severe depression with suicidal tendencies. It was her parents' constant nagging, negative comparison with her gynaecologist sibling and expressed disappointment at her choosing a course in Political Science and Economics instead of a professional course or a degree in science that hurt her deeply. It left her feeling worthless and unloved. She felt that her family did not appreciate her aim of appearing for the civil services. It required several sessions of counselling to get Shanti back her confidence, self-worth and ability to assert her career goal. Her parents were also counselled to help them understand their child better and the significance of their support in her life. Shanti has bounced back to life has again become one of the toppers in class and is earnestly preparing for civil service examination.

Mohan, a student in a city college got into trouble for violating several college regulations- shortage of attendance, delayed assignment submission, inattentiveness in class and skipping remedial classes. At the end of several warnings that went unheeded the authorities decided to rusticate him from college and inform his parents. However, the Vice Principal felt that Mohan needed help and should be given a fair chance. He referred him to the college counsellor. Looking distraught and dishevelled Mohan went to meet the counsellor, Mr. Nagesh. After a careful probing conversation, it emerged that Mohan who comes from very humble background works as a night shift operator in a private company to supplement family income. The earnings of his father, an auto rickshaw driver and mother, a domestic worker are insufficient to support his large family that include three other school going siblings and an aged grandmother. He wants to complete higher education to lead a better life but night work leaves him sleepy and tired making him often miss college and assignment deadlines. Mr. Nagesh empathized with Mohan, spoke to the college authorities and asked him to apply for scholarship. He also helped him earn through giving tuitions to a few school students. Mohan was also given tips on time management and study skills. Mohan is now a graduate working in a multinational company.

The above mentioned true cases of students are but a few of the many fortunate ones that received timely counselling interventions to cope with their problems and emerge successfully. However, there are many more that are not as lucky, either because they do not approach a counsellor or counsellors are not available. Students across gender, class, caste, community and region face different problems that they are unable to cope with leading often to fatal consequences. People around them like family friends, peers and teachers need to be vigilant, recognize the problems that some face and help them seek timely counselling services. With increasing psychological and behavioural problems seen among student population today, it is becoming mandatory to have in-house counsellors in every educational institution.

The vicissitudes seen in the last hundred years of the human history is unparalleled. No other century has seen such rapid changes occurring simultaneously in so many spheres - science and technology, economic, ecology, socio-cultural and, political. Scientific discoveries and technological innovations have made our lives a lot easier and more comfortable, medical advancements have enhanced our life spans and helped fight several infectious diseases, modes of communications has made it possible to stay continually connected with people and faster travel options have shrunk distances. At the same time it has drastically altered our socio-economic and political fabric. Rapid urbanization has waned the earlier concept of community collectives, village and neighbourhood bonding, roles of the elderly etc. Especially in the Indian society, three generations living under a single roof in a joint family system was the most common arrangement. Not only was the cost of living and maintaining household duty shared, bringing up children and caring for elderly were also a shared responsibility. Today, with fragmented family units, precious family bonding has been compromised. Each one of us has lost the possible confidante in grandparents or an aunt or perhaps a cousin.

These changes have had a direct impact on people's mental health and wellbeing. More number of people suffers from stress and stress related problems than ever before. In fact, depression has reached epidemic proportion and anxiety is commonplace. In the last two decades, the global suicide rate has increased from 7.9 to 10.3 per 100,000 persons. World Health Organization (WHO) reports that over half a million people die by suicide worldwide each year. India accounts for 33% of this number, more than twice as that of China. As per the June 2012 edition of The Lancet, 1, 87,000 estimated suicides occurred in India in 2010 alone. The actual figure may be far beyond this, since many go unreported. Poor mental health affects not only an individual's physical health but also has an adverse effect on interpersonal relationship, economic status, academic achievements and work performances.

Being a youth and a student in today's complex environment poses many challenges, making them especially vulnerable to emotional and psychological turmoil. Being at the crossroads of life they face academic pressure laced with hormonal changes, identity crisis, relationship upheavals and perceived guilt and shame on their economic dependence. In such a milieu, importance of psychological and emotional counselling cannot be overemphasized. Every educational institution is realizing the need for either appointing or outsourcing counsellors and setting up in-campus counselling centres. Since teachers undeniably have greater proximity to students it has also been found helpful to have them undergo basic counselling training to understand student behaviour and identify symptoms of emotional distress. This helps in early identification of problems and nipping them at the bud.

The Benefits of Teacher Counsellors

In modern times, aim of education and the way it is imparted has undergone a sea change. Besides, the very structure of college campus atmosphere and composition of students have altered irrevocably. These have led to redefining roles of teachers. Their job is no more limited to teaching and evaluation; they are required not only to shoulder varied responsibilities within the institutions but also competently deal with their students inside and outside classrooms. One significant emerging role of a teacher is that of a mentor and a counsellor. Historically this role of a teacher can be traced as far back as the times of Socrates. In several writings of Plato, Socrates is seen involved in counselling his students and followers. Likewise in the Indian Gurukul system a 'Guru' was not just a teacher, but was looked up to as a guide, mentor and a father figure. Today the concept of education has taken a full circle with rightful emphasis on overall development rather than on earning merely an academic qualification.

The role of teacher as counsellor involves a sense of power and influence alongside immense responsibility. The power base for counselling role comes primarily due to the personal and professional position and the likelihood of garnering positive influence on students. Unfortunately, many hesitate to take up this responsibility due to factors ranging from inability to understand the importance of counselling, lack of training, and prevailing stigma against mental health problems to reluctance for deeper commitment and extra work hours. However, these reasons are inconsequential in the light of today's pragmatic demand for a healthy campus environment. It cannot be emphasized enough that training teachers in counselling has manifold advantages. In fact, teachers are the most important persons who can bring about changes in campuses and possibly prevent many mental health problems and behavioural issues in students. They are in contact with students for the greater part of the day making it easier for them to know and observe students closely. Hence it is imperative that they understand adolescent behaviour well and act as wise guides. Timely counselling will help in preventing many of the mental health problems to appear at a later age. The teachers are considered to be most knowledgeable persons. Good teachers by virtue of their personal charisma and position command great trust and respect of the students. Therefore, possibility of students adhering to guidance provided by teachers is high. Furthermore, teachers are highly trainable and adept in picking up new skills. Alongside subject knowledge, developing sound ability in counselling is not difficult. Indeed, the teachers are most resourceful and capable of establishing network with a wide range of competent professionals and ensure providing referrals in times of need. Therefore, institutions that have teacher counsellors are better equipped to have higher mental health among students, better discipline, higher all round performance and a better campus environment.

What Is Counselling?

Counselling is both a science and an art. It is a very commonly used term in today's times to mean different things to different people. Most of us acknowledge that at some point in our lives counselling and advice are sought from persons we trust and revere. But casual advice is quite different from professional counselling. Before we know what counselling is, it is better to first understand what counselling is not.

Counselling Is Not

A. Advising, sympathizing or sermonizing; In all these acts there exists a hidden sense of hierarchy and patronage where a counsellor seems to take on a position higher than the one being counselled albeit inadvertently. This goes against the tenet of counselling and very often proves counterproductive.

B. Being judgmental and biased or trying to correct behaviour, the aim of counselling is not to find fault with the counselee.

C. Expecting or influencing counselee to behave in a way that the counsellor may have behaved when confronted with similar problems

D. Imposing counsellor's own value system without due respect and acceptance of the counselee

Counselling Is

A. Providing consultation and guidance while listening empathetically and 'being there' when one seeks help.

Establishing rapport and professional relationship where the counsellor remains unbiased and mutually agreed upon professional terms are set

B. Helping the person perceive the problems clearly and objectively and enabling to select different routes to solve problems

C. Helping the person to focus on inner feelings, experiences and strengths in order to bring about positive changes

D. It is a relationship of trust where maintaining confidentiality is of paramount importance

Is Everyone Capable of Being Counsellor?

Counselling is surely not an impossible task but it cannot be pursued and practiced casually either. It requires knowledge, specific skills, certain personality traits and definite attitudinal dispositions. Among these requirements, knowledge is perhaps the easiest to muster. But with due diligence, practice and zeal the other qualifications too can be gained.

Assessment of Counselling Ability

To find out how good a counsellor you can be, read the following statements carefully. Depending upon how you most often behave and what you believe, answer with 'yes' or 'no'. There is no wrong or right answer. To make an accurate self-assessment, answer them honestly. Do not spend too much time on any one statement; preferably give the first response that comes to your mind.

1. Students often come to me when in trouble and seek my assistance
2. Even when I am busy I somehow take time out to help them sort out their problems
3. I am vigilant and recognize when a student has problems
4. I refrain from judging people's behaviour and do not go by what others perceive as right or wrong
5. I treat everyone equally knowing that each individual student is different
6. When people talk about their problems I always listen patiently and carefully

7. I do not impose my beliefs and value system on anyone else
8. I believe that every individual can become useful human being with a little guidance
9. I have friends from different communities, castes, languages, religions and regions
10. I have contacts with various professionals including police, doctors, psychiatrist, counsellors, other teachers etc.
11. I continue to update my knowledge not just in my subject but other fields like mental health, suicide prevention, policies against discrimination, emerging social problems etc.
12. I do not get emotionally affected when someone shares very traumatic experiences
13. I am able to feel the pain of a person in trouble
14. If someone confides in me I do not share it with others and am able to maintain confidentiality

15 My friends and family find me to be a caring person.

[*Scoring:* Count the total number of 'yes'. 12 and above: excellent, 10-11: good, 7-9: average, < 7 need for development. However it may be noted that these scores are only indicative.]

Developing Competence in Counselling

Counselling is serving. Therefore, a will to help is the foremost requirement to be a counsellor. To a great extent training followed by continuous practice is essential for acquiring qualities required to be a good counsellor. Training in counselling involves several aspects which are discussed below.

Understanding Student Behaviour

Students studying in colleges are generally between the age group of 17- 23 years which represent most critical phase of their life. These years are marked by physical and hormonal changes, identity crisis, relationship problems, peer pressure, academic stress, insecurity and hypersensitivity. This is also an age when they are idealistic and try hard to establish their identity and belief systems. While it is common to find them join many human rights, social rights, environmental activist groups, they also run the risk of being sucked into many fanatic and rebellious factions and entering the world of crimes. It is also the time when hetero-sexual relationship is expected to grow and many suffer due to mishandling of these relationships.

In addition, near 10-30 per cent of them suffer from health impacting behaviours and conditions that need urgent intervention. This population is especially vulnerable towards nutritional disorders including both malnutrition and over-nutrition, tobacco, harmful alcohol and other substance use, high risk sexual behaviours, stress, depression, anxiety as well as injuries that include road accidents, suicides, and violence of different types. All these can have a long lasting impact. Very often multiple behavioural problems coexist in the same person that has a cumulative effect on their mental and physical health.

Although as students their prime focus is expected to be scholastic performance, unfortunately, it is this performance that suffers the most due to these complex factors. Lower performance in turn gives rise to various psycho-social problems forming a vicious cycle from which many find it difficult to emerge unscathed. Timely identification of the problem and counselling can certainly help in channelizing their activities well. Thus there are myriad issues that teacher counsellor need to deal with within the campus. They can be basically categorized into three groups:

(1) Intellectual or academic issues: problems with concentration, comprehension and memory, unhealthy competition, poor performance, information and guidance required for further studies or career, availability of scholarships etc.

(2) Emotional problems: managing anger, depression, fear, hatred, stress, anxiety, jealousy and rivalry, oversensitivity, heterosexual relationships, sexual harassment, ragging etc.

(3) Behavioural concerns: lack of confidence, poor communication, loneliness, absenteeism, fights and violence, discipline related issues, substance abuse, illegal acts etc.

Stages of Counselling

Professional counselling follows definitive process and follows certain well marked stages. This gives both the counsellor and counselee (student) a defined structure within which positive changes are worked upon, expectations from both sides are tempered and measurement of outcomes remains realistic and tenable. Primarily there are six stages of counselling, some of which will have to be sequenced while others are interlaced. For instance, from the following list, 1, 2, and 3 need to be followed in the order in which these are mentioned whereas, counsellor needs to employ 4, 5 intermittently and the counselling will end with 6 as the term suggests.

1. Identification of problem
2. Rapport building
3. Scheduling
4. Active listening
5. Interviewing or probing
6. Terminating

Identification of Problem

At the outset it is important to understand the kind of problem a student is facing and under which of the categories mentioned above can it be placed. Very often the problem cannot be placed under one particular category. For instance, a student complains of lack of concentration. Although it is an academic problem, it may turn out to be a relationship or an ethical issue that the student is facing which has affected concentration in class. Thus some deliberations are required to find out and list the actual problem(s).

Rapport Building

This stage is marked by careful and adequate communication which is an important prerequisite skill a counsellor needs to develop. Because without establishing a trusting relationship that puts the student at ease all other efforts and stages of counselling will prove to be an exercise in futility. In order to establish a trusting relationship the student at this stage has to be assured of not being under any scrutiny or judgement and that utmost confidentiality will be maintained. This is expected to help the student open up and explain the problem frankly.

Scheduling

Counselling is a professional commitment involving two persons, the counsellor and the student counselee; it needs to be conducted in a manner that sets the tone for proficient handling of issues. Right in the beginning, exact date and time of the counselling sessions may be planned and scheduled based on mutual convenience. The student counselee may seek an appointment to meet the counsellor well in advance with an implied promise of adhering to it. This ensures a sense of commitment and seriousness about the counselling process. On a case to case basis the number and frequency of the sessions may be determined.

Active Listing

A student counselee comes to a counsellor very often to be simply heard, which in psychological therapeutic parlance is termed as 'ventilation'. The least a counsellor can do is listen carefully and empathetically, which assures the student of having approached a kind and understanding individual. Active listening as against plain listening involves a lot more focus, right posture, eye contact, kind facial expression, occasional nods of acknowledgements, words like 'I understand', 'I know how you feel', etc. It conveys respect, empathy and concern for the counselee which does not go unnoticed furthering the relationship between the counsellor and counselee.

Interviewing or Probing

In order to understand the problems of the student counselee specialized interview method is resorted to by the counsellor. This is where the actual skill of a counsellor is put to test. It is done in the privacy of the counsellor's chamber or room without interruptions. Interviewing skills include properly worded questions, pace of questioning, voice tone, and body language like facial expression, posture, gestures, etc.

The questions asked need to be probing and leading albeit without showing undue haste or curiosity. If certain type of questioning is not able to get a clear response, counsellor has to be sensitive and vigilant to change the line of questioning. Both counsellor and student are required to work together in understanding and analyzing the problem, perceive it from various angles, search for probable solutions and agree upon certain doable actions that the counselee will undertake. Writing down these action plans and reviewing them jointly in every counselling session is helpful. Keeping records helps in easy tracking and also assessment of the outcome.

Terminating

Counsellor dependency is one of the many challenges. Hence, a counsellor needs to deal with sensibly. It very often happens that even after the said problem has been tackled well, the student counselee may not gather sufficient confidence to move on. He or she may continue to hold on to the counsellor and seek further appointments. Always there exists a possibility of the counselee developing emotional attachment to the counsellor and hamper professional relationship. It is therefore imperative that counsellor works towards smooth termination of the sessions without prolonging them beyond necessity.

Establishing Counselling Cell

Educational institutions have a perennial need for counselling, batch after batch and year after year. It is sensible to make counsellors available year round. It is now gradually becoming mandatory to establish counselling cells in all schools and colleges. This will create the right ambience, provide timely help to needy students and enable the counsellor to function effectively. Following are the prerequisites for the counselling cell:

(1) *Dedicated space*: People come to a counsellor only when in trouble, in a state of emotional trauma or when plagued with indecisiveness. It is therefore necessary to set aside a dedicated room as counselling cell that provides adequate privacy and is comfortable and soothing to troubled minds. The neatly kept room with requisite furniture, a few motivating quotations stuck on the wall, a few self-help books in the shelf, perhaps a fish bowl, a flower arrangement or a pleasant poster can do a lot to elevate mood of a visiting person while adding a professional touch.

(2) *Counselling register*: Counsellor needs to keep a track of all students who visit. A register with details of date and time of visit, name of student, problems reported, case details, counselling provided and future appointment has to be maintained. This helps in follow up as well as serves as a work diary.

(3) *Referrals*: A teacher counsellor often comes across complex cases. It is important for teacher counsellors to realize that

they may not have the expertise to deal with them. In such cases, professional ethics demand that without much delay and deliberations it should be referred to other expert mental health professionals. This will provide the much needed professional intervention and avoid further damage.

(4) *Continuous updating*: It will prove to be a good practice to keep abreast of current developments by reading available books, journals and articles on mental health, books on self-development and life skills. Counsellors can also attend workshops, seminars, and training sessions dealing with student issues to have a wider perspective.

(5) *Creating awareness*: many students are ignorant about counselling and are unaware of counselling facilities if any in their campuses. Some who know are either clueless regarding the problems for which they can seek counselling or shy away from approaching a counsellor. Also there exists a kind of taboo in the minds of many students and general public and therefore avoid going to counsellor. It is therefore important to create awareness and de-stigmatize counselling. Organising talks by experts on pertinent student problems, panel discussions, workshops, seminars, poster campaigns are some of the effective ways. The stakeholders of a college should be made aware of the importance of counselling.

Challenges for Teacher Counsellors

A teacher counsellor plays dual roles as a teacher and as a counsellor in campus. This often gives rise to some of the following challenges:

1. Dealing with ethical dilemma that arises between being kind and understanding and abiding by the discipline of the institution when a student seeks help for being pulled up for violation of institute's rules and regulations
2. Remaining unbiased and objective while dealing with issues that are against one's values, belief systems or prevailing social norms
3. Maintaining the promised confidentiality in critical cases like involvement with illegal activity or suicide attempt

4. Balancing between teaching and other academic activities with time and commitment required for counselling, since counselling is time consuming
5. Possessing adequate knowledge and training to understand and deal with the problems faced by students

In summary, counselling is both an art and a science. In order to be a competent counsellor one certainly needs to be trained, but that alone does not suffice. One has to be a continuous learner and a diligent practitioner of certain basic skills and endowed with compassion for fellow human beings, especially the students. It is the need of the hour to have in every college teacher counsellors who are not only competent but also dedicated to uplift the morale of students and bring them back on track. They can help students overcome depressions and loneliness. They can be great benefactors by saving the lives of students and help them shape their careers. It is desirable that every teacher has some capacity and appreciation for counselling and aware of its benefits. They can at least direct the needy persons to appropriate counsellors. Timely counselling can of students, for that matter even teachers and supporting staff will go a long way in making their life meaningful. As a matter of fact, every person in this modern stressful world needs counselling. Seeking counselling should be regarded as a perfectly normal idea and not as a taboo. A teacher counsellor in campus is that friend who unconditionally helps when a student needs most and when they feel that they have nowhere else to go. Therefore, to be a good counsellor is a God sent opportunity to serve the humanity.

Suggested readings

1. Hough, M. (1996): Counselling Skills. Longman, London.
2. Nelson, J. R. (2012): Basic Counselling Skills - A Helper's Manual, JBA, New Delhi
3. Sharma, R. N. and Sharma, R. (2013). Guidance and Counselling in India, Atlantic Publishers, India.
4. Wolfe, R. and Dryden, W. (2005): Counselling Psychology 3rd Edition, Sage, London.

All-round Development of Colleges

Chapter - 21

Resource Mobilization for Research and Institutional Development

—*A. B. Shanbhag and S. K. Saidapur*

Resouce mobilization is an essential constituent of higher education institutions (HEIs), especially the first grade degree colleges and the State Universities, to sustain growth, maintenance and expansion. The HEIs largely depend on the fee collected from the students, Grant-n-Aid provided by the respective State Governments and the University Grants Commission (UGC), to meet the financial needs. However, future role of UGC is uncertain. As per the media reports, the UGC Act of 1956 is likely to be repealed in the near future by passing an appropriate Bill in the Parliament. It appears that in place of the present UGC, two new bodies are likely to be created: Higher Education Council of India (HECI) and Higher Education Financing Agency (HEFA). Since the relevant bills are not yet passed, authentic details are not available. Therefore, the HEIs have to wait until the passage of relevant Bills pertaining to HECI and HEFA to know their mandate, specific role in governing academic and administrative matters, and guidelines pertaining to grant of funds.

The financial requirements have become graver in a scenario of ever expanding number of HEIs in response to the projected need to enhance Gross Enrolment Ratio (GER) advocated by the Education/ Knowledge Commissions, and also the pressing demands on people's representatives particularly in underdeveloped regions of their constituencies to meet people's aspirations. Also, most of the times HEIs get bogged down by the burden of inadequate financial resources to meet the legitimate, optimal needs of their developmental programmes, despite young energetic faculty members and supporting staff who are ready to shoulder the responsibilities, steer the projects through the thick and thins and take them to a logical conclusion. Furthermore, the unaided institutions do not get any support from the State Governments. Even the aided private institutions get generally support for only the salary of their employees and associated terminal benefits on retirement. But, the colleges need huge funds for establishment and support of infrastructure and its maintenance. Therefore, mobilization of funds from all available sources is quite essential. Here we present possible ways of mobilizing funds for sustenance of growth and development of colleges/varsities. Some of the resources for fund mobilization are as follows:

1. Students Fee
2. Opening Store for Sale of Books/Stationary/Uniforms
3. Raising Endowment Funds
4. Finance Reforms and Creating Corpus
5. Linkages / Collaborations with Industries / Institutions
6. Consultancy
7. Grant-in-aid from State Governments
8. University Grants Commission
9. Rastriya Uchchatar Shiksha Abhiyan (RUSA)
10. Other R & D Agencies

Having identified the possible major sources for mobilization of funds we can now take a look at each of these and evolve suitable strategies.

1. Students Fee

In most government colleges the fee collection is very low. Yet these colleges can survive because the State governments provide funds for basic needs (salary of employees, building and maintenance of infrastructure, consumables, equipment and running expenditures). On the other hand, the private (aided or unaided) colleges have higher fee structures but within certain limits specified by the State Governments. The private 'professional' colleges may not have serious problems as they often belong to the rich, and policy makers themselves who rationalize and fix the fee, generally on higher side. In essence, resource crunch is the problem of traditional, Arts, Science and Commerce Colleges who depend on student's fee to a great extent. However, a sudden raise in fee is unacceptable to the stakeholders. In rural and tribal areas, where mostly poor and not so well to do people dwell, raising fee often evokes hostile responses from the stakeholders. Therefore, the institution can only raise fees progressively in small increments annually or once in two years by evolving its own policy of revising fee structure. For instance the college may consider increasing fee by a small percentage each year (2-5%) or on alternate years (5-10%). This should also be made known through prospectus and other suitable channels, giving time to the stakeholders to get themselves mentally prepared for fee enhancements. Even small increments in fee collection can help meet inflations in the scheduled unavoidable expenditures.

2. Opening Stores for Sale of Books/Stationary/Uniforms

The colleges can open an evening store for sale of books, stationary and uniforms (where it is compulsory). The needed items can be purchased in bulk at a competitive rates and sold to students with a small profit but still keeping the prices lower than in the market. The store can be run preferably in the evening (1-2 hours) with the help of employees (retired or serving) and students who are willing to offer their services on voluntary basis. The entire sale-purchase and keeping track of the accounts should be properly structured and executed in a transparent manner with a service motto to help the students and create a kind of win-win situation for both college and the stakeholders. Even if this generates small amount it is worth the trouble and can gain confidence and appreciation of stakeholders.

3. Endowment Funds

There is enormous scope for raising endowment funds from the Alumni, philanthropists, non-resident Indians (NRIs) and other donors. However, two major requirements are to be met; a properly thought out, well structured plans (scholarships, free-ships, book grant, infrastructure development and other) that include details of execution. The institution should keep in mind the expectations of the donors. They always expect that their funds are judiciously utilized and accounting is totally transparent and displayed on the institution's website (including the annual audit reports). Once credibility gets established the donors will happily come forward and bequest generously, often in the name of their near and dear ones. The institution can set a target of say supporting 10 students each year through endowment funds. In service teachers and other employees can also contribute their might towards endowments.

4. Finance Reforms and Creating Corpus Funds

Judicious handling of funds is very important. The finance section should have appropriate software to handle and properly account for receipts and expenditures under various heads. Any unspent balance from any budget head that remains with the institution may be deposited in 'Corpus' funds in the first week of April each year. Initially the corpus can be created by donations raised from the stakeholders, employees and donors. The corpus funds should never be utilized. Only the interest amount earned on it could be utilized for all developmental works or other needs. Unutilized interest amount earned shall again be deposited to the corpus allowing it to grow over the years. A college may set an initial target of rupees one Crore or more for 'corpus fund'. A good corpus gives stability to the college.

5. Linkages and Collaborations with Industries/Institutions

In view of the complex higher education scenario linkages and collaborations have now become essential components of colleges and universities. Linkages and collaborations have both academic and financial implications. Experts from industries can help reorient academicians to the practical societal needs. Collaborations are certain to help in imparting good education by exchange of faculties between the institutions. The existing pitfalls / shortages can be overcome through functional collaborations, for teaching, research, execution of project works, sports, placement activities (through cluster formation), and extracurricular activities. Hence, avenues for appropriate collaborations should be explored by each HEI and also evolve formal mechanisms through Memorandum of Understanding (MOUs).

6. Consultancy Services

In principle it is possible to generate revenue through consultancy services. When successful, it also gives confidence to the students. However, consultancy may not be possible in all subjects. Yet, wherever it is possible, the institution and its faculty should make appropriate plans to offer consultancy services and generate some funds. Depending upon the competency and local needs, the faculty can undertake consultancy services in diverse areas. These include: translation of transcripts, water and soil quality analysis, filing income tax returns, training in yoga and meditation, courses on personality development, spoken English, functional English / Hindi / regional language, harvesting rain water and solar energy, mushroom cultivation, vermicomposting, bakery, tailoring, beautician courses and so on. The revenue generated after meeting the expenditures can be added to the corpus. To make the consultancy services effective the institution should have well defined formal mechanisms.

7. Grant-in-aid from State Governments

The State governments provide funds to government colleges and aided institutions as per their prescribed norms. Therefore, colleges have to raise additional funds for variety of other purposes. Quite often the Principals, especially the in-charge Principals of government colleges are hesitant to use the allotted funds fearing audit objections and delay in settling accounts and fixation of pension benefits. It is very desirable that finance rules are made user friendly by the respective State governments. In any case the Principals should ensure that all available funds in a given fiscal year are spent and there remains no unspent balance. Entire amount sanctioned must be utilized fully for the purpose for which the funds are released.

8. University Grants Commission

The University Grants Commission (UGC) ever since its inception in the year 1956 has played a major role in regulating and also funding HEIs, the Universities and colleges. It provided grants for infrastructure development, extension, renovation, maintenance of existing buildings and construction of new buildings, library development, scientific equipment needed for teaching and research, faculty development programs, research projects of faculty members, teacher fellowships to pursue research degrees, financial support for participation in academic conferences and visit of young faculty members to reputed institutions, organising workshops, seminars and conferences and so on. As per the recent media reports it appears that the UGC Act of 1956 is going to be repealed and UGC as such will be scrapped. In its place a new regulatory body called Higher Education Council of India (HECI) will be created by an Act of Parliament. The HECI will be entrusted with all academic matters governing the colleges and varsities with additional specific powers. New provisions may be made for improvement of teaching and research in colleges/varsities. Whereas, funding of higher Education Institutions is proposed to be taken over by the MHRD itself. May be MHRD will create another body called 'Higher Education Financing Agency' (HEFA) for disbursal of funds to colleges and varsities. The nature of funding, guidelines and other details are to be finalized and made known. Therefore, the faculty members and institutions desirous of seeking financial support should browse the websites of relevant governing/funding bodies for the latest information on the specific schemes and provisions before processing their proposals for funding.

9. Rastriya Uchchatar Shiksha Abhiyan (RUSA)

Declining educational standards in the recent decades, poor or obsolete infrastructure, crunches in funds and faculty, and big increase in the number of eligible youths seeking higher education appears to have prompted MHRD to initiate *"Rastriya Uchchatar Shiksha Abhiyan"* (National Higher Education Mission) scheme widely known as RUSA. It is meant to enable HEIs to build quality infrastructure for development of competency and skills to face challenges of globalization by strengthening colleges and universities to usher in good governance, academic, administrative and financial reforms as well as achieving autonomy, freedom, and flexibility for the institutions. The ratio of Central and State funding varies depending upon the institution; 90:10 for North-Eastern States, 65:35 for other States and Union Territories; 50:50 for private aided institutions. The funds under RUSA scheme are routed through the respective State Higher Education Councils for the following purposes.

1. Capacity building and preparation, Data collection and planning
2. Conversion of colleges to Cluster universities

3. Equity initiatives
4. Faculty improvements
5. Faculty Recruitment Support
6. Infrastructure grants to colleges
7. Infrastructure grants to universities
8. Institutional restructuring and reforms
9. Leadership Development of Educational Administrators
10. Management of Information System
11. New Colleges (Professional)
12. New model Colleges
13. New Universities
14. Research Universities
15. Research, Innovation and Quality Improvement
16. Up gradation of Autonomous Colleges to Universities
17. Up gradation of degree colleges to model colleges
18. Vocationalization of Higher Education

The RUSA funds may also be utilized for filling vacancies, creating new posts, faculty improvement, establishing specialized inter-university centres, innovation incubators, linkages with industries / varsities / research institutions / civil societies through Public Private Partnership (PPP) model and enhance overall quality of higher education: teaching, research and innovation.

10. Other R & D Agencies:

Other major funding agencies include CSIR, ICAR, DOE, DBT, ICHR, ISSR which support research in science and technology and social / historical sciences. Of course conditions apply. For instance, only those institutions having adequate staff and involved in good teaching and research activities can seek funds for strengthening infrastructure development in science and technology under the FIST scheme of Department of Science and Technology (DST). Any college/ varsity interested in seeking funds from Research & Development (R&D) agencies should browse the websites of various funding agencies regularly for latest information, guidelines, application formats and other needed details before preparing their proposals for funding.

Ideally, HEIs should strive to obtain funding for various activities like add-on courses, extension works and so on. Besides, there are some international organizations from which the HEIs can obtain funding. Ideally an experienced person who can provide information on various funding resources can help institutions greatly. Further, the colleges/varsities securing large number of grants from R & D agencies may evolve a mechanism for monitoring timely release and utilization of funds. The institution and the Principal Investigators should also ensure that entire sanctioned amount is utilized and not a single rupee is returned to the funding agencies. Certainly, leadership and encouragement from the Head of the institution matters considerably in cajoling the faculty members to apply and secure grants for their research, and utilize the sanctioned funds smoothly with minimum hassles. Research and publication activities by the faculty members will enhance respect for themselves and good reputation for the institutions. Growth and development of colleges largely depends on the availability of adequate funds. Therefore, there is no substitute for sound management, and mobilization of resources from all possible sources.

CHAPTER - 22

DEVELOPING A GREEN CAMPUS

— *A.B. SHANBHAG*

Nature holds the key to our aesthetic, intellectual, cognitive and even spiritual satisfaction. — **EDWARD O. WILSON**

Any practice considered as 'best practice' by practitioner or the practicing organization must have been designated so by its virtues or the dividends it must be yielding to the society at large. One such practice adopted by many educational institutions at various levels and especially those at tertiary level is the 'Green Campus' concept. This is a practice with global acceptance, naturally endorsed and promoted by United Nations' Environment program (UNEP).

Early alarms as to the climate change voiced since couple of decades by environmentalists were conveniently brushed aside by humanity blinded by affluent consumerist outlook. However, the phenomena such as ever soaring atmospheric temperatures, resultant receding alpine icecaps, and irregularity in long standing schedules of seasons, especially pattern of rainfall, flowering and fruiting of trees, unprecedented magnitude of draughts and floods have become inescapable reality.

Apparently, pace of Environmental degradation can be slowed down, fought back and overcome by concerted efforts of environment conscious citizenry. Hence, UNEP was mandated to inform, inspire and enable "Nations and people to strive to improve their quality of life without compromising that of future generations" in accordance with the 'Sustainability concept' developed at UN Conference on Environment in Stockholm in the year 1972. The understanding as to the finite nature of most of the essential natural resources on earth, environmentalists believe that "we have borrowed the earth from our future generations and not inherited from our forefathers"

Tertiary educational institutions - the Colleges and Universities obviously are the best grounds wherein young, energetic and receptive minds of their student population can be suitably sensitized and enthused as brigade of frontline soldiers to lead thc mission of environmental protection with commitment. These institutions have an added advantage for providing appropriate contemporary knowledge though suitably modified curricula with changing times, interdisciplinary laboratory backup for experimentation through funded projects towards generation of new knowledge, bio-incubators to test and make available economical and trustworthy technologies to regulate environmental quality and above all ever ready youthful band of student manpower eager to implement pilot projects on the campus to study their efficacy and demonstrate their advantages to society around. Hence the 'green campus' initiatives in these institutions can be the exemplary models to be emulated by the rest of the society around these islands. The green campus initiatives primarily revolve around sustainability principle based on efficient management of *Water, Energy, Waste* and *Pollution,* and *Biodiversity*. Relative importance of each of these parameters is described below:

Management of Water

Water is elixir of life, as no living being, plants, animals including we human beings, possibly with the exception of viruses can survive without water. Such an elixir of life, without which life is not sustainable, is taken for granted by the humanity and has been dealt callously. Net result is that many regions of globe are confronted with shortage of potable water, draught, failure of crops resulting in to famines. Unchecked pollution of water-bodies has been leading to heavy mortality of aquatic life including fishes, increase of waterborne diseases and epidemics costing quality of life, if not mortality per se. Increasing dependence on ground water through artesian wells for irrigation in rural areas and for daily use by urban populations has been driving water table to abyssal depths necessitating increasing costs to bank upon this resource too. Sum total effect is the interstate and international disputes in sharing water resources. No wonder that it is rightly said, God forbid, if at all any time the third World War is fought it would be for water. Therefore, it is imperative that we wake-up and understand the real value of water. In this direction we need to adapt measures to conserve, prevent wastage, recycle and augment/ recharge the water resources for the benefit of humanity.

The prevention of wastage of water is possible by giving a critical thought as to likely loss of water beyond the minimal limit in day to day chores in our routine, and consciously adopting simple preventive steps, if needed by adopting simple contrivances / devices as listed below.

Simple steps for containment of water wastage are:

(1) Using taps, faucets and showerheads with low flow/force

(2) Use of flush tanks with duel flush provision

(3) Running washing machines with full load rather than with partial load

(4) Turning off the taps while brushing the teeth, washing the hair, shaving etc.

(5) Inspecting the water pipelines and checking the leakages at regular intervals

(6) Avoiding use of toilet basin as disposal bin as it necessitates repeated flushing for clearance

Watering plants in the gardens and irrigation of farms also requires considerable amount of water. According to some estimates farming and irrigation amounts to 70% of total freshwater consumption by human. Good amount of clean potable water is also used for washing vehicles and so on in India. This is unfortunate. Therefore such practices constitute the fertile domains to look in to meaningful conservation steps such as those listed below:

(1) New plantations be carried out only during spring/rainy season

(2) Treated potable water supplied by corporations shouldn't be used for watering the plants in the garden, whereby excess cost involved in treating the water for potable purpose goes down the drain. Instead unprocessed harvested rain water or that stored from the surface runoff can be used for gardening or washing vehicles.

(3) Lawns and garden plants can be watered during early morning or late evening hours, specially the lawns by top mounted

revolving sprinkler heads to check the loss by evaporation and also to minimize on the total quantum used.

(4) Drip irrigation may be adopted in farms and agricultural lands in line with catchy pet slogan of our Prime Minister Narendra Modi "More Crop for Per Drop".

(5) Mulch could be used in gardens and farms to keep the root zones wet with minimum water

It is high time that we learn to reuse/recycle used water usage as well as harvest the rain water. These aspects are briefly dealt below:

Reuse /Re-Cycling

Recommendations have been appearing in the conservation literature as to the reuse of water once used, for which acceptability may not be easily forthcoming in all quarters. However, attempts are made to reuse the water from outflow of wash basins, bath room outlets and bath tubs for watering the plants and also to refill the flush-tanks in toilets. And, in rural areas the floor wash from cattle sheds and poultry farms is used to water the garden plants with an added advantage of enriching the fertility of the soil.

Harvesting Rainwater

The rain water is as good as distilled water, at least in areas relatively free of atmospheric pollution. The extent of rain fall also varies in quantum from region to region. Depending upon the porosity of the soil, part of the rain water gets absorbed recharging the aquifers, while much of the water moving as surface runoff through streams, rivulets, and rivers ultimately enter seas and oceans, turns salty rendering it useless for human consumption. Therefore, the rainwater if collected from clean surfaces such as roof tops and pavements and stored suitably can serve wide range of domestic uses like water for gardens, live stock, irrigation, carwash, laundry and indoor heating for homes. It can very well be used as cooling water in industries after preliminary filtration. Harvested water if it is filtered appropriately through filtration tanks with layers of coarse sand or metal meshes (20-40 mm pore size), it can be stored year round for domestic use or utilized for recharging the aquifers and underground water table. Such water after disinfection treatment can very well be potable. Already the rainwater harvest has been made compulsory for newly constructed households in several cities like Chennai, Bangalore and Pune.

Management of Energy Requirement

For quite some time global energy requirements have been met by fossil fuels such as the coal, natural gas, petrol and diesel. As these are the result of natural processes over long drawn geological past, they are categorized as non renewable sources. They are expected to last for another half a century at the rate at which they are consumed at present. Further, they are known to produce Greenhouse Gases (GHG) responsible for climate change; besides other pollutants like nitrogen oxide, sulphur dioxide etc. which get transformed in the atmosphere to nitric acid and sulphuric acid respectively and precipitate down along with the rains resulting in to phenomenon called acid rain in many parts of the world affecting aquatic life severely. All these concerns have made many countries to open up to nonconventional alternative energy options like Nuclear energy, Solar energy, Wind energy, Geothermal energy, and Bio-fuels like Biodiesel as they fall in the category of clean and green energy, and most of them are also renewable.

In the light of fore going analysis, campuses can very well bank upon solar energy which is in abundance, and also comes free of cost but for tapping expenses, especially for water heating in residential quarters and student hostels. Solar panels can not only be used for street lights, but also if they can be installed on a larger scale, meet other energy requirement on the campus. If stretched further, may turn out to be a source of income, to the institutions, if an agreement is reached to transfer access energy to the electric supply grids. Campuses in certain windy regions may draw on wind energy by wind mills.

Management of Wastes and Pollution

Dust pollution is common in most of the larger cities, either due to ever rising automobile density or location of industries in the neighbourhood. Four of the world's top 5 polluted cities are in India as per World Health Organization's (WHO) latest urban air pollution data base, based on the study of the 2,976 cities. These four cities are Gwalior, Allahabad, Patna and Raipur wherein particulate matter (PM -2.5), the dust particles in the size range of 2.5 microns suspended in the air ranged from144 to 170 micrograms per cubic meter per day, as against the permissible limit of 25 micrograms (suggested by WHO) per day. Over whelming impact of air pollution on stroke, heart disease, lung cancer and chronic and acute respiratory diseases is very much on records.

The waste management, especially of solid waste has gone out of control in most of the cities, mainly in metropolis. Amongst the solid waste, plastic is of major concern, as it is non-degradable in nature finding place in components of many manufactured goods, packaging material and also poly bags. Recent experimental study from Uppsala University, Sweden showed that exposure to micro-plastic particles at levels present in seas, inhibited hatching of fertilized eggs of European perch, stunted their larval growth and reduced activity levels making them susceptible to predators along with the associated rise in mortality rates. Bits of plastic within 5 mm from large plastic trash and manufactured micro-beads from products like soap, body wash and tooth paste are known to enter aquatic environment. It is also known that half hearted stray attempts in isolated places to ban poly bags thinner than 40μm has not really helped to tide over the scourge. The problems out of decomposable as well as hazardous wastes such as corrosive chemicals, nuclear waste, and e-waste are also of great concern.

Simple steps in the form of segregation of waste into wet and dry category, recyclable matter, and hazardous matter may go a long way in dealing with the problem. The decomposable matter may be dealt by organic manure production in green manure pits or wormy-compost pits or biogas plants located in the campus. Recyclable waste like plastic, glass etc can be stored aside and sent to recycling plants through the appropriate agencies. Hazardous waste should have to be dealt through certified contractors according to the laid down procedures through state/central Pollution Control Board.

Nurturing Biodiversity

India is one of the mega biodiversity countries with two biodiversity hot spots; Western Ghats and Eastern Himalayas with large floral and faunal composite and many endemic species. Expected forest cover is 33 % of the land area, and always afforestation drives are undertaken by various Educational institutions, NGOs, apart from Government

Departments in the form of 'Vanamahotsava', during spring/rainy season. Tangible results are not very evident possibly because monitoring of survival rate and post plantation care is often wanting. In the process, easy alternatives like planting hardy exotic species such as Acacia and Eucalyptus are undertaken. This leads to monocultures. The mono cultures are branded with some inbuilt problems such as allelopathy to the indigenous varieties, low support to the undergrowth, allergic problems because of the enormous quantity of pollen grains released from exotic species. Further, the monoculture habitats adversely affect local microhabitats and diverse indigenous species with flowers and edible fruits. Also, some of the monoculture species such as Eucalyptus are said to deplete underground water table because of heavy rate of transpiration. Therefore, some environmentalists brand the monocultures as 'Green Deserts'. In this background, the best environment friendly alternative is to undertake plantation programmes using indigenous plants, only using monoculture exotic plantations as transient measures in raising soil fertility of fallow lands prior to afforestation by indigenous varieties.

The heterogeneous patches of greenery with extensive microhabitats are expected to shelter variety of fauna including insects such as honey bees, butter flies and beetles many of which are beneficial and complimentary for the growth of forest and commercial crops because of their role as pollinators and the support to insectivorous birds doing away with crop pests. Hence, institutions having adequately large campuses must be able to nurture greenery with indigenous flowering and fruiting plants in combination with apicultural practice. The colleges can also generate sufficient manure through wormy-compost practices to suffice the needs of the institution. In this process, NCC/NSS volunteers can play an important role not only in plantation but also in nurturing the plants and enjoy seeing them bloom over the time. Large shade giving trees can be convenient places for study even in summer. Besides, properly managed greenery not only beautifies the college campus but it can also effectively reduce ambient temperature and ground water evaporation.

Chapter - 23

Involving Alumni in College Development

— *A. B. Shanbhag*

Nobody is bothered about an institution more than its alumni.
— N. R. Narayana Murthy

Alumni Association (AA) is a union of graduates or more broadly of former students (alumni) of a given educational institution. Naturally these associations are formed, and function around the nuclei of institutions of higher education, such as colleges, post graduate departments, independent schools of studies, universities, and institutions of research and training. On practical considerations, as a matter of convenience, central offices of these associations are based within the institutional campuses. Most of the graduate students passing out from any of these institutions are likely to be dispersed far and wide across the globe, in pursuit of further training or in search of greener pastures for higher attainments in career. Alumni of any institution are likely to be congregated in greater numbers in cities and metropolis with more centres of education and research, industrial belts, business hubs, trade centres etc. Thus, there is scope for these larger groups in bigger cities/ metropolis to form Alumni Chapters with regional tags affiliated to parent AA working in tandem and in close association towards common goal.

Objectives of Alumni Association

AAs serve as vital links between the alumni, contemporary students under training in the institution, and the institution for benefit of all, and in turn the society. Thus, they pave the symbiotic pathways amongst all the stake holders related to the institution, significantly contributing to the enhancement of its visibility. Therefore, the viable AAs and their developmental activities have been categorised as an important best practice by assessment and accrediting bodies of educational institutions. The principal objectives pursued by most AAs are outlined below:

1. To keep the flame of gratitude, spirit, love and affection of the alumni to the alma-mater glowing
2. To provide a forum for the alumni to come together, renew and refresh their ties amongst themselves and with the institution
3. To further the cause of education and training in their respective fields, in turn promoting the unstinted progress of the institution, human resource trained by it, and nation at large
4. To promote alumni in social and professional networking, facilitating their placements and entrepreneurial opportunities
5. To engage in such academic and social activities that shall catalyse prosperity of the alumni in their academic and professional career

Launching Alumni Association

A new establishment requires an earnest beginning, careful planning, and appealing framework that can enable to design and also sustain number of viable programs, envisaged by the founder members. Obviously, the AA must remain in a state of vibrancy year on year. As a rule, new formations pass through the birth fangs during their inception and thereafter for quite some time. Often the programs and projects started with considerable pomp and fanfare lose steam, fall apart and disappear without any tell-tale signs over a period of time when their reigns fall in wrong hands. This is true with the AA also. Therefore, successful formation and prolonged meaningful viability of the association requires a group of committed active alumni members residing in the easily accessible geographic limit of the institution to come together with an earnest desire to contribute to the noble cause. Alumnae/alumnus or employees of the organisation who are (a) willing to work with their institution, (b) willing to contribute time for the cause, (c) possess high level of energy and enthusiasm, and (d) ability to motivate others can contribute to the sound establishment and smooth functioning of AAs. Alternate and welcome proposition for forming AA is an initiation made by the institution itself. Initially, the Head of the institution may formulate a core team consisting of a few senior faculty members (serving or retired), one or two members of the administrative section, and some alumni, who might have attained necessary visibility in the social circles of the region. This team may direct their efforts to raise a preliminary list of alumni and their contact details, to begin with from the neighbourhood of the institution through the information gathered from various sources and their contacts of known friends and relations of alumni.

To facilitate starting AA the institution should provide space for housing an Office of 'Development of Alumni Affairs' identifying place for its functioning/address within the premises, and nominate a person each from its administrative office and the faculty as the nodal link persons to initially co-ordinate and set the ball rolling. The basic logistic support like some furniture, computer with Wi-Fi facilities, printer, and a part time attendant for maintenance of the office room (as and when needed) could be also provided by the institution besides all other needed support and encouragement. As soon as a group of highly interested persons come together should quickly register the AA under a suitable Act (e.g. Society's Act) and formalized. The AA should have its own bylaws and rules/regulations to guide its functioning: election of office bearers, enrolling members, membership fee if any, contact details, programs to be undertaken etc. Once the AA is fully set up, and got number of membership in place, it can function on its own with basic logistic facilities of the institution. The following aspects need serious consideration before launching the AA.

Constitution and By-Laws

Before registration of the AA, it is necessary to frame the Bye laws, business rules and regulations. The ad hoc Committee constituted during the first meeting of the Association can formulate the By-laws within a prescribed time frame providing all needed details for registering the AA and its proper functioning. The details include aspects like: objectives, memberships, election of officer bearer and their powers and functions, formation of committees, meetings and programs, matters related to resource mobilization and utilization of funds and so on.

Getting Organised

Soon after crystallizing the ideas about forming AA, meeting of interested alumni could be convened to deliberate and list out the objectives of the association, structure of the format for seeking membership, annual membership fee if any, design of the website, and constitution of committees to further the work smoothly. Below listed items may be looked into.

(a) Constitution of an ad-hoc committee to draft Constitution / By-laws for proposed AA
(b) Aims and Objectives of the Association
(c) Functions of the Association (e.g. communications, directories, mailings, newsletters, fund raising, instituting scholarships etc.)
(d) Identification of short and long-term needs of the institution
(e) Areas of interest and capabilities
(f) Projected expenditure and dues structure
(g) Nomination/election of office bearers
(h) Appointment of other required committees (e.g. communication, recognition of distinguished alumni, organizing various events etc.)

Reaching out to Prospective Alumni

Communications through regular mail, e-mail, news paper advertisement, telephonic calls with the known alumni, intimation could be disseminated to the prospective alumni from the list already raised, introducing them to the leader, requesting them to update their contact information, inquiring their interest to volunteer to help on various committees to be formed and so on are part of reaching out mechanisms. First, a website with all needed details and provision for interaction should be created. It is better to prepare format for seeking information with all needed contact details for future use. The objectives and need for such an AA should be clearly spelt. It can highlight how the AA is going to be made a dynamic organization for frequent meetings and retaining close link with the alma mater. The correspondence should include details of permanent and present addresses, telephone numbers. Email ids of the office bearers, website details, objectives, details of registration, bylaws etc.

As a first step, the AA can enrol the final year students of UG courses as members with a minimum of say Rs 50/- or so as membership free. Those who are unable to pay can also be enrolled as members without the voting rights. The AA should also create provision for online registration and payment. These components may be embedded in the byelaws of the association. The AA over a period of time can enhance its communication system with members, plan to bring out News Letter etc., which can be part of the website or publish its activities in the college magazine and attract future members. The AA may plan for instituting scholarships and fellowships, awards for deserving meritorious or poor students in the area of their studies, sports, cultural activities and so on in the name of donors or philanthropists as per their desire by securing more and more endowment funds. Sky is the limit for AA activities. Annual gatherings to discuss activities, income and expenditures incurred, and future plans of the association can go a long way in promoting strengthening AA and its credibility.

Having a large membership size for the AA is important. This can be accomplished by making it free initially say for about 5 years. Then the AA can prevail upon its members to contribute regularly say Rs 500/- per annum after they secure jobs. In due course of time it can result in a huge corpus funds for the association. Efforts should be made to raise endowment funds so that AA can effectively contribute to the growth of the alma mater and also help the needy and deserving.

Possible Activities of AA

A dynamic AA can undertake many activities. Listed below are some of the concrete activities by the active AAs of leading institutions within the country with the proven track record of two-way benefits to the institution and alumni.

(a) Involvement and Services

An active and engaged alumni network can empower the college and the alumni towards attending the events, participating in various projects or serving as volunteers in academic, social and cultural programs of the institution.

(b) Career and Networking Services

If a strong global membership base is established, it can in the long run, provide helpful links to the fresher with senior stalwarts working in various capacities in different parts of the globe. Alumni can participate in seminars, workshops and technical events and showcase their skills and accomplishments and thus take advantage of opportunities to interact with specialists and captains of corporate bodies and industries.

(c) Continuous Learning

Alumni can enjoy benefits of lectures, discussion sessions, on campus conferences by eminent alumni and current as well as emeritus faculty.

(d) Student-Alumni interaction

AA can support current students through different mentoring opportunities either by being a part of on campus lectures or through online commitments, provide internships, recruit fresh graduates, present career programs etc.

(e) On-going benefits

Alumni can avail benefits of their Alma mater in various ways like Access to online alumni directory, free email account and forwarding services, part concessions in accommodation charges in the guest houses of the institution while on transit or on visit to the city of their training, concession in library membership, play-ground, swimming pool, jogging track, and other facilities.

(f) Events and Reunions

Alumni can actively participate in the events in the institutional campuses and also in those of the active regional chapters established in different parts of the country or world. AA members can also be invitees to campus events like foundation day, convocation day, musical programs, cultural events, picnics, outings, sport events and meetings of special interest groups. Expert Alumni members can help the current students of the alma mater in conducting filed works, survey works, trekking and so on.

(g) Alumni Chapter activities

Alumni may have opportunities to participate in the events organised by thriving city chapters and have opportunities to renew old friendships and start new ones.

(h) Travel

Head-out on weekend jaunts, an educational voyage or expedition with alumni, friends and family members.

Opportunities to Repay

Being a member of an active AA is a unique opportunity. Besides, it also provides opportunities to repay back the obligations and express the gratitude to the Alma-Mater. In fact, every alumnus must do something for his/her alma mater. Some examples are given below:

(a) Replenish

Very often, in every batch sizable student population can be from socially and economically challenged segments, not having enough financial support for meeting legitimate day to day needs. Interest earned on the alumni generated corpus funds can help meet such needs by instituting the educational loan facility on a nominal rate of interest, to be paid back after completion of education and acquiring a suitably earning job. This gesture will be of paramount significance for deserving students from under privileged sections of society in pursuing education that is becoming dear year after year. Recovered money can be reinvested to replenish the fund to be used for later batches, thus extending the helping hand to more of needy students and wider section of the under privileged society over a period of time.

(b) Support to Hostel Mess

The hostel messes are the only affordable venues catering the nutritional needs of many students from far-away places residing in hostels. They may also be manned by workers from needy sections of the society, who might also be caring and kind to students staying away from their parents and near and dear ones at home. There can be programs to invest reasonably from the alumni funds towards infrastructural improvements in hostel and also to extend needed support to mess staff whose income might be meagre and insufficient to meet their family needs which in turn will turn-out to be caring and considerate gestures of kindness towards both the segments in the hostel mess.

(c) Support to Village clusters

It is well known that India lives in villages rather than in cities. Therefore, suitable development projects will go a long way for their growth, also reducing unchecked migrations and exodus of people from villages to cities. Successful and prosperous AAs and AACs can adopt certain rural village clusters in their neighbourhood for specific development plans and programs like establishment of sports ground, village library, conducting educational and skill development training, open air amphitheatre to hold village level cultural activities, evening schools for adult education can play a beneficial impact in the life of these villagers. Other such programs including providing awareness about the new initiatives floated by State or Central governments regarding loan facility and diverse schemes for self employment etc. can be thought of by the AA using the location specific advantages.

(d) Other Activities

Arranging lectures on current affairs at National / International arena, Science and technology, Skill development and Entrepreneurship programs, Value based education related programs and so on. The AA can think of instituting many awards (e.g. Institution and disbursement of "Distinguished Alumni" award, Honouring Senior 'Gurus' etc.), organize sports meets, reunion meetings and so on.

Thus, successful AAs can become the important tools and drivers of nation building through their impressive and imaginative programs towards the growth of their alma-mater, students passing-out of their portals and providing sense of contentment to their fellow alumni contributing their might for the national progress. Large numbers of alumni (especially the non-resident Indians) are willing to donate generously to their alma mater especially after they are well settled in life. All they need is an opportunity and assurance that their contributions are judiciously used and accounts are maintained in a transparent way. Therefore, working of the AA should be democratic, transparent and efficient. It should be known for its work and nobility in the region. A dynamic website can be a great boon in remaining connected with all alumni. In any case, in this globalized world, it is quite essential that the higher education institutions have a vibrant AA considering its immense utility. Some may not have AA and others may have their AA in a dormant state. Therefore, establishment of a new AA or early revival of dormant one as the case may be is essential to harness its immense potentiality, and establish a good linkage between the institution and its alumni for development of the college. Involving Alumni in developmental activities will go a long way in ensuring good health of the institution.

Suggested Reading

1. https://en.wikipedia.org/wiki/Alumni
2. http://alumni.iisc.ernet.in
3. www.odaa.iisc.ernet.in
4. www.iitbombay.org

Future Prospects

CHAPTER - 24

EDUCATION IN THE 21ST CENTURY

— *S. K. SAIDAPUR*

"Education is not about filling bucket but lighting a fire"

— W. B. YEATS

Human society has been undergoing rapid changes due to formal education, scientific progresses, technological advancements, innovations and industrialization particularly in the past three centuries. Growth and development of a nation largely depend on the quality and relevance of higher education based on which industrial revolutions (IRs) take place worldwide which constitute the backbones of the country's prosperity. The IRs impact prevailing education systems as well and, compel them to evolve in response to the industrial needs. The first IR (coded as IR 1.0) took place in late 18th century (around the year 1780). This was chiefly characterized by the *mechanization* of production using water and steam power and weaving looms. The second industrial revolution (IR 2.0) manifested around the year 1870 enabled *mass production* using electrical energy and division of labour (assembly lines). Again, a century later, around the year 1969 further automation in the production of goods became possible due to technological advancements in electronics and IT leading to IR 3.0. The 3rd IR was thus dominated by *automation, computers, electronics and internet*. It used 'simple' digitization technology. Now we are witnessing the fourth industrial revolution (IR 4.0) which utilizes 'complex' digitization technology (cyber-physical systems). Importantly, the IR 4.0 is more powerful than the previous ones both in speed and impact due to great breakthroughs in fields like Robotics, Internet related developments, Autonomous (driverless) vehicles, 3-D Printing, Quantum Computation, Data storage, Energy Storage,

Material Science, Nanotechnology, Biotechnology, Artificial Intelligence (AI) and so on. A rapid progress in IR 4.0 has enabled mass manufacture of products for better quality life as well as increase in global income levels. At the same time, the 4th IR that is fully empowered with technology has already made many presently existing jobs redundant; and more of this is sure to follow. To illustrate this point let us take a common example, the smart phone. The little smart phone performs numerous tasks. The examples include: telephonic communication, call recording, messaging and sharing information instantly (SMS, Facebook, Twitters, Blogs, WhatsApp, Instagrams, personal or institutional websites), video conferencing for business meetings, PC, TV, Radio, alarm clock, music system, GPS, Organizer, Calculator, Mobile banking, Dictionary and Thesaurus, Camera, Torch, online shopping, booking tours, travels and hotels, accessing e-books, e-papers, e-journals, content sharing, active participation in social media (Facebook, Twitters, Blogs etc.), data storage, games and so on to name only a few. With specific apps in place a smart phone can perform large number of functions. These are too well known and hardly need elaboration. As a result, possession of several coveted instruments and equipment has become meaningless. Yet, communication, sharing information, business transactions have become unbelievably simple and fast. Hence, imagine how many kinds of instruments, industries and number of personnel working in such industries may have been affected by this one innovation, the making of a smart phone. The example of smart phone eminently explains what technology driven job disruption is all about.

In spite of the job disruptions one need not be excessively pessimistic or lose hope. All new technologies do create new opportunities and new jobs. For instance, maintenance and up gradation of technologies and making new innovations remain important at all times but require new skills. The major drivers of IR 4.0 are: new media literacy, super-structured organizations, globally connected world, rise of smart machines and systems, increased use and application of computational systems, new media ecology that requires new communication tools, and increased human longevity. All these have a far reaching impact on the labour market, income of workers, and displacement of workers by the machines and AI. The onset of IR 4.0 was recognized close to a decade ago though its formal announcement came in the year 2016 in Germany. The "Industry 4.0" epitomizes alignment of man and machine and many unforeseen opportunities by exploiting the potential of digital technologies, personalized data, and open sourced contents etc. Evidently it demands a change in the kind of top skills needed in future: dealing with complexities, critical thinking, creativity, emotional intelligence and cognitive flexibilities, ability for co-working, co-creation with both men and machine together to name a few. Basic elements of IR 4.0 are therefore creativity and innovation. Use of 'Internet of Things' (network of physical devices, vehicles, home appliances and other items embedded with electronics, software, sensors, actuators, and connectivity which enables these objects to connect and exchange data) will become very common and in doing so many challenges will surface at workplaces. Hence, the future youth (Gen-Z population – those under 20 years of age) need to be adequately prepared.

It is quite imperative that we prepare ourselves to face the technology driven loss of jobs on one hand, and emergence of new ones on the other as IR 4.0 progresses. Therefore, education for 21st Century needs to be redesigned on priority. Before addressing the nature of future higher education let me first recapitulate evolution of education systems.

Pattern of Changes in Education Systems

The *Gurukul* system practiced in India from time immemorial is a classic depiction of Education 1.0. It typically employed traditional methods of teaching where a teacher represented ultimate embodiment of knowledge gained over centuries of experience and memorization. The education process was unidirectional; from teacher to the taught. So, teaching meant speaking and learning meant listening. Knowledge was limited to books available in the library. Essays, assignments, tests, occasional group works within the class room were the broad norms. Interaction with other institutions was uncommon or absent. Passive absorption of knowledge by the learner was by and large the mode of learning.

Education 2.0 began at the turn of 20th Century thanks to the internet facility. This enabled learning, sharing knowledge through variety of means of social media like, emails, wikis, blogs, Facebook, in recent times, twitters and WhatsApp facilitating production, collaboration, publication and social book marking. These are now the new components of education. This education system was heavily digitized but it still operated essentially within the same framework of education 1.0. Hence, education 2.0 is often regarded as evolution and not revolution. In any case, it enabled transition from passive to active learning, E-learning, collaborations with other institutions (national and international), open access to teaching-learning and sharing educational and research materials. Finally, technology enabled management of governance, teaching, learning and evaluation became possible. In this changed scenario the teachers had to take up some new roles like guiding, mentoring and helping to an extent.

The Education 3.0 is used by education theorists to describe integrated approach of technology in teaching-learning processes. It is a confluence of neuroscience, cognitive psychology and education technology, using web-based digital and mobile technologies including apps, hardware and software etc. Also, it is characterized by formal collaborations for cross institutional prospects for learning and exchange (knowledge-producing education). It is worth noting that the learners themselves could become creators of knowledge and share it by social networking and enhance social benefits. Thus it provided avenue for producing as well as consuming knowledge, strengthening collaborations and, pave way for reforms in teaching, learning and evaluation processes as well as administration of educational institutions.

Embracing New Education System

As stated before, the impact of fourth IR is more forceful which makes use of complex digital systems and 'internet of things'. Hence, redesigning the future education to match the requirements of IR 4.0 is an urgent necessity. A primary concern of the new education system (4.0) is to provide a blueprint for future learning: blended learning, lifelong learning as well as playing a constructive role in the society. It is a model that is aligned with the future trends and needs and focuses on 'empowering education to produce innovation'. It envisages a change from 'brain as storage' to 'brain as processor' model. It focuses on interactive and applied learning with question and answer sessions, reviews and quizzes, discussions, problem solving, labs and project based learning. It provides scope for customization and personalization so that educational content is planned to meet the needs of specific students (slow or advanced learners). Further traditional classrooms may transform into a virtual and flipped classrooms wherein lectures (theoretical aspects) are conveyed online (video conferencing) and assignments (practical components) are done together in classrooms through interactions between teacher and the taught and among the taught as well. But, are we ready? How shall we prepare for this? Do we have will to change?

The major drivers of future education are: Future skills, 100 year Life, Millennial mindset, Digital networks and Devices, Personal Data, Collaboration Platforms, Talent Investment, Shared Content and Resources and Social Progresses. A movement towards Education 4.0 therefore entails a change in the *mind* and *mindset* of teachers, learners and educational managers. As far as the 'mind' is concerned it is no serious issue. Indian mind is often superior in several aspects to that of the Anglo-Saxon or Caucasian or any other. Many seminal contributions, in the area of science and spirituality have origins in India. Today we talk about the 'Global Village' which Indians knew as *Vasudhaiva Kutumbakam* (World is one family) much before the Christian era. What about the 'mindset'? It refers to the attitude. Fixity in the attitude on the part of teachers can be a great hindrance in the implementation of future education policies. This can happen often due to the digital divide between the teachers and the learners. In India one in thousand persons has a PC. However, the current generation of learners especially the Gen-Z population of youth (those under 20 years of age), more and more of them have access to smart phones and computers and as such they are more advanced in their skills of handling these devices compared to the teachers. Therefore, reluctance on the part of teachers to accept digital mode of education is natural but unfortunate. Large section of the teaching community still feels chalk and talk is the best method of imparting education. There is no denial that it is a good method and good teachers even taught under the banyan trees effectively when the information was limited. Today we are lost in the ocean of information. That is not all. With the availability of facilities like epidiascopes, over head projectors and PPT teaching became more and more teacher centric rather than learner centric. More often than not, teachers projected their write-ups and read it in the class. However, the times have changed. We now very clearly need learner centric teaching. A teacher needs to meticulously plan to promote, creative thinking, making innovations, group learning, blended learning, lively discussions, projects and home assignments, quizzes and so on. In short teachers ought to be creative themselves and also continue lifelong learning.

In any case, there is a pressing need to fast forward our mindset to 21st century situation. We need to accept the future challenges with all sincerity to empower our growing youth population (considered demographic dividend) to face the challenges of the ongoing IR. We have a moral obligation too to provide not only 'right to education' but 'right education' and 'right way of education' as opined by R. A. Mashelkar. Education in innovation and innovation in education will be the hallmarks of 21st century education. Therefore, the new education system needs to focus its attention on imparting sound knowledge and skills that help build confidence and self esteem in the minds of learners. This in turn will enable them to face challenges and sail through the future IRs. Thus, the sole purpose of new education revolves around facing the challenges of technology driven disruptions in the jobs and future employability. The Universities, State and Union governments, the Ministry of Human Resource Development (MHRD) and State Education Ministries should therefore undertake needed reforms in higher education on priority and forestall the possible disasters. Any complacency in preparing our youth to the new norms of education and industries can only demolish the demographic dividend that India boasts of. Being professionally competitive both in knowledge and skills is the only way to succeed in globalized world that is witnessing rapid industrial revolutions and technology driven disruptions in jobs. Therefore, it is imperative that the education system metamorphoses in response to the colossal developments in science, technology, knowledge base and rapidly undergoing IRs.

Future Teaching-Learning Processes

Education is a dynamic process in which adoption of innovative ways of teaching and learning, and weeding out the obsolete ones take place on a continuous basis. The teachers need to go beyond the prescribed curricula. Skill based learning and group learning should become the prominent components of education. Teaching has to be more and more student centric and in tune with the ability and aptitude of learners. The teachers have to learn new methods of teaching: Self learning, Group learning, Blended learning (a combination of offline and online learning to complement one another using LMSs the learning management systems, mobile devices like smart phones and tablets), Flipped class rooms, Monitoring individual progresses, Problem solving, Use of internet based tools and technology etc. The traditional classroom lecturing methods have become obsolete and need redesigning to accommodate latest technological innovations, new education contents for stimulating creative thinking and making innovations. Learning through project works and field studies need to be impactful. Apparently, a future teacher will have to serve as a facilitator, mentor, guide, and confidence builder. They have to be lifelong learners so as to minimize the digital gap between them and the learners. It may be noted that by 2020 half of the world population will be linked by internet. There is no escape from the digital literacy in the modern world.

Novel reforms in examination system are also needed. System of examination based on one correct answer (often taught by the teacher) is no more the best way. Problem solving to find multiple solutions must become priority. Let me give an example. Ask kindergartners 'A' for? All will say 'apple'. All children will give one (correct) answer. They are all taught that way. It is not their fault. However, if we change the question a bit we can get multiple answers by making the children think. For instance, we can ask the children to write words starting from 'A'. There will be at least a dozen or even more words coming from the same children because it makes them think! Lastly, a continuous evaluation of students' progresses is more desirable over one time (semester end) examinations. Performance in routine day to day academic activities like seminars, quizzes, assignments, and discussions should form the basis for gradation rather than a single examination. In fact, Universities should do away with the practice of deciding the fate of students based on one single semester end examination. Further, provision for online examinations needs to be in place wherever feasible.

The above paradigms clearly call for a change in professional profiles of teachers so as to remain relevant and enhance their own social status. These may include: openness to adopt new teaching strategies, becoming technologically more and more literate, integrating technology in teaching, guiding students for self actualization, serving as a friend, philosopher and guide to learners and help them to acquire new knowledge and skills using diverse teaching pedagogies. At the same time, promotion of ethical and moral values leading to citizenry cannot be ignored. In summary, focus of the new education system is strengthening four pillars of learning: 'Learning to know; Learning to do; Learning to be, and Learning to live together' (*source*: 'International Commission on Education for 21st Century'). Finally, the teaching fraternity involved in 21st Century education ought to prepare their minds and the mindsets to accept new teaching pedagogies at the earliest and, embrace new education norms. There is no scope for reluctance to change our education system or being apologetic about it.

Suggested Reading

1. http://www.mashelkar.com/convocation-addresses/175-science-2-0-education-3-0-and-industry-4-0 Education 3.0 from Wikipedia
2. www.unesco.org/education/pdf/15_15.pdf
3. International Commission on Education for 21st Century- 1996.
4. www.unesco.org/education/pdf/15_62.pdf

CHAPTER - 25

REDESIGNING HIGHER EDUCATION: A FEW TITBITS

— S. K. SAIDAPUR

Having been associated with the higher education system for over 5 decades I had the opportunity of seeing progression of several universities/colleges in the country including a few newly established varsities carved out of postgraduate centres. In general, the universities started prior to the country's independence (1947) or soon thereafter had the good fortune as they enjoyed considerable autonomy and were headed by illustrious visionaries as Vice Chancellors whose personal charisma brought reputation to the universities. They could appoint members of the teaching staff based on merit by inviting them from any part of India or abroad. This provision is now limited to Central Universities and certain premier institutions. The faculty was one of the best at that time which enabled sustenance of higher education institutions (HEIs) till late 1970s or so. The professors of yesteryears were thus scholastic with good basic training, and experience of working with eminent scholars from abroad. They were effective communicators, highly disciplined, meticulous in their work, and committed to the profession. They strived hard in establishing the undergraduate (UG) / postgraduate (PG) departments from scratch; built museums, equipped laboratories with best possible scientific equipment available then for use in teaching and research. More importantly, they conducted themselves with great dignity and exuberant aura of scholarship. They mentored their students and the institution exceedingly well. In those days, the PG classes were composed of students from local areas as well as from different parts of India, especially from the neighbouring as well as from far-off States. Those who came from other States returned after procuring their degrees and became ardent brand ambassadors of the alma mater. Apparently, such ambassadors played an important role in building brand name for the institution, be it a college or university. At present the State Universities mostly admit students coming from their own affiliated colleges.

The first few generations of local students in the free India who availed the collegiate and varsity level education also performed very well. A few of them even pursued research and obtained their doctoral degrees. Of these a few went abroad for further training in technologically more advanced countries of Europe and North America. Many such students settled abroad for good. However, some of them returned to occupy positions often in their own Universities. Thus, the second generation began to take over roughly in 1960s. They also carried out good research. Furthermore, they strived to become good teachers as they were competing with their own teachers who were still around and exemplary. They had perhaps a point to prove. Unfortunately, later on over a short period of time, entire faculty became homogenous following rampant inbreeding; a need to prove one better than the other lost relevance. Furthermore, the inbreeding trend in the appointment of faculty, often without postdoctoral experience and exposure to the outside world, seems to have contributed to the loss of hybrid vigour in Universities to a great extent.

It is a matter of great concern that the quality of education with regard to both knowledge and skills has been declining rapidly which has led to a loss of credibility of the varsity degrees. It is no secret that a good majority of teachers lack professionalism, teaching and mentoring skills due to poor competency, commitment and values. The reading habits of teachers and a craving for new knowledge have faded over the years, at a time when the world is witnessing knowledge explosion, complex digitization, development of technology and making innovations. Furthermore, a visible rot in the knowledge of fundamentals among teachers is a matter of serious concern; such teachers can hardly inspire and mentor their students in any significant way. Modern teaching aids have helped the teacher more than the students.

A fallout of the above concerns is glaringly reflected in the performance of students in NET / SLET which is shockingly dismal over the years; the pass percentages rarely touch double digits despite the fact that those who appear for these tests often hold first classes, distinctions, ranks and Gold medals in the varsity examinations which in turn depicts rather excruciatingly a loss of standards in university teaching, evaluation, marks and degrees. Therefore, it is not surprising that marks and degrees fail to match with the performance of candidates in competitive exams, eligibility tests, and interviews. Relying more on publications rather than competency for promotions has contributed significantly to a boom in the number of research papers and journals with least regard to quality and credibility. Repetitive research and plagiarism have become sickeningly common. Thus, barring a few institutions, the quality of education and research are in a dreadful state. Obviously, a strong will, sincere efforts and hard measures are needed to ensure reasonable standards in higher education and build public credibility.

Dismal performance of faculty or students is not all. Look at the reputation of Vice Chancellors and other authorities of the Universities in recent years. Often they are men and women of very low calibre and competency besides their love for nepotism, favouritism and corruption. The buck does not stop there. Water percolates down from the roof to the living areas. In the same way, when Heads of the HEIs are appointed on considerations other than merit, malpractices and corruptions flow down the line reaching all the way to research scholars, students and other stakeholders. In some State Assemblies, the legislators have also openly raised the issue of corruption in the appointment of Vice Chancellors. Even the Chancellors, the highest authority for appointing Vice Chancellors are not free of such accusations. So in effect, the governance system is progressively becoming corrupt in which corruption and nepotism are favoured and honesty is punished. In such a scenario, *natural selection* (a Darwinian principle of evolution) favours the corrupt and eliminates the honest. Yet, I advocate the readers to be optimistic. A time will come when there will be demand for honesty to honestly manage the assets of dishonest people! We can only hope that this will happen soon.

A need for reformation of higher education is felt fervently and unequivocally especially in the past 2-3 decades because most HEIs stand impoverished in terms of faculty, supporting staff, infrastructure, finance, autonomy, governance and leadership. Furthermore, production of unemployable graduates (including the professional courses) is glaringly staring at the utter failure of the education system and education planners. Sadly, any cognizance of a close relationship between education system and industrial revolutions is grossly overlooked. However, education and IRs impact each other in a very significant way as described earlier in Chapter 24. Obviously, prevailing education system must match with the demands arising out of IRs. As we are in IR 4.0 now, we need drastic revolution in our education system. However, redesigning higher education is by no means an easy task, considering the diverse complexities that include primarily the quality and quantity of faculty, geographic location (metropolitan, urban, rural, tribal area and so on), inadequate faculty, inapt infrastructure, library and laboratory facilities, background of students (urban, rural, tribal, first generation learners etc.), virtual lack of leadership, and political interferences to name a few. Also, the issues and constraints differ vastly between institutions as we have affiliated or constituent and autonomous colleges on one hand, and government, private- aided and unaided colleges on the other. Each type of institution has its own constraints. In addition, there are many newly started colleges without infrastructure or faculty and sometimes no students either. And, there are many old colleges where buildings and furniture are more or less in a dilapidated condition. Likewise, when it comes to Universities, there are Central / State run universities, private and deemed or deemed-to-be universities and in recent times, foreign universities. Now the MHRD is contemplating the idea of 'world-class universities'. There is nothing like 'world class'; all universities need to be of global standards.

In the foregoing passages I have attempted to emphasize the expediency of redesigning the ongoing education system despite many complexities and difficulties that discourage taking bold steps. So what is the way forward for making our colleges / varsities the vibrant centres of higher education? After all, education is not a mere luxury of gaining knowledge; it should remain relevant to the contemporary needs of the industries, jobs and society at large. Initiating hard measures requires courage of conviction and a goal of long term good for all. A strong desire, sincere efforts, hard measures, freedom from politics and politicians are needed to ensure (near) global standards in higher education and meeting the challenges of IR 4.0 described before in

Chapter 24. It is high time that our legislators realise that amount spent on education is actually an investment for the progress of any nation and therefore apportion funds liberally.

Major parameters in the form of *titbits* are described below to facilitate bring in changes in the higher education system as a whole. These are, however, representative in nature. Additional, institutional specific parameters may be evolved by the concerned HEI to accomplish the set goals in a given time frame.

1. Setting Institutional Goals

Setting goals is a typical attribute of industries. To the best of my knowledge the educational institutions are not known to set goals and time frames for achieving the same. This is in stark contrast with the private industries and entrepreneurs. It is only after the initiation of assessment and accreditation (A&A) processes in the year 1994, HEIs have started displaying 'vision and mission' statements though often with little distinction between the two. Evolving 'vision and mission' and setting up the time bound 'goals' is not same. In order to further the interests of the institution (or the nation) and the stakeholders, setting up time bound goals is a basic requirement without which it is like wandering aimlessly in the dark, that too in a wild forest. Ideally, all HEIs must first deliberate on 'goals' and fix a time frame (say 5 years) to guide achievement of intended results. Annual review of successes and failures in reaching the set goals can help in undertaking needed corrective measures.

2. Leadership is Key to Success

Any institution that aspires for a directed growth and development, it must have a leader with vision, honesty, integrity and competency to play the crucial role in building credibility and reputation of the organization. For universities, it is the Vice Chancellors, and for colleges, it is the Principals who are to provide the leadership. Evidently, leadership qualities are innate and do not come by seniority, religion, cast or creed. Therefore, appointing persons for steering an institution to greater heights should be purely based on their competency, commitment and leadership qualities. Therefore, persons of national/international standing should alone be considered for these positions. Considerations based on other criteria and justifications made under the political or religion based guises will only result in a stunted growth if not disaster for the institution. Such practices have already led to alarming proportions of disrespect to the institutions. A bad leader has all the attributes to ruin the institution in a remarkably short time. In fact, we commonly encounter even private colleges with good infrastructure and sound financial status but sadly they are also in bad shape due to the leadership crisis. As far as the government colleges are concerned, the less we say is better. A mediocre leadership will only lead to mediocrity. After all 'like begets like'.

For a college to bloom into an excellent learning and man making centre it is absolutely necessary that most competent persons are appointed as the Principals on the basis of a transparent selection process purely on the consideration of merit-cum suitability of candidates out of a national pool. Competency, honesty and integrity should outweigh other considerations while appointing principals. It is desirable that a person with at least 5 years of service to spare is appointed to head the college, on selection rather than on mere seniority basis. Autonomy and incentives may attract good souls to this position even from distant places. Unfortunately, in most colleges, senior most faculty member is compelled to work as in-charge principal. He is neither interested nor will he provide any leadership. Such stop-gap arrangements over long periods will merely ensure downfall of the institution.

3. Competitive Faculty is a Must

The most important element of higher education system is 'faculty'. Primarily, it is the teachers who shape and mould the career of students, inspire them and help build character and citizenry. Therefore, HEIs need to appoint the best faculty purely based on their aptitude and competency for teaching and research that involve creative thinking and making innovations. The institutions also need to nurture faculty empowerment. Some of the concerns that relate to faculty appointment and their jobs are listed below:

- Teachers ought to be of national standards for colleges and of global standards for varsities; inbreeding must be avoided at any cost.
- Newly appointed teachers as a rule should teach all core papers of the course in the first 5 years.

- Each teacher may be assigned 5-10 students per semester for mentoring (academic, personal issues).
- Appointing 2-3 eminent visiting faculties will inspire students / teachers as well as enhance academic ambience.
- Encourage faculty development
- Avoid commissioning teachers for non-academic assignments like the hostel warden, gymkhana, bursar and so on; they can be members of the academic committees
- Promotion of sports, games, athletics, yoga, meditation, placement, and such other works are better done by outsourcing using unemployed and superannuated personnel who have the passion for such undertakings.
- In government degree colleges teachers are often transferred. This is a serious issue and requires clear rules, regulations and proper implementation.
- The teachers have to be life-long learners and prepare themselves for changing roles as highlighted in the previous chapters (Chapter 2, 24).
- Teachers may volunteer to adopt one or two students annually and support them. This will enhance their image and respectability among the student community. Teachers should strive to become role models.

4. Focussing on the 'Relevance of Education to IRs'

As discussed in Chapter 2 the entire education system is set to change radically from traditional classroom teaching to modern methods that ensure learner centric teaching using modern infrastructure and technologies. We need to train our students to acquire new skills and promote creative thinking and making innovations. As we traverse through the fourth industrial revolution, numerous kinds of the presently existing jobs will vanish and in their place new jobs requiring new skills will emerge. For this reason education system needs to be well designed so that it can produce employable graduates and entrepreneurs, the job givers. The new education system of the 21st century focuses on technology development, innovations and empowering learners to make innovations. These are indeed the hallmarks of education 4.0 in tune with the ongoing industrial revolution. Any lethargy in radicalizing education to new requirements may create more social problems, like unemployment, unrest and wastage of demographic dividends. If not, God forbade, the demographic dividend has all the potential to contribute to growing numbers of antisocial elements in the society. It is imperative that all HEIs (colleges/Universities) redesign the curriculums to tune education fully to the needs and consequences of the ongoing industrial revolution, keeping the Gen-Z students of the 21st century in mind.

5. Redefining Role of Teachers

The conventional classroom teaching method allowing the learner to passively absorb knowledge has outlived its utility. Now teachers need to adopt strategies that will enhance creative thinking, group learning, making innovations, project and field study based learning besides providing basic and fundamental knowledge of a given subject area. Hence, the mindset of teachers, their competency and approaches have to change enormously. Future teachers have a significant role as facilitators, mentors, friends and philosophers. The teachers' profile will accordingly change. The colleges/varsities therefore need to quickly adopt flexible curriculums and teaching processes with new paradigms described earlier. The teachers have to continuously work to keep the digital gap between them and the learners to the minimum and avoid becoming redundant.

6. Redesigning Academic Staff Colleges

The Academic Staff Colleges (ASCs) are typically involved in providing 'Orientation' (OC) and 'Refresher' (RC) courses to college/ varsity teachers. Unfortunately, these courses have not been very effective due to faulty design and functioning of ASCs and uninspiring leadership of the ASC Directors with few exceptions. Often the resource persons are asked to lecture on topics of their choice which may or may not be relevant to the participants. This does not help. Ideally, there should be a definite curriculum for the OC and the training provided must help every participant in shaping the teacher and creating awareness on various dimensions of higher education. For instance, the OCs need to sensitize teachers on: history of higher education India, various education commission reports, objectives of higher education, governance of HEIs, conduct rules, role of teachers and their obligations. They must also be sensitized about creative teaching, learner centric teaching, self learning, lifelong learning, blended learning, problem solving, group learning, project based learning and continuous evaluation. As far as the RCs are concerned, they should be thematic and only resource persons having great experience in the field of a chosen theme should be invited for delivering lectures. Eminent resource persons with high reputation can indeed inspire the participants. And, this is exactly what is needed. The lectures need to be foundational in nature; starting from the basics they should cover recent developments in the field. Resource persons delivering talks on their own research work is often uninteresting and therefore not well received by the participants. The ASCs need to go a step further and redesign the refresher courses such that the participants not only learn recent developments in a subject, but also, learn how to teach a particular subject, how to be student-centric in their approach, how to promote students to think, how to learn through group discussions and so on. The RCs may have broad titles like: 'Physics Education', Biology Education', 'Commerce Education' and so on. In short, the design of orientation and refresher courses should be such that teachers are trained to be learner-centric, promoters of creative thinking and life-long learners, and innovators. Finally, course completion certificates should be given only if the participants score 70% or more in the evaluation based on continuous or online.

7. Promoting Life Skills

It is impossible to list all 'life skills'. Also, they are difficult to explain in short as they encompass a very broad canvas. In brief, any skill that helps a person to lead his life comfortably is a life skill. For example, fishing is a life skill for some while preaching is a life skill for some others. The GOI has taken many initiatives for promoting skills and entrepreneurship as outlined in Chapter 18 of this book. This is indeed a great step that will go a long way in self support and sustenance of growth of the country. In addition the entrepreneurs will also become the job givers. It is now very relevant for every HEI to have a separate department or a wing that is actively involved in sensitizing students, providing possible skills on one hand and bringing awareness about the initiatives of the GOI for self employment through entrepreneurship. This can be easily done by outsourcing or through linkages with industries/institutions, with minimum expenditure. In any case, one must seize such opportunities to better the lives of vast mass of youth swiftly. It is also a noble venture in which HEIs can participate actively and fulfil the societal obligations. The future education system is certain to revolve around IR 4.0 and its consequences. Evidently this calls deafeningly for acquiring new skills, creative thinking, innovating and entrepreneurship.

8. Fostering Women's Education

In recent decades, in most colleges and varsities, the number of woman students is progressively exceeding the number of boys. For this and variety of other genuine reasons the girl students deserve more attention. Also, in recent times more girls' colleges and, women's universities have sprung up. Unfortunately, the women's universities are not really women centric as they run same courses as in other traditional varsities. These institutions, at best serve to segregate girls from boys. The benefits of such separation however remain debatable. Ideally women's colleges/universities should run mainly women centric 5-year UG-PG integrated programs with exit and lateral entry options after 3 years/graduation. The examples of women-centric courses include: Fashion Designing, Interior Decoration, training to become Air hostess, Secretarial Assistants, undertaking Corporate Social Responsibility (CSR), Nursing, Palliative Care, Catering, Bakery, Hotel management, Handicrafts, Computer Application/Programming, Music, Tourism, Translation of Scripts, Yoga and Meditation. Add-on courses may be designed for training in communication skills, self defence and gymnastics. These are representative examples. These trainings may be offered in the form of Diploma or Certificate or courses. Such courses have huge potential for securing jobs and self-employment. Therefore, the women's universities should provide entrepreneurship training to female students with the help of the newly initiated GOI's skill initiative projects (see MHRD website for details).

It is a matter of great pride that presently a women defence minister (Ms Nirmala Sitharaman) is taking care of the country. Likewise, our present Minister for foreign Affairs is also a woman (Ms Sushma Swaraj) who is doing an excellent job. It is also heartening to note that a few railway stations and aircrafts are completely managed by women.

Apparently, given an opportunity, women can be equal partners in building the country. All they need is self esteem, encouragement, support and special care. Furthermore, it is time that the HEIs change their mindset about the girl students and make sincere efforts to empower them. It is time to move on from women development to women lead development.

Sadly, in most HEIs the needs of girl students are often neglected; may be because they do not resort to protests, strikes and so on. In almost all colleges/varsities that I have visited I have generally encountered a namesake ladies room that is shabby with no amenities and, grossly unworthy of inhabiting and uninspiring. Shifting emphasis from boys to girls needs high priority. That girl students indeed deserve special attention in institutions of higher education is unequivocal. The basic needs include providing a big and cosy hall with inspiring ambience (soberly painted and well lit) with refreshing window drapes and portraits of women achievers in various fields (sports, science, music, literature etc.) from India and abroad, The various amenities include: decent furniture, provisions for resting, dining, small library with inspiring books and women's magazines, browsing, some indoor games, vending machine for sanitary napkins, toilets and so on to name a few. A namesake girl's room in a pathetic condition is not only depressing and inhuman; it is belittling the girl students and a crime on our part. Perhaps, MHRD directly or through its funding bodies should seriously consider providing grants specifically for developing model girl's rooms in colleges/varsities. In the past, the UGC gave considerable funds to colleges for building girls hostels and ironically most of these buildings seem to be either unoccupied or used for other purposes. In contrast, creating best facilities for academic and holistic growth of girl students will go a long way in furthering the prospects of building *women power* in the country as well as attracting more girl students to main stream and higher education.

9. Institutional Mentoring

Often persons lacking leadership qualities and competency are appointed as Principals and Vice Chancellors due to variety of reasons (seniority, nepotism, political compulsions etc.). Generally, merit, competency, aptitude and leadership qualities do not constitute essential qualifications for the appointment of the heads of the institution. In an context of corporate world, long ago Dr. Laurence J. Peter, the Canadian education scholar in his book titled "The Peter Principle" (1968) asserted that "every position in a given hierarchy will eventually be filled by employees who are incompetent to fulfil the job duties of their respective positions." This appears to be unequivocally true in most situations be it corporate world or educational institutions. To overcome this, it is good to appoint 'Mentors' for the HEIs. However, mentors so chosen should be eminent persons of high calibre and repute in their own fields of study and proven competency and, experience of building institutions or known leadership qualities. The mentors could visit the institutions 3-4 times in a year or as may be needed and provide guidance. The host institution may provide travel support, local hospitality and suitable honorarium.

10. Holistic Development is Hallmark of Education

Being a literate person possessing degrees is not necessarily the hallmark of educated person; it simply means that a person can read and write. No education is meaningful if it does not ensure holistic development of a person. "Education is the training of mind, heart and soul" said Sri Aurobindo. A great thinker, Swami Vivekananda said, "Education is the manifestation of the perfection already in man". In essence these quotes call for all-round development that is beyond acquiring skills in chosen fields or bookish knowledge, to be called *educated*. It is widely believed that in the colonial days, natives were thoroughly brainwashed so as to revere everything foreign or English as superior and everything eastern (Indian) is inferior and hence deserves to be looked down. Unfortunately, this dogma nurtured over the years ranging from pre-colonial to postcolonial era has ruined us enormously and killed our thinking processes, education, research, lifestyles and most importantly, the self esteem. Indian contribution to true education and philosophy as well as sciences only constitutes insignificant proportion of our curricula. Even when it comes to history, often we are stuck with distorted history and obliterated truth. India has certainly made enormous contribution in several areas that can make us feel proud and hold our head high. But, this is possible only when our students understand, appreciate and feel proud of country's contribution to diverse fields including science and spirituality, they can develop national pride and respect for Indian culture and ethos, traditional knowledge (e.g. Ayurveda, Unani), knowledge enshrined in Veda, Upanishad, Bhagavad Gita (ancient scriptures), contributions of our great sages and thinkers who were several centuries ahead of the rest of the world even before the Christian Era. Indian contribution to spirituality is indeed ultimate; evident from the fact that Westerners visit India in large numbers round the year seeking spiritual pursuits and happiness. 'Spirituality' is India's greatest gift to the world. If students have to feel proud of the country's achievements in diverse fields they ought to be taught about these things in schools and colleges as well as varsities. That Indians are not inferior intellectually to any other race needs to be instilled in the minds of our students and help build their self esteem, confidence and national pride. Moreover, studying everything on western style and western books will take us nowhere. In short, it is high time that schools and colleges as well as universities incorporate the components of holistic development in the curricula that inspires and generates respect for Indian ethos, culture and scriptures, and finally national pride. Likewise, all educational institutions must adopt a prayer song of the state (in the regional language) or the national anthem (preferably instrumental in nature) and play it each day at a specified time when everyone will stand still as a mark of respect. An imported song in foreign language can hardly inspire the Indian soul.

In summary, a proper management of higher education is crucial for nation's growth, development and security. Knowledge is power. Education is for providing knowledge and skills, building self esteem, confidence and national pride. It must also be remembered that a major aspiration of learners seeking higher education is employability. In view of the fast changing scenario globally following the fourth industrial revolution and its impact, it is imperative that education for 21st century is redesigned with flexible curriculums. The teachers will have new role in the future education. Unfortunately, most colleges depend on the affiliating universities for curriculum. The universities with no set goals and no visionary leaders seldom consider revamping curriculum to the global standards and changing needs. Even the autonomous colleges which have the freedom to prescribe their own curriculums seldom take initiatives for redesigning education system. Often, provision of autonomy in colleges/varsities is used for diluting the syllabi. It is sad but true that in most universities the curriculums framed are meant to suit to the mediocrity of the faculty. The result of all this is production of graduates who are unemployable as they are not fully trained for specific jobs. At the same time, the world over, people are facing 'technology driven disruption of jobs'. Nevertheless, development of new technologies also creates new jobs that require additional skills. Therefore, a revamped education system is ought to consider emphasizing skill development, creative thinking, making innovations and entrepreneurship. It also calls for lifelong education. The teachers will have to assume new roles; a shift from traditional classroom teaching to flipped classrooms, student-centric teaching that involves creative thinking, blended learning, group learning and project based learning, self learning and so on. One major challenge for future teachers is keeping the digital gap between them and the learners to minimum as the latter are more likely to be ahead of teachers. Also, new role of teachers in future is to function more like a facilitator, guide, mentor and friend and philosopher.

A massive redesigning of education system, infrastructure and attitude of teachers and administrators is not easy. One basic problem is that over a period, our HEIs have successfully built hierarchy of incompetency rather than competency and merit. As a result, the stakeholders are paying the price. There are no easy solutions to fix this monstrous development. Any attempt to set right the situation requires great amount of courage, conviction and concern for making the higher education relevant to the changing needs: making innovations and facing challenges of industrial revolutions. It also requires support from the general public. The policy makers, the various regulatory bodies, and the respective State Higher education Councils should launch massive resurrection programs by redesigning education system before it is too late.

Lastly, the present education system needs overall redesigning to meet challenges of technology driven disruptions in industries and jobs and demand for new skills. Therefore, the new education system must be designed such that it promotes creative thinking, making innovations, acquisition of new skills in relation to the technological advancements; and these shall be the hallmarks of 21st century education system.

Suggested Reading

1. The State Universities: Problems and Perspectives. University News 51, No. 17, 2013; pp 114-119.
2. Applying Education Reforms in True Spirit. Deccan Herald. August 28, 12014. *[Article on RUSA scheme of MHRD]*
3. Revamping Higher Education. *Guest Editorial*: *Curr. Sci.* 113, pp 831-832, 2017.

ABBREVIATIONS

A & A = Assessment & Accreditation
AA = Alumni Association
AAA = Academic and Administrative Audit
ACAR = Indian Council of Agricultural Research
AI = Artificial Intelligence
AICTE = All India Council of Technical Education
AIU = Association of Indian Universities
ANS = Autonomic Nervous System
AQAR = Annual Quality Assessment Report
ASC = Academic Staff College
ASDP = Aajeevika Skill Development Program
ATI = Administrative Training Institute
ATM = Automated Teller Machine
BARC = Bhabha Atomic Energy Research Center
BCI = Bar Council of India
BT = Biotechnology
CAL = Computer Assisted Learning
CAN = Campus Area Network
CBCS = Choice Based Credit system
CCMB = Center for Cellular & Molecular Biology
CDC = College Development Council
CGPA = Cumulative Grade Point Average
CPWD = Central Public Works Department
CSIR = Council of Scientific and Industrial Research
CSR = Corporate Social Responsibility

DAY-NULM	=	Deen Dayal Upadhyaya Yojana-National Urban Livelihoods Mission
DBT	=	Department of Biotechnology
DCI	=	Dental Council of India
DDU-GKY	=	Deen Dayal Upadhyaya Gram Kaushal Yojana
DGT-MES	=	Director General of Training-Modular Employable Skills
DIC	=	District Industries Centre
DOAB	=	Directory of Open Access Books
DOAJ	=	Directory of Open Access Journals
DOAR	=	Directory of Open Access Repositories
DOE	=	Department of Environment
DOES	=	Department of Employment Services
DST	=	Department of Science & Technology
EDII	=	Entrepreneurship Development Institute of India
EDP	=	Electronic Data Processing
EMS	=	Environment Management System
ERP	=	Enterprise Resource Planning
GATE	=	Graduate Aptitude Test Engineering
Gem	=	Government e-Market
GER	=	Gross Enrolment Ratio
GMAT	=	Graduate Management Admission Test
GOI	=	Government of India
GPS	=	Global Positioning System
GRE	=	Graduate Record Examination
HEC	=	Higher Education Council
HEI	=	Higher Education Institution
HELINET	=	Health Library and Information Network
HR	=	Human Resource
HRD	=	Human Resource Development
ICAR	=	Indian Council of Agricultural Research
ICHR	=	Indian Council of Historical Research
ICMR	=	Indian Council of Medical Research
ICSSR	=	Indian Council of Social Science Research

ICT	=	Information Communication Technology
IHE	=	Institution of Higher Education
IIM	=	Indian Institute of Management
IISc	=	Indian Institute of Science
IISER	=	Indian Institute for Science Education and Research
IIT	=	Indian Institute of Technology
ILL	=	Inter Library Loan
IMC	=	Indian Medical Council
INDEST	=	Indian Digital Library in Engineering, Science and Technology *(now merged into e-Shodh Sindhu)*
INFLIBNET	=	Information and Library Network
INFONET	=	UGC-INFONET Digital Library Consortium *(acronym for the e-Journal Consortium managed by INFLIBNET. Now renamed as e-ShodhSindhu)*
IP	=	Internet Protocol
IQAC	=	Internal Quality Assessment Council
IR	=	Industrial Revolution
ISRO	=	Indian Space Research Organization
IT	=	Information Technology
KMS	=	Knowledge Management System
LIC	=	Local Inquiry Committee
LMS	=	Learning Management System
MAN	=	Metropolitan Area Network
MANREGA	=	Mahatma Gandhi National Rural Employment Guarantee Act
MCI	=	Medical Council of India
MES	=	Modular Employable Skills
MHRD	=	Ministry of Human Resource Development
MIS	=	Management Information System
MoLE	=	Ministry of Labour and Employment
MOOC	=	Massive Open Online Courses
MoRD	=	Ministry of Rural Development
MOU	=	Memorandum of Understanding
MSDE	=	Ministry of Skill Development and Entrepreneurship

MSME	=	Micro, Small & Medium Enterprise
MSME-DI	=	Micro, Small & Medium Enterprises, Development Institute
NAAC	=	National Assessment & Accreditation Council
NCC	=	National Cadet Corps
NCHER	=	National Council for Higher Education & Research
NCI	=	Nursing Council of India
NCL	=	National Chemical Laboratory
NCTE	=	National Council of Teacher Education
NET	=	National Eligibility Test
NGO	=	Non-Governmental Organization
NISER	=	National Institute of Science Education and Research
N-LIST	=	National Library and Information Services Infrastructure for Scholarly Content *(now- merged into e-Shodh Sindhu).*
NRLM	=	National Rural Livelihood Mission
NSDA	=	National Skill Development Agency
NSDC	=	National Skill Development Corporation
NSDF	=	National Skill Development Fund
NSS	=	National Social Service
NT	=	Nanotechnology
OA	=	Open Access
OC	=	Orientation Course
OPAC	=	Online Public Access Catalogue
PCI	=	Peripheral Component Interface;
PCI	=	Pharmacy Council of India
PG	=	Postgraduate
PIO	=	Public Information Officer
PMKVY	=	Pradhan Mantri Kaushal Vikas Yojana
PMR	=	Progressive Muscular Relaxation
PPP	=	Public Private Partnership
PPT	=	Power Point Template
QA	=	Quality Assessment

QAC	=	Quality Assurance Cycle
QE	=	Quality Enhancement
QR	=	Quality Radar
QS	=	Quality Sustenance
R & D	=	Research & Development
RC	=	Refresher Course
RPL	=	Recognition of Prior Learning
RUDSETI	=	Rural Development and Self Employment Training Institute.
SDI	=	Skill Development Initiative
SLET/SET	=	State Level Eligibility Test
SLQAC/SQAC	=	State Level Quality Assurance Cell
SSR	=	Self Study Report
STEAM	=	Science, Technology, Engineering, Higher Education& Mathematics
STR	=	Student Teacher Ratio
SWOC	=	Strength, Weakness, Opportunity and Challenges
TIFR	=	Tata Institute of Fundamental Research
TM	=	Transcendental Meditation
TOEFL	=	Test of English as a Foreign language
UG	=	Undergraduate
UGC	=	University Grants Commission
WAN	=	Wide Area Network
Wi-Fi	=	Wireless Fidelity